A Counsellor for School
A Child Mental Health Perspective

A Counsellor for School
A Child Mental Health Perspective

Dr H L Kaila

MD Publications Pvt Ltd
New Delhi
www.mdppl.com

Published by :

MD Publications Pvt Ltd
"MD House", 11, Darya Ganj,
New Delhi - 110 002
Phone : +91-11-41563325 (Customer Service)
+91-11-41562846 (Editorial)
E-mail (orders): order@mdppl.com
Website: www.mdppl.com

ISBN: 978-81-7533-299-7

Published and Printed by Mr. Pranav Gupta on behalf of **MD Publications Pvt Ltd** at Times Press, Delhi.

PREFACE

Child Mental Health in Indian Schools is a serious concern for educationalists, mental health professionals and policy planners. The schools are applying content-based, syllabus-pressurized approach in educating children; they have not given a choice to students to ask what they would like to learn. In the present structure of the schools; the children have no influence or say on matters what concern them. Teachers victimize students in order to discipline their classroom, as they don't know better ways of managing the classroom. Teachers are not aware as to how they harm emotional health of children. Peers bully their friends as they seek fun and thrill, they are not aware as to how they are affecting their friends emotionally. The teachers in schools crushed the natural personality of the children so badly that the children lost their self-esteem and self-trust in school so much so that even they grew up, they could not face the real life situations in bold manner. The students got the education at the cost of losing their precious self.

The schools are killing creativity in them. We can promote bright economy of India only if we promote creativity in children. Children's contentment lies in the use of their own creativity which is in abundance in them. The 17.0% students in school experienced one time that someone talked about sex and they didn't like it. The 10.4% students experienced the same a few times. The school principals are not aware of the magnitude of children being victimized in school premises and the effects of victimization on children. We must stop victimizing children at the earliest, and allow children to raise their voice by democratizing schools. Teachers need to be educated for caring mental health of children. The schools need to invest on teachers to upgrade their mental software to deal effectively with the emotional health concerns of children. On one hand, while the mental health of children is a State responsibility, the child-in-school is to be heard for his/her choices and concerns. *The children need a big change in schools.*

Child abuse is endemic in nature in Indian schools. This obnoxious practice has affected the mental health, learning process and knowledge level of students in large numbers. Obviously, urgent measures by policy makers in government and professional educationists assume significance to prevent a disaster of gigantic proportions. The book provides a broad child mental health perspective for counsellors in schools in favor of child development.

Child mental health in school is a very wide-ranging study, this book carries a perspective limited to certain relevant topics such as mental health issues, traumatic experiences, educational culture, academic stress, learning disorders, depression, eating disorders, autism, mental retardation, resilience, juvenile delinquency, parenting, democratic education, and victimization in schools.The manuscript intentionally does not include counselling process or skills as these are covered in earlier reference books.

I am very grateful to Mr Pranav Gupta, Director of MD Publications Pvt Ltd, New Delhi, for his kind cooperation and support for this book.

Dr H L Kaila

ACKNOWLEDGEMENTS

Author is grateful to the following Professors and Professionals from different Universities/ Institutions for their guidance in preparing this manuscript:

1. Cecilia Bradley, Sydney
2. Dr Anjali Chhabria, Mumbai
3. Dr K. B. Kushal, Mumbai
4. Dr. Harish Shetty, Mumbai
5. Jerry Mintz, New York
6. John Loflin, Indiana
7. Mrs. Bharti Gandhi, Mumbai
8. Prof Reeta Sonawat, Mumbai
9. Prof Usha Nayar, Mumbai
10. Prof Usha Ram, Pune
11. Prof. A. K. Srivastava, Kanpur
12. Prof. A. K. Srivastava, Varanasi
13. Prof. Abhijit Gangopadhyay, Mumbai
14. Prof. Aruna Broota, Delhi
15. Prof. I.L.Singh, Varanasi
16. Prof. Jitender Mohan, Chandigarh
17. Prof. Meenakshi Arora, Varanasi
18. Prof. Prakash Padakannaya, Mysore
19. Prof. Shejwal, Pune
20. Prof. Surinder Jaswal, Mumbai
21. Prof. Vibhuti Patel, Mumbai

Contents

1

Mental Health Issues of Children in Schools

A. S. Neill said he'd rather have a HAPPY street cleaner than a neurotic scholar.

This chapter reviews literature on mental health issues of children in schools since 1974 till date. It touches upon certain researches on school climate and frustration of children, school fright and phobias, academic burden on school students, PTSD in children, segregation and school violence, psychological disturbances in school-going adolescents, peer abuse, alienation among adolescents and the need of providing mental health services in schools.

Introduction

In the new millennium, there is an increasing emphasis on the mental health perspective in the globalizing society. More and more people are in need of such help due to changing family structure, prevailing environment at home, parental values, societal values, cultural values, relationships between wife-husband, parent-child, school-student, child-peer, individual-society.

The outcomes of mental health problems are stress, frustration, irritability, mistrust, isolation, and alienation. Many children and adults resort to socially destructive and personally devastating ways of coping this stress as evident by increased rate of crime, alcoholism, drug addiction, suicides, accidents, self-harm, running away from home, depression, stammering, bed wetting, nail biting etc. The manifestations of the outcomes range from simple behavioral problems to varying degrees of psychiatric problems. The chances of such problems show up more or found in broken homes, marital discord, one or either parent suffering from mental problems, death of either of the parent.

Children suffer from depression and severe anxiety especially when the time of examination approaches. They feel that if they do not perform well, family and friends might shun them. The result is self-harm feeling of intense shame and even suicide in extreme cases. Many a psychologist and educationist agree that the rising psychosomatic, learning and behavioral problems of children can be attributed to a number of factors, the most important one being over-ambitious parents (Hindustan times, March 1988).

Teenage girls studying in Mumbai schools reported significantly higher percentages of parental nagging in the form of being reminded to study, being asked to reduce their leisure time and being told that they were not utilizing their abilities to study. Perceived parental pressure was found to be negatively associated with academic interest and self esteem. Mehta (1999) and Sebastian (1997) reported that if parental expectancies are too high, children might feel frustrated, causing a dislike for studies and would experience stress during examination time.

According to a W.H.O. report, at least 3% of school children suffer from mental illness such as depression, suicidal thoughts, psychosis, serious attention or obsessive-compulsive disorder. The Indian children are no exception. Psychologists dealing with young children and teenagers agree that present generation from various quarters is facing these problems in their life (Bombay Times, January 1999).

Stress and Mental Illness among the Young

The sociological and psychological literature almost

uniformly suggests that young boys experience more stress than young girls, in part because of social expectations and in part because of different rates of biological development and other physiological factors. But it also suggests that with advancing age, the sex difference in experienced stress tends to disappear and by late adolescence the situation of girls appears to be at least as stressful if not more so than that of boys. On the premise that the differences in experienced stress would be reflected in rates of treated mental illness, the national rates of males and females in psychiatric treatment between ages five and nineteen are compared. The data consistently show preadolescent males to have higher rates of mental illness, while by late adolescence, females appear to have as high if not higher rates of mental illness than males (Walter R. Gove; Terry R. 1974).

Impact of School Structure on Self-Esteem

The purpose of this study was to examine the impact of the movement into early adolescence upon the self-esteem of children. Which children are most vulnerable to this role-transition and what is the effect of changes in school environment, pubertal development, and social behavior? With repeated survey interviews and nurses' measurements, 798 school children were followed from sixth into seventh grade in two different types of school systems. Findings indicate that, in seventh grade, white adolescent girls who have entered the new environment of junior high school appear to be at a disadvantage in comparison both to boys in general and to girls who do not have to change schools. Among the girls, the ones with lowest self-esteem appear to be those who have recently experienced multiple changes, that is, who have changed schools, have reached puberty, and who have also started to "date." Among boys, in contrast, early pubertal development is an advantage for self-esteem. These data thus demonstrate the way in which coping with a major role transition can be significantly affected by environmental context, level of biological development, and social behavior (Roberta G. Simmons; Dale A. Blyth; Edward F. Van Cleave; Diane Mitsch Bush, 1979).

School-Based Intervention to Promote Coping in Rural Teens

Jacqueline M. Lamb in her paper summarized that there are a number of biologic and environmental stressors that place the high school student at risk for maladaptive coping, depression, and self-destructive behavior. The findings in this study support the investigators' previous work, which indicates that this nurse-led assessment and intervention program provided in the natural setting of the school can identify high-risk students and has the potential to promote mental health among high school students, especially females. Results of this study have demonstrated that nurses who work with adolescents are in an ideal position to lead and/or coordinate such programs (Jacqueline, Pennsylvania).

School Organizational Climate and Reactions to Frustration of Children

School Organizational Climate, a relatively enduring quality of the internal environment of a school, is characterized by the resulting conditions within the school from the interpersonal relationships among the teachers and between teachers and headmaster and it influences the organizational behaviors of incumbents (Sharma, 1978). Analytically, school organizational climate is characterized by the pressure of such elements, as disengagement, alienation, morale, intimacy, psychological hindrance, controls and humanized thrust at different extent.

This paper attempted to find out relationship between the organizational climate of school and secondary school children's reactions to frustration (Directions and Types of Aggression and Group Conformity Rating). Sharma's S.O.C.D.Q was administered. Sample: 700 boys (N=354) and girls (N=346) belonging to sixth (N=235), Eighth (N=251) and Tenth (N=214) grades of ten uni-sex secondary schools situated in the districts of Nadia and 24-Parganas (North) in West Bengal served as the sample. Multistage random sampling technique was followed. Mean age ranged from 11 to 15. The teacher of those ten schools who served their respective schools for continuous 2 years was considered to perceive the climate were used for diagnosing the school organizational climate. Total number of teachers included in the study was 219. The following variables were assessed: (a) reactions to frustration, (b) school organization climate, (c) open climate, (d) autonomous climate, (e) familiar climate, (f) paternal climate, (g) closed climate. The result revealed a significant relationship between the variables and it was found that the paternal as well as open climate was congenial to the healthy development of children's reactions to frustration and the autonomous climate had some adverse effect on the development of subject's reactions to frustration. The other climate types did not reveal any significant influence on the subjects' reactions to frustration (Pares Chandra Biswas, 1990).

Stress and Mental Health in Childhood and Adolescence

Kapur (1990) in a study of 150 normal rural and semi rural pre-school children elicited certain emotions and responses to situations in the child's daily life. Rural children felt sad when no food was given, while their semi-urban counterparts felt sad when they were beaten up, scolded or their demands were not met. Majority of them responded by crying or keeping quiet. The children feared animals, insects, strangers and punishment by parents. Rural children responded by avoiding the situations and coming home while semi-urban children became quiet or cried. Anger was provoked when they were beaten or were denied something. The rural children responded by being quiet, whereas semi-urban boys hit back: girls in general became quiet or threw temper tantrums. This study made use of mostly mother's observation of the children. According to the mothers, expression of happiness shown was by jumping, smiling, kissing and hugging in these pre-schoolers. The parents belonged to low socio economic families. The children were screened for malnutrition. In this predominantly rural community, these stable though poor families protected their children from need to observe nature of emotional responsiveness to the various situations, in the very young children and how the information can be elicited from the mothers.

In an epidemiological study of 1,535 school going 5 to 8 year olds from middle class urban background, Shenoy (1992) studied a sample of 164 disturbed children and 171 normal children and reported chronic stressors in the disturbed group. These stressors consisted of alcoholism in the father and neuroticism in the mother. The fathers were often indifferent while the mothers were hostile rejecting or overprotective or over-ambitious. In addition the siblings were hostile and the disturbed children had difficulties with the peers. The study suggested that chronic stressors at home with peers had significant association with psychiatric problems. From an epidemiological survey of 408 urban middle class 8 to 11 years old school children, the effects of recent life events were studied on 18 psychiatrically disturbed and matched sample of 18 normal children (Sarkar, 1990). She reported the number of stressful events in the past one-year being significantly larger in the disturbed children. There were significant correlations between stressful life events, behavior problems and adjustments. Academic problems were present in 60%, poor acceptance by the peers in 50%, illness or operation in 40%, and change of residence was reported with equal frequency in both the groups.

In an epidemiological study of 663 adolescent girls, Dalal (1980) in a group of 79 disturbed girls found the number of stressful events to be significantly higher when compared to a control group of 78 non-disturbed girls. The checklist of 20 developmental and 20 non-developmental stressors were equally high in the disturbed groups. This group of adolescent girls from middle class background showed little preoccupation with heterosexual matters or sexual pre-occupations.

Arukmani (1989) in a study of 15 disturbed and 15 competent adolescent boys from extremely impoverished background, found both the groups to have equal number of stressors in most of the areas. However the disturbed adolescents had higher stressors in interpersonal relationships and pertaining to self. Coping behavior patterns of the competent adolescents had high flexibility and they had larger repertories of coping responses. Their copying styles included seeking social support, self control, accepting responsibility, planned problem solving and positive self-appraisal. This disturbed adolescents used escape avoidance as the main coping response. The study appeared to suggest that a healthy family matrix was essential for effective coping even under extreme adverse circumstances.

Studies in clinic settings

Sonpar (1982) studied 40 non-psychotic psychiatrically disturbed and 40 normal controls, divided equally, into early and late adolescent groups, from urban middle class, on the Vincent and Rosenstock modification of Coddington scales. She found that the greater number of stressful events in the disturbed adolescents was more of daily hassles than major events. Early adolescent boys had significantly higher number of stressful events than girls, while girls had significant history of anxious personality. Thus, the interplay of temperament and stressful events proved to be an important ingredient of psychopathology in adolescence.

A study by Rangaswamy and Kamakshi (1983) on 30 adolescent hysterics in the age range of 13 to 17 years, using Coddington scales, reported that 88% of the hysterics had significant life stress before the onset. The onset was preceded by unpleasant personal experiences, impersonal life events and school problems. In these 30 adolescents, in 13% there was death of parents, and in the other 13% hospitalization while breaking of friendships was present, not being allowed to participate in extra-curricular activities by the parents in 23% and increased arguments between the parents in 10%. Kaur (1987) found similar trend in somatoform disorders.

Uma (1988) in a clinical group of 70 hysteric children in the range of 8-12 years reported that stressors had significant role to play in precipitating hysterical symptoms. The precipitating home events were parental quarrels and punishments or scolding by the relatives. It was observed that though the events were not severe by themselves. But they experienced for the 1st time by the children. Precipitating events at school were change of school, punishment by the teachers, fights with peers and stress of academic work. The third group of stressors consisted fearful experiences when the child was alone, such as seeing ghosts, skeletons, dead bodies and feeling of being pushed - when no one was around. In addition to fearful experience with strangers or mentally ill person and sexual assault or conflicts also have been encountered especially in adolescents (Ninan and Kapur, 1989). Chronic stressors have been reported to be significantly high in school and in the family context being disciplinary styles, discordant relationships, over- involvement, anomalous family situations and mental disturbance in the family. Thus, in the Indian clinical settings there is a strong association between stressful recent life events and onset of hysterical and somatoform symptoms.

Daniel (1989) studied the psychological stressors in 33 conduct disordered, 33 with mixed disorders of conduct and emotion, and 33 emotion disordered 8 to 12 year old children, and compared them to those of normal controls. There was significant marital disharmony in the parents of 3 clinic groups. Parents of the conduct disordered were hostile and rejecting, while the parents of the emotion disordered, and those with mixed disorder of emotion and conduct, were over protective. High sibling rivalry was present in all the three groups, more so in the conduct disordered group. Peer interaction was especially in the emotion disordered but not in the other three group.

Malhotra, Kaur and Nehra (1992) in a study of 80 psychiatrically disturbed and 100 normal children in the age range of 4-14 years, using Monagham modification of Coddington scale found the psychiatrically disturbed had significantly higher stress scores, though the number of recent life events was somewhat similar in both groups. However, the younger children showed higher association between number of life events and disturbance. In addition, normal children showed significant increase in the number of life events and stress scores with increasing age. The study suggested closer association between psychiatric illness and recent life events in the younger age than in older age groups.

Psychological disturbances in school-going adolescent girls

Adolescence is recognized as a stage in the developmental process. The crucial issues in the study of adolescent populations are the methodology employed to assess them. The pattern of disturbance, and the role of psychological stressors in generating and maintaining psychological disturbances. The aims of this study were to find out the prevalence and the pattern of psychological disturbances in adolescent girls studying in classes 8 to 10 Std. To assess the type and number of stressful events, behavior problems and adjustments. The sample consisted of girls studying in classes 8 to 10 Std in the age group of 12 to 16 years, in two English medium schools in Bangalore. Both the schools being girl's schools and catered to the lower middle-class / middle socio economic strata. Tools used for the study are [a] socio-demographic data sheet was administered to obtain the background information of the students. [b] Goldenberg's health questionnaire [GHQ] [the 30 item version of the GHQ 1972]. It was used to find out 1). the prevalence rate 2). to identify the disturbed sample from the population 3). to screen the normal sample [c] Achenbach's Youth Self Report (YSR). The YSR is the revised version of Achenbach's Child Behavior Checklist. YSR is designed to be filled by youngster's own behavioral description of competences and problems. There are 112 items divided into subscales, categorized into two broadband scales, Internalizing and externalizing scales. Pre-adolescent Adjustment Scale (PAAS). The 40-item scale by Pareek, Rao, Ramlingaswamy and Sharma (1975) - Stressful life Scale events (SLES). A compilation of SLE from the available Indian and Western scales suitable to the age group of 12 to 16 yrs was made. The Indian tools included the scales developed by Sonpur (1982) and Revathi (1986). The Western scales included Swearingen and Cohen (1985) and Compass Davis and Forsythe (1985). The compilation yielded a total of 77 items, including the "any other" category. The final scale had 60 items of which 20 were development stressors.

Prevalence rate was found to be 31%. When the cut off score GHQ was 6 in patterns of psychological disturbance, it was found out that a significant difference between the disturbed and non-disturbed existed, comparing the finding with the mean scores of boys on the YSR in Rozario's study showed that there was a significant difference in boys too, but comparing the two results it was found that the mean score of girls to be relatively lower on YSR, compared to the boys of similar age group. On the SLES the median reported of stressful events was 11. Showing that disturbed group had significantly greater number of stressors both developmental and non-developmental in the 6 month period. It also shows that the two groups differ significantly in their adjustment in various areas with the disturbed group being poorly adjusted. In comparison with boys it was found that girls had better adjustment than boys (except in the area of home). Thus taking the prevalence rate and the mean scores on the various subscales YSR and PAAS the difference between the two sexes indicate (a) The adolescent girls have a higher prevalence rate of disturbance (b) The degree of disturbances is much lower in girls, compared to boys, during the early adolescence. The various correlations indicate that there could be a strong association between the stressors and the disturbance, and the nature of adjustment and disturbance.

The study results implicate that certain theoretical issues emerge. As conceptualized, adolescent turmoil does seem to be manifested in mild forms of depression, anxiety and minor disagreements with authority figures. Also as postulated in various theories the adolescents in the present study do report experiences related to concerns about physical change, the changing roles and expectations; and the cognitive development leading to increased concern for academic achievements and the changing nature of interpersonal relationships. Comparing the Western counterparts in the groups studied, there was minimal to nil reporting of any preoccupation with sex or concern about heterosexual relationships. Indian middle class families could hold this because of the cultural differences and values.

The present study throws light on the behavioral problems, the number and type of stressors and the adjustment pattern seen in the group of early adolescent girls in India, which is also found similar to that of the early adolescent girls in the West. In the conclusion it was found that the prevalence rate in early adolescent girls was found to be 30.92% GHQ with a cut off of 6. Psychological disturbances and stressful life events were found to have a significant positive correlation, while disturbance and adjustment were found to have significant negative correlation. The pattern of adjustment was significantly poor in the area of home, school and peers and teachers in the disturbed group (Dalal S., Kapur M. and Subbalakshmi D. 1990).

Pushing kids into neurosis

At school the teacher frowns if he hasn't completed his homework. Back home mummy wants him to score over his cousins and all the neighbours' brats. Daddy only likes to hear that he is always at the top in the class. Why can't he leave cosmonauts like Rakesh Sharma by the wayside, they argue. These days the child registered for admission at half a dozen prestigious schools even before he is born. The day he learns to take the first step in life, pressure on him starts building up to memorize nursery rhymes, count numbers, articulate letters of alphabets of at least two languages, recognize objects, shapes and colours, etc. all this is supposed to prepare him for the momentous interview he will face on reaching the age of three. That will be the take off stage in his educational career. Among the things he is expected to know are human anatomy, animal and birds names and sounds, nature's products such as trees, flowers, fruits and vegetables, the national flag and anthem, etc. The ordeal for parents is no less trying. The admission months turn into a nightmare. Approaches are made in quarters that matter. Subterfuges are resorted to. The principals of the most sought after schools often behave like highbrow bureaucrats, while parents act like supplicants before them. The child himself cannot but be affected by the anxiety writ large on his or her parents faces and that, too, on his account. And if he fails to qualify for admission to a preferred school, it might really have an adverse psychological effect on him, besides making the parents feel unhappy. Not a good omen at the threshold of an academic career. Is all this really needed? Is the criteria applied to test the intelligence of a child justified? And does the school really get the best of the lot who knock at its doors? Children subjected to this kind of stress often lose weight, develop abdominal disorders and show distaste for food. They also become victims of diseases such as stuttering, mental retardation, sporadic outbursts of temper. Japan where excessive emphasis is laid on achieving excellence at too early an age, which is the cause of high rate of suicide among children.

It is a myth that a child who shows early promise will in later life turn out to be a genius. Not necessarily, some of the world's greatest intellectuals, scientists and writers such as Einstein, Newton and Ramanujam were no prodigies and came from ordinary social backgrounds. Recently, studies sponsored by the Inner London Education Authority showed preclude academic success. The quality of teaching, curriculum planning, classroom environment and wise utilization of school funds, among others, are the factors that influence achievement of educational goals. A humane and child-centered approach should envisage easy entry into school, care and affection by all concerned, less burden of books and subjects taught, total elimination of homework, and lots of opportunities for play and interaction with other children. What the child needs most is a reassuring pat by his parents and teachers, a few breaks from the routine and greater understanding of his needs. Parents should try to see things from his point of view. The irony of the situation is that the teachers are aware that what they are telling the children. But they are pressed for time since they have to complete before the session ends.

The National Council of Educational Research and Training itself has acknowledged in one of its reports that the curriculum load at each grade level is excessive. However no effort has, so far, been made to lighten this burden. In days of fast technological progress, child learns from listening to radio, watching television and films, reading comics, playing with mechanical toys. But most of this is a feature of the urban scenario and is largely related to the upper and middle classes. The social divide is children of the rural poor and urban lower classes. These schools are ill-equipped, under-staffed and overcrowded. Chaupals and panchayat ghars are often used as classrooms. In some rural areas, students have to walk five to 10 miles to reach the schools. There it is the load of poverty and not the burden of the schoolbag that they carry. The concept of a national system of education as laid down in the Indian Constitution and reiterated in the 1986. Is this objective anywhere in sight? (Mani Pande, 1994).

Sexism in Secondary School Classrooms

This study investigated how engenderment (socialization to gender) operates in three types of independent secondary schools—boys' schools, girls' schools, and coeducational schools. Observational data were collected in 86 classrooms in 21 schools in specific curricular areas. The study found that teachers initiated most of the incidents in six categories of sexism. Furthermore, although the frequency of incidents was similar in the three types of schools, the forms of sexism were different. Chemistry classes were the major locus of sexism in coeducational schools, and the severest form of sexism was found in boys' schools. Although girls' schools exhibited the most gender-equity events, they also perpetuated a pernicious form of sexism: academic dependence and non-rigorous instruction. Schools with policies that actively promoted gender equity in enrollment, in the hiring of faculty, and in personal relations were the least likely sites of sexism (Valerie E. Lee; Helen M. Marks; Tina Byrd, 1994).

Peer Abuse and Its Effects

This qualitative study focuses on peer abuse as a sociocultural phenomenon. Peer abuse emerged from the analysis of students' written recollections of what had made them the unhappiest at four stages in their earlier lives. The sample consisted of two student cohorts (1974 and 1989) including 90 respondents each. Far more negative peer treatment than negative parental treatment was reported, along with reports of serious and lasting developmental problems generally attributed only to parental causality in the literature. These results were even more salient for the 1989 cohort than for the 1974 one. Moreover, the data illustrate how peer abuse impacted negatively on the victims' parents. Answers are suggested for the question: Why is peer abuse not a more prominent research and social policy concern? (Anne-Marie Ambert, 1994).

Dynamics of Inclusion and Exclusion in Preadolescent Cliques

A critical structural form organizing the social arrangement of children's lives is the clique. This primary group colors the character of children's preadolescent years and shapes their socialization to adult life. In this study, longitudinal participant observation and in-depth interviews with advanced elementary-school children to explore the central feature of clique dynamics: the techniques of inclusion and exclusion. Cliques are circles of power wherein leaders attain and wield influence over their followers by cyclically building them up and cutting them down, first drawing them into the elite inner circle and allowing them to bask in the glow of popularity and acceptance, and then reducing them to positions of dependence and subjugation by turning the group against them. The generic features of these inclusionary and exclusionary dynamics, the characteristics of this cyclical pattern, the implications of this socializing experience for the broader societal dynamics of power and manipulation, and the kind of in-group/out-group differentiation can lead to prejudice and discrimination (Patricia A. Adler; Peter Adler, 1995).

School fright and student phobias

Research shows that subjecting very young children to the rigours of formal education could be detrimental to them in later life. According to a clinical psychologist at Kalavati Children's Hospital. VR Nigam, "When children are forced to go through the rigours of early education, they develop symptoms such as class fright, enuresis or upset stomachs. Other symptoms are "school fright" which is characterized by an aversion to go to school." These are children who have been "pushed out" by their parents, in a desperate attempt "to leave no stone unturned to secure admission to a good school", psychological ill-effects of early format schooling have been amply demonstrated by research in developed countries. In these countries, children at the age of three go to kindergarten but formal education begins at age seven. The research shows up the whole gamut of problems faced by children in the first four years shapes the child's early years as well as its adult personality. A child needs an "unbroken day" i.e., a day without too many social and locational changes and full of emotional contacts with peers and adults to develop all its five senses. If too many social or locational changes take place in child's early childhood, it can manifest as distortions in the adult psyche. Dr. Nigam according to this rush to push kids to learn is really of the parents massaging their own egos by sending their children to good schools, doing well and building a career.

Children at different stages of development, have different requirements, explains Uma Gaur at the department of anatomy of the Lady Hardings Medical College. Real socialization begins at two-and-half years of age when a child starts locating people and places, speaking unconnected words. There are lots of gaps in information about the early socialization of children and the role played by education. This is due to the fact the two streams of professionals – pediatricians and sociologists – have different approaches, which are never synchronized. A flip side to all this research. Parents have little choice when it comes to educating their children. They prefer private schools given the poor state of Government schools. The great disparity between standards of education in Government and private schools breeds disparity and drives a wedge between children attending these two types of schools. The Integrated Child Development Scheme (ICDS) has two lac people working on child development schemes, including the welfare on preschool children. The committee according to the linkages between ICDS and early childhood care and education exist only on paper. Education in ancient times was considered as the third eye to give human beings an insight into the world we live. But the way things have turned out, putting the very young through the rigours of formal schooling is proving to be detrimental to their proper socialization (Sujata Sahai, 1994).

Ecological Approaches to Mental Health Consultation with Teachers

This article argues that ecological issues are at the core of concerns about the violence among U.S. students, particularly those in low-income urban communities, are exposed to or experience within or outside of school. Consequently, it suggests that ecological systems theory-based mental health consultation for teachers should be an essential component of school violence prevention services. Further, it outlines a broad framework for generating teacher- and school-based interventions based on empirical data from the youth and school violence literatures, ecological systems theory, and consultee-centered consultation models (Ron Avi Astor; Ronald O. Pitner; Brent B. Duncan, 1996),

Emotional Disturbance as a Stress Reactor among Students

The term "Stress" refers to the psychological state, which derives from the persons appraisal of the success with which he or she can adjust to the demand of the environment. In other words, it is the reaction of the mind and body to change. How one responds to stress is determined by how he or she evaluates the change. The present study aimed at screening the students seeking admission to an academic institution so as to identify individuals susceptible to emotional disturbance under stress and to suggest coping skills training programme for them as a preventive measure. The sample consisted of 372 students seeking admission to post graduate and research programmes. Tools used were: Personal Information schedule Subjective well being Inventory (SUBI), developed by Sell H. and R. Nagpal (1992). It consists of 40 items, which measure 11 factorial dimensions. The data obtained was scored and analyzed. Of the total sample 21% students scored below average indicating their susceptibility to manifest emotional disturbance while they are exposed to special stress. It was evident significantly that more number of students scored low on negative items. Sell and Nagpal (1992) suggest that negative factors items are more likely to be affected by transient adversity and circumstantial changes, whereas a significant impact on positive factors would envisage a more serious and irreversible impact on personality. The SUBI score distribution among 372 students revealed a mean score of 92.06 with a SD of 8.55. The findings suggested that coping skills training programme in the following lines would benefit them: training in effective time management, relaxation training and use of recreational and social activities as a means of releasing day to day tensions.

A study revealed that student aiming for higher academic achievement, ensuring postgraduate and research programmes face specific stresses and can become susceptible to emotional disturbance. Susceptible students can be identified so as to help them in developing coping skills as a preventive measure (Dharitri R. 1996).

Need of providing mental Health Services in the Schools

Schools play a crucial and formative role in the development of personality, cognitive development, emotional development and social development. Although only small number of school mental health services has been carried out in our country, there is considerable clinical data about the extent of mental health problems in the school going population. In a survey conducted by Sethi *et al.* (1967) mental health problems were found in nearly 10%; of the conducted by Lal and Sethi in 1977, the extent of psychiatric problems in the school going population was found to be almost 1/5th (17.3%); and surveys conducted by Verghese *et al.* (1974) and Nandi *et al.* (1975), however, reported a lower percentage of psychological problems. Further in an I.C.M.R. sponsored multi-centre study of child and adolescent disorder (1983), analysis of 1983, 5 children attending child guidance clinics revealed that 37% had behavioral disorder, 12% had mental retardation, 7% had specific developmental delays, 14% had epilepsy and 25% had psychosis.

Behavior disorder has been reported in 10 to 40% cases attending child guidance clinics in the country depending upon the geographical areas and several other factors, undoubtedly the diagnostic sub-classification of psychiatric disorders in children causes several practical difficulties and that is why different reports show conflicting rates of various childhood psychological problems. The differences could be largely on account of the diagnostic criteria adopted in different studies. That is why the generalization is quite often difficult on account of methodological issues or non-representative nature of samples. The entire group of children should be studied in terms of age, reference e.g., pre school children, school going children and adolescence; because the psychological problems are entirely different at different age levels.

In a recently published book on child mental health in India, edited by Savita Malhotra and others, it has been pointed out that nearly one third of the world population belongs to the age group of less than 15 years and 5-15% of the children are affected with persistent mental disorders. Strikingly enough, 80% of the world's children live in developing countries but mental health services so far available in these countries is still very meager, malnutrition, communicable diseases and inadequate health care delivery system further complicates the problems of mental health.

In India, children constitute about 40% of the population (about 350 million children) and it is pathetic to observe that we do not have even 40 child guidance clinics to provide psychological care to emotionally distributed children in the country. Most of the clinics are rendering services to the mentally retarded children and you would agree with me that their psychological care is entirely of a different nature. There are still only a few departments of child psychology and child psychiatry in the whole country. Of course NIMHANS, Bangalore and few other centers like K G Medical College, Lucknow have been providing excellent services. The greatest problem which requires hardly any elaboration relates to the facts that in the schools and colleges every section of the school is likely to have around 15-20% students, who are not able to maintain a satisfactory scholastic progress which often is the result of some kind of school maladjustment or emotional or adjustment problems. It is ironical that parents in India usually have to face a lot of economic hardships to provide suitable education to their children resultantly they develop a very high expectation and on the other hand there is no system in the schools and colleges where students facing emotional problem or stress could seek the required psychotherapeutic help. Keeping in view that the number of trained clinical psychologists in our country is relatively meager, the only plausible solution is that there should be training institutes to provide short-term psychotherapeutic orientation or orientation in mental health care.

The trained personnel of the institutes could serve as counsellor or school psychologists. What should be the exact curricula and the period of training is a matter of thorough discussion and I think our association should hold a workshop to elaborately discuss and format counselor's training programme. However, some are of the opinion that teachers of the schools could be provided a few days or few weeks training to work as counselor. I personally feel that such a proposal would hardly meet the requirement as the teachers in majority of schools are overburdened with the task of teaching. The pupil teacher ratio in most of the schools is so unreasonable that they can hardly do justice with their existing assigned duties. Moreover one has to look into the motivational aspects of the programme. In general, the school teacher is a rather frustrated lot in the present socio-economic milieu of the society. One more point, which I could like to greatly emphasize, is that school children are very much burdened with the existing syllabus and it is highly pathetic to see small kids carry 6-8 kg school bags on their backs. Yash Pal commission appointed by the Government of India in the recent past has expressed a great concern about this inhuman burden on the backs of these small children.

The clinical psychologists should build up a pressure through the available print and audiovisual media and try to impress upon the authorities to make concerted efforts to reduce the burden of the syllabus upon the young children so that mental health of children as well as parents could improve to a substantial level. Permit me to say that burden of the school bags and prolonged hours if the school study only subdues the intellectual caliber and creativity in our children. There is hardly anytime to them to involve in expressive and recreational activities. In the end, I would like to propose that our association should take initiative in devising certain specific solutions to the problems of mental health care of our children and for this purpose a workshop involving senior professional members, leading educationalists and effective government representatives should be held to sort out the issues and suggest feasible recommendations to enhance the mental health of the future generation (Mata Prasad, 1996).

Creating Safe and Caring School Communities

This article asserted that school wide interventions have

the greatest potential for buffering students from violence outside of schools and for preventing violence within schools. It examines critical aspects of one such intervention, the Comer School Development Program (SDP), and explores the ways in which this program directly and indirectly impacts both the level of violence in the school and children's, parents', teachers', and school administrators' responses to it. By embracing children within a web of prosocial relationships and activities, the SDP is shown as creating a "safe heaven" that supports their healthy development, fosters optimal learning, and discoura_es interpersonal violence (Norris M. Haynes, 1996).

Educating Children in a Violent Society

Child abuse, domestic violence, and interpersonal/ community violence are leading causes of injury and death for specific gender and racial sectors of the U.S. population, especially young ethnic minority males. Responses to this public health issue have brought together leaders in medicine and education in the design of interventive curricula and programs for classrooms and communities. Health providers have played a nontraditional role in the design and implementation of some of these initiatives. This article reviews some of the interdisciplinary collaborative strategies that have been offered and presents evaluative commentary on the success and challenges of this new partnership (Renee R. Jenkins; Janice G. Hutchinson, 1996).

Waging Peace in Schools

Drawing upon recent research and the authors' extensive field experience, this article describes a program which recognizes that the ability to manage emotions, resolve conflict, and interrupt biases are fundamental skills that can and must be taught. It further asserts that schools can play a critical role in stemming youth violence; however, a new vision of education is needed if the nation is to create safe, caring communities of learning for children. Toward these ends, a plan is offered for the successful implementation of the Resolving Conflict Creatively Program (RCCP), a comprehensive, nationally disseminated and evaluated school-based model (Linda Lantieri; Janet Patti, 1996).

Reducing academic burden on school students

Children and adolescents are often victims of several kinds of stress in school and are not aware of how to cope with these (Nathawat and Gupta 1990). Systematic studies in this area in our country are not too many. This research gap needs to be fulfilled. Among several sources of stress in adolescents, information load and parental expectation are important, besides these sources of stress; adolescent's academic pressure or burden seems to be the most obvious source of stress in teenagers. Gifted students create their own pressure by setting high standards and unrealistic goals. Another common daily stress among teenagers is their concern over future.

R. K. Narayan, noted novelist and former member of Rajya Sabha pleaded for abolition of the school "by ordinance if necessary". Based on his observation he reported that child aged six carried a bag of not less than six to eight kg with lunch box and water bottles. Also those students couldn't leave book behind at home as teachers would then terrorize them if not brought to school. He also adds about the senseless regulation regarding uniform, ties, and socks irrespective of climate. He submitted before the house and honorable members to think over and advice a remedy by changing the whole educational system and the outlook so that childhood has chance to bloom rather than perish within the dreadful process of learning.

Yash Pal committee report emphasized the need to lessen the burden or load of the school bag in the early stages of school. The committee also made a statement as "a lot is taught but little is learned and understood" therefore if inferred that the load of non-learning or non-comprehension is the real load one should be concerned about. The above statement challenged "memorizing with understanding" would prove burdensome on children. Thus the committee suggested that attempts should be made to reduce or overcome stresses in school going students. Learning without burden is possible if recommendation of the committee were implemented and some resistant does appear in its implementation. Issues such as age of entry in school, teaching day, classroom facilities, strengthening of professional support system etc. should be considered in reducing school burden [academic] on students. Study by Ashok Gupta (1994) "success in life and its correlation with early educational background" came up with the suggestion and conclusion that good academic school achievements do not guarantee success in life in the later life and poor performance does not necessarily mean failure, on the other hand over expectation from parents may result in emotional disturbance problems including depression and suicide in many adolescent.

Gehlot and Nathawat (1983) observed that suicide was a result of over expectation of parents, which then were labeled as "performance suicides". Thus stress in school-going teenagers may lead to serious consequences including several psychiatric aliments. Thus making a conclusion that unnecessary and excessive pressure to perform should be reduced and the emphasis should be on sharpening the talents and aptitudes of the students in whatever field they look potential (Nathawat S. S. 1997).

Overburdened Child

The children are a pleasure to watch. They are so happy and carefree. "You're better off as you are. Wait till these little carefree innocents have to go for their school interviews". Admissions into primary schools have become a nightmare for parents, and for their little ones. According to a psychotherapist and parent of a four year-old. "Children are forced to begin life on the wrong foot – forced to face failure when they are not yet ready for competing or proving". Tapasi Bajaj, principal, Bal Vikas nursery school. "A child's attention span is small, maybe just about three minutes. Why are such small children forced to sit in a classroom? They are treated like a herd, when what they really need is to be given the freedom to develop as individuals". This much pressure is not enough, there are also special tuition classes conducted to further prepare the child for the crucial admission tests. According to Meera, the mother of a three-year-old boy, " I suppose I am due for worrying right now. My son will be appearing for admission tests from the end of this year. I think it is very cruel – to force him to sit on a chair and push him to study the alphabet and numbers, when he is not psychologically ready for them yet. I don't want to do this to my child. But sooner or later, I will have to start pushing him".

Some schools like Bombay International have a more relaxed admission procedure. They also have limited seats, but the interviews aim only at gauging how well adjusted the child is and how well he/she communicates. Some schools, however, expect children to know their numbers. The child is expected to be confident without his/her parents. In fact, a lot of children cry and cling to their parents, unwilling to be taken to an unfamiliar place, to meet unfamiliar people. As a consequence, the child goes through tremendous strain and there are times when it may just refuse to perform. For a little child to behave for a whole hour without getting fidgety is almost impossible. According to Tapasi Bajaj, "Children today are forced to perform. In order to be accepted, they do perform, but develop strain they are under. Bed-wetting, stuttering, becoming moody, are just some of these". Aruna Thakkar, principal, Sunflower school, "Frankly, it is parents who push their children beyond measure". According to her, " Writing and reading is so much a part of doing. The fun element in it should be so pronounced that the tedium is absorbed. The idea is to leave the child free and then help him do a little more every time. Bal Vikas believes that a child should be allowed to play whenever he/she wants to. The children are well adjusted and happy here. Sunflower has an organized system. There is play-time swim-time, cook-time, gym-time, outdoor-time, indoor-time, study-time and art-time. But everything is organized. Children here are also well adjusted and happy. A particular mother wanted her son to get only into Cathedral. She and his teachers put pressure on the child, making him work extra hours. He got his admission. One wonders whether he suffered under the pressure? Or does it matter? Have parents wondered why a lot of children wake up in the morning moaning, "Please Mummy, I don't want to go to school". Is it normal?

Primary education has become quite relaxed nowadays, and the curriculum comes across as being very interesting and enjoyable. But by the time the child gains admission to it, he may be so sick of the very word school. The answer to the problem perhaps lies in a standardization of the primary school admission testing system. The method could be simplified so that the child does not go through torture in the name of preparations (Anita Sharan, 1998).

Perceived Stress and Adjustment in Adolescents

This study aimed at exploring the nature of the stressors perceived and adjustment in different areas among thirteen to fifteen year old, school-going early adolescents. Stress, coping and adjustment is emerging as an important vehicle for examining adolescent mental health by psychological theorists. Two hundred and sixty early adolescents from the same school studying in IX th Std. was the population from which the sample for the study was drawn. Majority of them came from nuclear families. Two male and two females class teachers participated in the study. Tools used were (1) General Health Questionnaire (GHQ-30 item), (2) Interpersonal Competence Scale (ICS) - It is an 18 item rating scale for teachers which yields three primary factors: aggression, popularity and achievement, (3) Checklist of Stressful Life Events (CLSLE) - It is an 74 item stressors checklist tapping 8 areas of stress-school, peer interaction, parents, siblings, family, self, socio-cultural issues and general, (4) Pre-Adolescent Adjustment Scale (PAAS) - It is a 40 item scale that measures adjustment in areas of home, school, teachers, peers and general and gives a total score for overall adjustment.

The results of the study indicate that the disturbed adolescents had significantly greater number of stressors in areas of school, peers, siblings, self and general. However, no significant differences were observed in the area of 'parents' and 'family' in comparison to the competent group. Relationship between stress and adjustment - There is significant negative correlation between number of stressors perceived and the adjustment in each area. The number of stressors perceived by the disturbed adolescents is greater than the competent. This finding suggests that the disturbed adolescents perceive more problems in their environments with which they need to cope effectively. There was no significant difference in the area of 'parents' and 'family' between the two groups of adolescents. The altered relationship with parents faced by the adolescents is specific to this stage. Difference in adjustment between the competent and disturbed adolescents- poorest adjustment in the area of 'teachers' by disturbed group is a significant finding of the study. The current study suggests that some kind of mutuality of perception exists between teachers and students with both groups rating each other in the negative as seen on ICS ratings by teachers. This finding is of significance as positive school environment is viewed as an important protective factor. Relationship between stress and adjustment - the relationship between perceived stress and level of adjustment has been implicated in previous studies. Increased stressors and poor adjustment can lead to psychopathology. When faced with major life stressors, factors such as good coping skills and positive parent-child relationship have been indicated leading to positive outcomes. Conclusions - (1) There is difference in the nature of stressors perceived by the competent and disturbed adolescents, (2) The disturbed adolescents show poorer adjustment in all areas, (3) There is a relationship between number of stressors perceived and adjustment in different areas, (4) The above findings have implications in planning organized mental health services in school settings (Nandini, 1998).

Exams Stress

Summer's heat brings on the examination fever, which acquires epidemic proportions in the student community. An 'achiever', with a merit list academic track record, she now lies unconscious on a hospital bed with glucose and saline drips. The reason: dehydration due on excessive vomiting triggered off by the fear of the impending science practical exams. The pressures have mounted to such an extent that "there has been a definite upsurge in the number victims to exam stress in recent years," according to Dr Dayal Mirchandani. Without the emotional psychological apparatus to cope with this stress, psychosomatic problems- "physiological reactions to psychological tension", as Dr. Mirchandani puts it – surface in several children. Bed-wetting, asthma, dizziness, fainting, stomach cramps, severe headaches and recurring nightmares are some of the disturbances.

The emphasis in most schools today is on polishing cognitive processes and not on character and personality building. Faulty practices followed in the formative years of the school life of a child can undermine his psychological well being, making him vulnerable to stress in later life. The beginners face the brunt. Disturbance can be observed as early as in kindergarten. Later, even five and six year olds are overburdened with a load of homework and the "essential" evil of tuitions, thus becoming ensnared in the all-work-and-no-play-makes-Jack-a-dull-boy trap. As Dr. Mirchandani points out, "parents often do not realize the importance of play in character building: plays helps children deal with fears give vent to their feelings of aggression, to interact and learn the lessons of competition and co-operation and cope with various difficult situations. A healthy emotional psyche, which will help the child, tackle stress effectively in later years. Her parents to grab first position were egging on the child a third ranker in class. Her conscientiousness was, in fact, an overpowering anxiety that had robbed her off sleep. This pinpoints the destructive role of excessive parental pressure. "When the pressure to perform comes from within it is easier to cope with than pressure from outside. Self-created expectations competing with and attempting to better one's own previous performances can be handled more effectively than external pressures. In fact neurotic trends and phobic reactions to failure such as loss of self-esteem, a feeling of effectiveness, self devaluation, anxiety, depression coupled with aggression that 'I will never be successful' make nervous wrecks of healthy, happy children. In certain instances psychomotor retardation, clumsy movements, lack of co-ordination, slurred speech and bad handwriting can be sad result. Suicidal tendencies may also surface in adolescents who are haunted by morbid, dysphonic thoughts or self-condemnation and alienation. They are also the first child takes music lessons, attends karate classes and is a member to various libraries in an effort to prove that extra-curricular activities can compensate for academics. Lack of preparedness then leads to examination stress.

A self-confident child of average intelligence has a greater chance of succeeding in life than a child of average intelligence who has a poor self-image. Peer pressure can also be a hurdle especially in high school. Dr. Udayan Patel pointed out, "Our educational system spawns children who have set answers to the set questions. The all-important process of learning is totally ignored" (Veena Mathews, 1999).

Alienation among adolescents

The stresses and strains due to physical and physiological changes affect the adolescents' interests, social adjustment and feelings about themselves. Four hundred adolescent subjects in all were included in the present study. Their age range was from 13½ to 17½ years. Keeping in view the aim of the study, top 25% scorers and the bottom 25% scorers on the total alienation scores were selected as those high on alienation and those low on alienation respectively. The following standardized tests were used for measuring different variables selected in relation to the present study. (1) Dean's Alienation Scale (1961) (Public Opinion Questionnaire) was used to measure alienation. (2) Eysenck's Personality dimensions viz. extraversion, neuroticism, psychoticism and lie (social desirability) scale. This has been standardized in India by Mohan and Associates (1987, 1988). (3) Study of Values (Allport, Vernon and Lindzey, 1960). This scale was used to measure six types of values i.e., theoretical, economic, aesthetic, social, political and religious. (4) Bell's Adjustment Inventory (1937) was used to measure adjustment in four areas - home, health, social and emotional. (5) Rosenberg's Self-Esteem Scale (1965) was used to measure self-esteem. (6) Rotter's (1966) Internal-External locus of Control Scale was used to measure subject's internal - external locus of control. (7) For Academic Achievement, scores of last annual examination were taken as the index of academic achievement. The aim of the present investigation was to study the differences in the personality characteristics, values, adjustment pattern, self-esteem, and locus of control and academic achievement of adolescents high on alienation and low on alienation. Results reveal that there are significant differences between the high-alienated adolescents and low alienated adolescents on personality, adjustment and self-esteem (Jitendra Mohan, Nisha Mahajan, Neeraj Kakkar, 1999).

PTSD in children

Children, similar to adults, are profoundly affected by traumatic and stressful events and consequently may develop symptoms of Posttraumatic Stress Disorder. Historically, PTSD has been studied in children who have survived natural disasters, bereavement, chronic illnesses, and child abuse and neglect in the home (Brown and Kinchen, 2001; and Terr, 1991). However, few researchers and child advocates have recognized the prospect of PTSD developing from traumatic experiences in the school (Hyman, 1997). The main reason for the lack of recognition is that many people have failed to admit that schools have practices that could harm the child socially and emotionally. Hyman and Snook (1999a) describe in great detail how schools have adhered to many punitive disciplinary strategies that cause severe damage to a child's mental health. These disciplinary procedures include time-out, preventing students from using the bathroom, sarcastic remarks, and paddling. In addition, Hyman and Snook (1999a) outline various school practices that not only are proven to be unproductive and psychologically harmful, but are also infringements of children's civil liberties. The authors demonstrated that numerous school policies such as corporal punishment, strip searches, random urine testing, and censorship that violate a child's civil rights and alienate the child from school and the democratic process as a whole.

All these practices of maltreatment can be experienced as traumatic events, alienate the students, and lead to aberrant and destructive behavior. Further, when schools become a place of stress, and when victimization predominates a student's experience, it is likely that the victim will develop a range of negative emotional reactions, including anger, hostility, and aggression (Hyman and Snook, 1999b).

The consequences of hostile school environments are reflected in a recent report indicating that 2/3 of school shooters felt bullied, threatened, or persecuted prior to carrying out violent acts at school (Vossekull, Reddy, Fein, Borum, and Modzeleski, 2000). Given the recent focus on school violence, there is a pressing need to explore the factors which may lead to various types of school violence, and the effects this violence can have on the emotional well being of the students.

Originally, the description of PTSD focused more on adults. However, most psychologists now acknowledge that children can also develop PTSD. The new revised edition of the Diagnostic and Statistical Manuel for Mental Disorders-Fourth Edition (DSM-IV-TR) recognizes that Posttraumatic Stress Disorder can develop in childhood. PTSD is a psychological condition that can severely affect children's daily functioning, including their performance in school. Children experience traumas everyday, and there are psychological repercussions to this mental condition.

The occurrence of childhood trauma and the resultant symptomatology of PTSD not only adversely affect the daily functioning of the children, but will also influence the future social, psychological, and emotional status of the adult. Many researchers have proposed that PTSD symptoms in childhood factor into determining the existence of PTSD and other psychological disorders in adulthood (Terr, 1991). PTSD in childhood has been shown to lead to various problems such as anxiety disorders (Chu and Dill, 1990), borderline personality disorder (Herman, Perry, and Van der Kolk, 1989), and even multiple personality disorder (Kuff, 1985). In addition, PTSD has been shown to result in various aberrant behaviors that are "non pathological" such as drug use and criminal behavior (Burgess, Hartman, and McCormack, 1987).

Poverty and child emotional and behavioral problems

Using a sample of four to nine year-old children from the 1992 wave of the Children of the National Longitudinal Surveys of Youth data set, we evaluated racial and ethnic differences in the effects of current poverty and the persistence of poverty on child emotional and behavioral problems, and in the variables responsible for those effects. We considered three sets of variables in the latter analysis-mother's early characteristics and behaviors; correlated socio-demographic characteristics; and mediators (neighborhood problems, mother's psychological resources, and characteristics of the home environment) and evaluated their relevance across three racial/ethnic subgroups (blacks, Hispanics, and non-Hispanic whites). Consistent with our expectations, we observed a significantly stronger effect of the persistence of poverty on child problems for whites than for blacks, an effect that is attributable to the relatively strong association between poverty and mother's prior history of delinquency and current marital status among whites. The effect of poverty on child problems was substantially explained for blacks by mother's early self-esteem, whereas mediating processes took on greater relevance for Hispanics and non-Hispanic whites. Our results support the conclusion that there are racial / ethnic differences in the selection processes and proximal conditions that are responsible for the diminished psychological well-being of poor children (Jane D. McLeod; James M. Nonnemaker, 2000).

School Mental Health in Mumbai

The majority of schools in Mumbai do not have counselors on their staff. They are busy doing routine. Child guidance and counselling services in schools are unstructured and happen on an irregular basis. Research indicates that children and adolescents have high educational and vocational anxiety, and they have indicated problems such as low self-esteem, difficulties in managing anger and sexuality. Mumbai parents are supportive, and emphasize upon discipline, character building, and achievement in their growing-up children. The recommendations of WHO (1994) to introduce 'mental health programme in schools' have not impacted schools. The recently introduced PTA forum in schools by the State Govt. is a welcome feature but the role of PTA in schools is undefined. The individual MH professionals, CGCs, NGOs and professional associations are active in promoting mental health in schools and organizing awareness programmes for parents, teachers, principals, students and counselors towards better child guidance and counselling services in schools. The media coverage of children issues is appreciable. The process of what has moved the school mental health in Mumbai has been highlighted (Kaila, 2002).

Segregation and School Violence

While research exploring the consequences of desegregation and resegregation for academic achievement and intergroup attitudes and behavior has been prolific, scant attention has been paid to the impact that school segregation differences has had on school violence. Using data from the state of Florida Department of Education and the U.S. Bureau of the Census, we attempt to adjudicate between competing hypotheses about the nature of a relationship between segregation and school violence: (1) that segregation is associated with increased school violence; and (2) that segregation is associated with decreased school violence, especially under conditions of racial inequality. Results from a multilevel analysis show that increased school district segregation has a substantive negative association with school violence, particularly in contexts of greater community inequality, consistent with Pettigrew's (1971) observations about the contact hypothesis (David Eitle; Tamela McNulty Eitle, 2003).

Mental health issues among adolescents

According to Dr. Harish Shetty, a renowned Mumbai psychiatrist, most children and adolescents, with mental illness remain untreated not only in India but also in western developed countries. In India this issue attained sharp focus as a result of increase in suicide among the youth, addiction to drugs among teenagers, development in the burgeoning middle class, changing paradigms in teaching, rapid social change, better understanding of the child and change in attitude towards the female child. Violence and child abuse has also made policy focusing attention on adolescent mental health issues.

Problems: It is a direct lack of proper training in these issues in teachers training course; lack of sensitivity among policy makers whose formative years had no exposure to the subject; another hindrance in understanding story is spiritual side of things that undermine the understanding of human mind.

Factors influencing adolescent mental health: the rapid change our societies are experiencing is one of the most important factors for affecting the health of adolescents. Alienation experienced by all, more so in the urban areas. Unequal opportunities: the wide variance among communities, cultures regions and opportunities available to the student.

Lack of understanding: the advances in researches in the field of mental health have not only yet percolated to other relevant systems such as the educational system, other health systems.

Ignorance: condemning anything that comes from the west and believe everything that has evolved within the country is the common rhetoric heard at all the levels.

Emerging concepts: in school, brain is equated with intelligence and the health of the school is equated with marks of its students. Schools rarely evolve mechanisms where emotional hygiene becomes a debate among teachers, policy makers or students.

Understanding mental health and emotional problems should not be done in isolation. It should be linked to health education, value education, sports, sex education etc. In isolation, emotional problems can never be tackled and all the efforts to understand this problem or evolve answer should be done in relation to all human issues.

Some strategies: though psychological issues are part of B.ED or D.ED courses in reality, the manner of training is poor. Understanding is limited to answering the exams, curriculum of teachers should have an effect and input on mental health for better understanding. Small skills to large masses: India being a large country providing small skills to large numbers, thereby promoting the concept of barefoot counselors. Counselors should be sensitized to respect the beliefs of whom they help and should know cultural limitation.

Corporal Punishment

A school survey by 'Parent Teacher Association United Front' from Mumbai on March 15, 2005 reported as following. This included nearly 1000 boys and girls from 50 schools of south Mumbai with medium of instruction as English/Urdu/Marathi/Gujarati.

Use of scale...72%
Slapping the children.... 42%
Use of the duster 1%
Hitting with the corner of the book....20%
Use of cane...12%

Pinching.....24%
Twisting hand...2%
Hitting with knuckles...4%

The corporal punishment was observed more in the vernacular medium and more in boys school than in the girls school.

Segregation and detention in schools

Segregation is when children are divided into different groups on the basis of their marks. All the high scoring and bright children are put in one class and poor or low performing students are placed in other classes. This normally happens in Indian schools when they wish to concentrate more on bright students and achieve a 100% result in 10th grade examinations. As a result, the schools start detaining or failing under-achievers in lower classes such as 8th or 9th grades. Some schools go as far as expelling poor performers from school. Segregation and detention practices are "educational crimes" that carry on presently in Indian schools (The Times of India, 2004).

Segregation and detention lead to inequality, discrimination, prejudice and bitterness in students and parents. Much of the time students and parents feel helpless and do not know how to react to this situation. Segregation is like introducing a caste system into schools. We need to ask schools whether they want bitterness or betterness in their children.

How do teachers behave when the bright and average students are segregated in schools?

- They pamper bright students and at the same time they make the average students feel low.
- They call bright students scholars whilst they call average students dull, duffer or nuts.
- They pay more attention to bright students and they don't bother with average students.

- They mark bright students high and average students low in their tests and exams.
- They don't talk properly with average students.
- The teachers become partial and prejudiced towards poorly performing students.
- They become selective in choosing children for extracurricular activities.
- The teachers make average students feel that they are lesser.
- The teachers also get segregated in the school. The bright teachers teach bright students and average teachers teach low performing students.
- The teachers are not aware of the extent to which a child feels bad due to their discriminating and negative behaviour.

How do children feel and behave when they are segregated?

- The bright and average children also start segregating among themselves.
- The bright students feel happy, they do not make friends with average students, and they look down on average students.
- The average students feel low, depressed and lack interest in studies.
- The average students lack confidence.
- The average students feel anger and hate towards discriminating teachers.
- The average students feel helpless and alienated.

Segregation and detention are the ills in schools, the mental health effects of which are not known to the teachers and principals. They need to be made aware of how segregation and detention adversely affect children's creative mind. Schools need to be equally concerned about all children with regard to academic and non-academic activities. Schools, which are temples of learning, should not discriminate between the gifted and less gifted (Kaila, 2005).

All work, no play

'All work and no play for kids' is emphasized at play schools in Delhi (Times of India, 2005). The children are prepared for admission to nursery interviews. A series of these mock interviews are based on fixed curriculum for the kids below three years of age. Parents also go through the how-to-tackle-interviews drill. Principals and teachers are of the view that these play schools actually are doing more harm to children than any good.

Conclusion

The schools are heterogeneous in terms of management and standards of teaching-learning, student-teacher ratio, and the interaction between children, teachers, and parents. The scenario of schools put a challenge for offering child mental health and counselling services in terms of: access to school management for counselling; attitude towards counselling as a "service"; is it another financial burden or support for 'children and the school system.'

What Needs Attention? Teachers need to be educated for caring mental health of children. More hotlines, help lines are needed. State Govt. needs to put efforts on mental health education. It should conduct mental health surveys and make mental health education compulsory in schools. What is required is the collective vision on part of the mental health professionals. They need to create a collective vision on what the concerns of the young people are, and direct their efforts towards better understanding of those issues / concerns for making a healthier society.

According to Kaila (2005), children are searching for a baseline meaning for their life. They need an open environment in which they can express and experiment with their original and novel ideas. At present most schools and teachers are unable to tap and develop the creativity in children, which is in abundance in them. Informal and formal structures of the school do impact on the child's learning, creativity and the way they absorb values, which they will unconsciously use when they grow into adults.

Schools need to be democratized where children have the right to decide over matters that concern them in learning and education. The world needs democratic schools where children no longer suppress themselves but instead feel free to experience life the way they wish, and develop the natural potential they are endowed with and that suit their individual personality. Democratic schools offer a lot of opportunity for creativity and innovation in the school that the children enjoy.

Question for Readers

How are 'Mental Health' and 'Economic Health' of a country related?

2

Traumatic Experiences of Students in School

"The teacher was going on and I asked the teacher to give permission to me to go to toilet. He refused and told me to sit there. It was a very serious problem to me. So at the last moment of the period I ran away from the back door to the toilet". . A student.

"During my 11th standard when my exam was about to come I was really upset because that incident happened to be my worst experience. One girl from my class told me that she liked me and loved me but I did not listen much. But she used to come and tell those words almost everyday when I go for class. And she cried and told me that she was going to die if I didn't love her. I agreed to be in love with her. But after a month I found that she was just trying to do something so that I fail my exam. She informed me of the boys from her class that I was always after her. And 4 boys started searching for me and warned me, so I told them I didn't like her she had forced me to do this. But the guys came frequently. So I left for the home. As I was afraid that they would even kill me". . A student.

School bullying or victimization of children in schools is going on over the past many years, as it has remained unquestioned and unchallenged by any school or education authorities; the mental health effects of which are not yet clear to the teachers and principals. Here are the details of such a study.

The Purpose of Research

The general purpose of this study was to expand the current knowledge of students' victimization by both educators and peers, and to explore the nature and extent of PTSD caused by student victimization. THE STUDENT ALIENATION AND TRAUMA SURVEY (SATS) developed by Hyman Irwin. (1999b) was utilized to identify the nature and extent of traumatic events.

The specific research questions are as follows:

1. What types of traumatic events do students experience and how frequently do these events result in PTSD?
2. What is the relationship between school stressors and stress symptoms and how do patterns differ?
3. What percentage of the sample has reported symptoms of PTSD as a result of their worst experience in school?
4. Are there significant differences concerning the nature and extent of stress symptoms caused by educator victimization as compared to peer victimization?

School, college and university students were selected from Mumbai and around. A total of 966 students from nine educational institutions became sample of this study. Mainly the age bracket of students was 16 to 22 years.

Most students who participated in the research belonged to the family income bracket that was either considerably better off than most households or slightly better or about the same as most households. The students who participated in the study belonged to high school and college. The number of years of formal schooling completed by the study participants was mainly between 11 to 16. Out of 966 students, 33.6% of male students and 65.5% of female students participated in the study.

Instrument

This study utilized the *STUDENT ALIENATION AND TRAUMA*

SURVEY (SATS) in English, which is a two-part self-report survey developed by Dr. Irwin Hyman that measures students' worst experiences in school. Part 1 of the SATS, which is the focus of this research project, provides a list of 54 traumatic events that occur in schools such as bullying, physical assaults, and psychological abuse. It also includes an open-ended question where participants are asked to write about their worst school experience.

Part II presents a list of 105 stress symptoms. The SATS represents a revision of the earlier *MY WORST SCHOOL EXPERIENCE SCALE* (MWSES) to now address issues of peer victimization. The symptom checklist of the MWSES and the *MY WORST EXPERIENCE SCALE* (MWES), which is now incorporated into the SATS, is a psychometrically sound scale. It has been validated to aid in the assessment of PTSD for children and adolescents who have experienced a variety of stressors. These stressors range from maltreatment by caregivers and interpersonal assaults to natural disasters (Hyman, Snook, Berna, Ducette, & Kohr, 2002). Part II of the SATS is identical to Part II of the MWES and the MWSES and thus the psychometric properties of the symptom checklist are identical for each scale.

Statistical Analysis

Using SPSS, the descriptive statistics have been gathered on the types of traumatic stressors and types of victimization by adults and peers for frequency and duration.

TRAUMATIC EVENTS STUDENTS EXPERIENCE

We would like to learn more about bad things that happen to students in school. Many people have had at least one bad thing happen to them in school that involved an adult(s) or other student(s). This chapter tells us about your worst school experiences.

There are 58 such worst things that happened to male and female children and adolescents in school as described on the following pages:

1. I was teased ....

The 42% students were teased in schools a few times, whereas 35.4% said it did not happen to them. In the words of a student, "Once in my school one student who teased me a lot not behaved well with me. Taking my things like note books and something else and throw here and there. I gave a one or two warnings but he did not stop, so I was angry and had fight with him". Another student said, "I was teased in standard 6th. The boy teased me commenting on my body colour. He used to call me in different ways. This was my worst experience". The 45.9% of male students and 40.1% of female students were teased a few times.

2. I was yelled at ....

The 41.7% of male students and 36.1% of female students are yelled at a few times in school. A student stated her experience, "she was my class teacher. With nothing wrong in me she started yelling at me in front of the whole class". Another student said, "the teacher yelled at me really badly as I was only physically present in the class but my mind was somewhere else. It was my mistake but she had yelled at me very badly. For once, I felt like crying but I did not want to cry in front of my friends and embarrass myself afterwards". On an average 38% of students are yelled at in schools.

3. I was embarrassed ....

The 30.8% of male students and 30.1% of female students got embarrassed a few times in school, which means one out of every three students experience embarrassment in schools. A student quoted, "it was normal day at school in 9th standard. I was being late for 2-3 days. So on that day I was late again for the 4th time in a row. So my class teacher embarrassed me by saying that, 'you come from slum, you don't take bath, that's why your hair are so dry,' in front of whole class. I felt so bad; I didn't enter the class and went back home. So teacher sent two boys to bring me back and I finally attended the lecture, but was deeply embarrassed in front of whole class".

4. Someone threatened to do something bad to me or to someone I care about ....

The 8.5% of male students and 5.9% of female students said that a few times someone threatened them to do something bad to them or to someone they cared about in schools, whereas 17% of male students and 9% of female students said it did happen to them at least one time. In the words of a student, "When I was in 9th std, after finishing the drawing exams my friend handed me a bag and asked me to keep near the school office. Next day our class teacher threatened me very badly and also slapped me. Then I realized that my friend had put me in trouble by giving me the bag of our class teacher".

5. Other students were allowed to hit, push, or slap me .....

The 8.8% of male students and 3.7% of female students said that 'other students were allowed to hit, push, or slap me' at least one time. "When in 10th std one boy who was very jealous used to hit me in the class, and in the tuition class as well because he was also going to the same tuition class as I was"... a student.

6. I was given detention ....

The 10.2% of male students and 6.5% of female students were given detention a few times. "I was punished few times for no reasons or mistakes but because I didn't join tuition with my teacher in the 9th std. I was detained and forced to go for SSC privately or by correspondence"... a student.

7. I was suspended ....

The 7.2% of male students and 3.1% of female students were suspended one time in school. Two students expressed, "I was suspended from the class as I was in fight with friend during the lecture time". "I was suspended for 12 days because of my few friends. Although I had done nothing wrong but the teacher still punished me. I also tried to talk to the principal but it did not help".

8. I was expelled from school ....

A student said, "The principal of my school asked me to clean the classroom, which I had made dirty. I was also threatened that I will be expelled from the school. But I was not". The 2.2% of male students and 1.9% of female students expressed that they were expelled from school.

9. I was not allowed to be part of special subjects or activities ....

The 11.3% of male students and 8.3% of female students were not allowed to be part of special subjects or activities one time. A student said, "In 12th std I was not allowed to stand for the CR election. But I didn't let it affect me and set the aim to do in the next year CR election. And very next year I had chance to stand and I got elected".

10. I was not allowed to go to the bathroom ....

In the words of a student, "I wanted to go to the bathroom urgently but I was not allowed. I was upset as the teacher thought I was lying". The 11.3% of male students and 6.6% of female students were not allowed to go to the bathroom a few times.

11. Things like a book, eraser, or something else, were thrown at me ....

The 20.7% of male students and 11.5% of female students expressed that things like a book, eraser, or something else, were thrown at them a few times. A student said, "It was a very silly reason for which I was slapped. I was writing the notes being dictated in class when suddenly my partner just grabbed my notebook and threw it on other side. Afterwards I stood up and requested him whether I could take my book back and the whole class bursted out laughing. He thought I was trying to crack a joke in class and slapped me in front of everyone when I tried to justify myself by telling him the truth I was thrown out of class". Another student said, "It was my school day when I was in 9th std. we all were playing regularly in our P.T. period. In that game a person from the opposite team had thrown the ball on my face, which broke my specks. The purpose was only to hurt me not to winning the game. Because he felt jealous all the time. When my specks were broken than I broke his nose by giving a fight on his face. This created problem to me a lot. Our head of P.T. teacher took the action against me". *Chi-Square results reveal that significantly more number of boys experienced things like a book, eraser, or something else, being thrown at them than girls in schools.*

12. I was beaten up ....

A student said, "when I was in 10th standard my science teacher had beaten me a lot because I made a minor mistake in the answer paper and because of this, most of my marks were cut down, because of this experience I was afraid of my teacher. After beating teacher explained me how I wrote the paper. I felt that if she told me this before, I would have understood more". The 19.2% of male students and 13.1% of female students stated that they were beaten up a few times.

13. I was pinched or squeezed so hard that it hurt ....

A student said, "our miss pinched me so hard during the dictation, when she could not make out 'e' from my writing". Another student said, "Sir pinched me when I was not able to answer him well so he pinched me. It hurt me very badly and blood started to come out from it. I felt that if she told me this before, I would have understood better". The 17.8% of male students and 11.5% of female students stated that they were pinched or squeezed so hard a few times.

14. I was slapped ....

The 18.4% of male students and 6.3% of female students expressed that they were slapped a few times. A student said, "one of my friends slapped me during the class and in front of everyone for no reason whatsoever. I got angry but I controlled my anger. But after few days things were back to normal". Another student said, "When I was in 9th std I had also joined tuition class after the school. One day on my way to the class after the school, I took an apple and part of it stuck between my teeth as I was entering the class I was trying to remove that piece by my tongue and just at that time the teacher entered the class and she thought that I was making faces on her and she immediately slapped me. I could not understand what was my fault that she had to slap me hard and I will never forget her face for the rest of my life". *Chi-Square results reveal that significantly more number of boys than girls were slapped in schools.*

15. I was pushed ....

A student said, "When I was in school, someone pushed me into the muddy water and all my clothes got dirty. Then my friends started teasing me". Another student said, "We had the general practice of queuing while proceeding to the seminar hall, when I was pushed out of the line and I, kind of abused the person who did that. At that moment the vice-principal was present and I was penalized for the same. The student colleague who pushed me was left free while I was caught. The rest of the day I had to kneel down and had to get my parents signature on a note given by the vice-principal, which was unjust and embarrassing. The 25.4% of male students and 16.3% of female students articulated that they were pushed a few times. *Chi-Square results reveal that significantly more number of boys than girls were pushed in schools.*

16. I was grabbed very hard ....

The 7.9% of male students and 3.8% of female students articulated that they were grabbed very hard a few times. A students aid, "We were enjoying and doing 'masti' (having fun) and then they (other students) grabbed me, but it didn't bother me". In overall, 5.1% of students experienced being grabbed very hard a few times.

17. I was shaken ....

The 11.2% of male students and 11.5% of female students expressed that they were shaken a few times.

18. I had my ear or hair pulled ....

The 25.9% of male students and 11.8% of female students

had their ear or hair pulled up a few times. *Chi-Square results reveal that significantly more number of boys than girls experienced their ear or hair pulled up in school.* A student said, "I was studying in 10th std. When I was shouting and our teacher entered our class and I was called out of my place and teacher pulled my ear and hair very badly. This happened with me in front of whole class. And I was upset little because these types of cases happen with me few times. Another student said, "My worst experience was when I was in 9th std. and my class Miss pulled my hair and ear and took me to the principal's office in front of whole school that was only day in my life when I was upset.

19. I was hit with a ruler, paddle, or something else ....

A student said, "I was in standard 10th and my science journal was incomplete, so the Miss had put me and my friends out of the class. And at the same time our principal was on a round. He started inquiring about the matter and hit us". Another student said, "When in 6th std I had taken new admission in school, and no one talked with me. One girl teased me and showed me her shoe and hit me with it and I cried but no one helped or talked to me. Later on my mom spoke to teacher and everything is fine now". The 34.1% of male students and 18% of female students expressed that they were hit with a ruler, paddle, or something else a few times. *Chi-Square results reveal that significantly more number of boys than girls were hit in schools.*

20. I was chased ....

The 10.7% of male students and 8% of female students expressed that they were chased a few times. A student said, "A boy chased me from our school till my home, he was my classmate. I was so scared to inform my parents about it. But next day I made complain to our school principal about that boy and he was punished by the principal and stopped chasing me again".

21. I was picked last ....

A student said, "During the inter-school contest I was picked as a substitute to other student despite my good show in the studies. And I thought myself as a scholar so it hurt me that I was picked up as a substitute. This was the worst experience of my school days". Another student said, "I felt very hurt when I was picked last because the person who ignored me was supposed to be one of the close friends. Now, it so happened that a teacher came to our classroom and asked each one individually about our papers because it was our exam that day. But she completely ignored me, I felt very hurt as well as depressed because at that time my friend was also not speaking to me. This happened many times to me that whosoever became my close friends, they started taking me for granted and when I protested they stopped talking to me but I always could cope up with it within a month. But this time it took me 1 year". The 9.7% of male students and 7.8% of female students expressed that they were picked last a few times.

22. Other students stopped talking to me.............

The 8.1% of male students and 10.5% of female students expressed that other students stopped talking to them a few times. A student said, "My friends used to tease us about my friend and me by sexual comments. She was very much like my sister and they have a wrong impression about us. It really hurt us a lot and after sometimes we stopped talking to each other. That was really my biggest, worst experience I ever had". Another student said, "This happened to me when I was in 8th std. A friend of mine had linked me to a teacher, in classes, who was young. She was jealous of me, as the teacher was friendly to me and not to her. I think she liked him but she said all rubbish about me to other friends and everybody stopped talking to me and I was completely taken aback when I heard this".

23. Someone got others to not like me.............

The 12.1% of male students and 9.5% of female students expressed that someone got others to not like me a few times. A student said, "One of my best friend stopped talking with me. I felt very bad when she did that she always has to ignore me. When I asked her the reason. She refused to explain, it to me. I was totally upset on that day. From that day onwards I have decided no to make best friends. After few days I came to know that she did not like me, because she had joined some other group".

24. I was tripped..............

A student said, "I was tripped and my knee was dislocated, and when I asked principal to let me go home, he didn't allow me and also denied visiting the doctor". The 13.2% of male students and 6% of female students stated that they were tripped a few times in school. *Chi-Square results reveal that significantly more number of boys were tripped than girls in schools.*

25. Someone talked about sex and I didn't like it ....

A student said, "the worst experience was the one, which related to a friend talking to me about sex. At that juncture, I was focused on my studies and during the spare time occupied in sports. The untimely conversation disturbed me greatly". The 17.0% students in school experienced one time that someone talked about sex and they didn't like it. The 10.4% students experienced the same a few times.

26. Someone lied about me and I got into trouble ....

The 25.5% students in school experienced one time that someone lied about them and they got into trouble. The 16.7% students experienced the same a few times. A student said, "The worst experience came about when I was fairly matured and in the 9th std. A friend lied about me and made up a story of how a bad and characterless girl I was. It made me feel extremely ashamed of myself for no fault of mine. My parents were also shocked as I studied in a girl's convent, didn't attend any other classes beside the ones in school. Didn't go out too often except with my female friends! This upset them to a great extent as they had complete trust in me and they continue to have till today. It made me angry and embarrassed only because of the tension in the family and I had to work really hard to gain back the faith and trust of my parents".

27. No one helped me when I asked for help ....

The 11.5% students in school experienced a few times that no one helped them when they asked for help. Significantly more number of girls (12.5%) than the boys (9.7%) experienced so a few times. A student said, "When I was in 4th standard till then no one was helping me like my school friend. Whenever I asked him to teach me Math then no one was helping me because that time I was not in a position to go to tuition".

28. I was made to stay alone, away from everybody ....

A student said, "I was traveling by bus at the age of 15 years. I was sitting alone on the last seat of the bus, and the bus conductor came and sat next to me and then it happened. I got scared at that point of time for a couple of days. But now I laugh at it every time I remember it". Another student said, "I was beaten badly for my bad handwritings. I was punished to write a full chapter in good handwriting after the school and left alone with peons. I had cried a lot for this unfair punishment given to me. My father was waiting downstairs for me and he came upstairs after all the students were gone and he took me home". The 5.7% students experienced that they were made to stay alone, away from everybody a few times.

29. Sexual comments were made about me ....

The 5.2% students in school experienced that sexual comments were made about them a few times. A student said, "Someone wrote sexual comments to me on notes and I felt really embarrassed and did not tell anyone about it and forget the whole thing in few days".

30. I was touched sexually ....

A student said, "One of my uncle's friends who becomes my uncle, used to try to have a sexual touch with me". Another student said, "A senior student sexually touched me during the brake in the extra lecture. I felt little bit upset and different at that time but I didn't react to it, as I did not know anything about sex. I did not come to know what he was doing and was it right or wrong. But later when I passed 12th std and came in Degree College and heard about sex I remembered this incident and then felt guilty about it". The 5.6% students experienced sexual touch one time in the school. The 3.4% students stated that they were touched sexually a few times.

31. I saw something really bad happen ....

The 18.1% students one time saw something really bad happening and the 12.5% students experienced the same a few times. A student said, "I saw something bad happened to someone and I feel bad when I see poor people sitting in-group and smoking. Chi-Square reveals that significantly more number of boys (15.8%) than the girls (10.6%) saw something really bad happening a few times.

32. I was punched.............

The 7.8% students were punched in school one time. The 3.2% students experienced the same a few times. Chi-Square test reveals that significantly more number of boys (14.5%) than the girls (4.4%) were punched in school one time.

33. I was forced to have sex ....

The 1.9% students were forced to have sex one time and the 1.3% students experienced the same a few times. A student said, "My worst experience was that I was sexually harassed first when I was in Sr. KG. This occurred in the school. The person tried to catch my hand. Touched on the parts, forced me remove my clothes. The same incident also occurred when I was kept at baby sitter. It was her son who was a quiet boy above 20 yrs. He forced me remove my clothes and thus harassed me forcibly when there was no one at home.

34. I was locked in a closet or small room ....

The 5.5% students (one out of twenty) were locked in school one time in a closet or small room. More boys (6.9%) than the girls (4.7%) experienced so one time.

35. I was tied up ....

The 4.0% students experienced being tied up one time in school. The 2.0% students experienced the same a few times. It occurred to more boys (6.5%) than the girls (2.7%) one time.

36. I was strip-searched ....

The 4.1% students in school were strip-searched one time and the 2.0% students experienced the same a few times.

37. Someone stole something from me ....

The 22.0% students reported that someone stole something from them one time. It occurred to more boys (27.1%) than the girls (17.9%) a few times. The 21.1% students experienced the same a few times. A student said, "Someone stole my computer project and then did not permit me to do it again. So vice-principal asked me to do some another project.

38. I was left out ....

A student said, "I was hoping to be selected for the school cricket team but it turned out to be a bad show where good players were not selected and left. Another student said, "I was teased and usually left out in group activities because of the way I looked. The 14.3% students in school experienced one time that they were left out. The 9.6% students experienced the same a few times.

39. Someone made fun of my clothes ....

The 11.9% students in school experienced one time that someone made fun of their clothes. The 10.8% students experienced the same a few times. It occurred to more boys (14.0%) than the girls (9.0%) a few times. A student said, "Once my friends and I were going for a movie. All were dressed by their own way. Even I was dressed well. But I was told that you look funny. Even in the party we were told to wear a party dress. I did not have a good dress. I had worn a simple suit; again my friends teased me, made fun of me. I felt very bad and hurt.

40. Someone made up a story about me ....

A student said, "My worst experience was during my school time. This happened when I was in 8th std. somebody made story out of me, that I am not an obedient student. He was scholar, all rounder of my school so each and every teacher used to favour him. At that time I got very upset. This was a time when our projects were going. At that time I was asked to prepare a diagram, which was to be submitted after 2 days. But that boy told teacher that she would not be able to prepare or she is not that much intelligent to make a circuit or diagram. But as time flew, my sincerity proved my talents. This experience happened, when I was newly admitted in my school". The 17.7% students experienced one time that someone made up a story about them. The 9.8% students experienced the same a few times. Chi-Square test reveals that it occurred significantly to more boys (13.7%) than the girls (7.6%) a few times.

41. I wanted to be friends with someone who did not want to be friends with me ....

The 14.8% students in school experienced one time that they wanted to be friends with someone who did not want to be friends with them. Significantly more boys (17.4%) than the girls (13.2%) experienced the same one time.

42. Someone took out a gun, knife or other weapon ....

A student said, "This boy in school, who had fallen into bad company, took out a knife and threatened the teacher who was reprimanding him". The 8.1% of boys and 2.4% of girls experienced one time that someone took out a gun, knife or other weapon. Chi-Square test reveals that significantly more boys than the girls experienced it.

43. I saw someone get badly hurt or killed ....

The 21.7% of boys and 19.4% of girls in school experienced one time to have seen someone get badly hurt or killed. A student said, "I was coming home from school at nearly 6 p.m. A driver came and just poke a knife in the stomach of a person. The road was empty there were few people it was a winter evening so it was becoming night. I was so afraid after the incidence that at that night I had no eating anything and I did not sleep but as the day gone by I forgot it. But till it is my worst experience because it hurt my heart".

44. I was hurt so badly that I had to go to the hospital ....

A student said, "I was hit by one person. I was hurt so badly that I had to go to the hospital". Another student said, "We were crossing the lane when one girl suddenly pushed me and the car coming from behind hurt me for which I was hospitalized. The 12.2% of boys and 6.6% of girls experienced one time that they were hurt so badly that they had to go to the hospital. Chi-Square test reveals that significantly more boys than the girls experienced it.

45. Someone picked on me on my way to or from school ...

The 5.0% of boys and 2.8% of girls in school reported that someone picked on them on the way to or from school a few times.

46. Someone said bad things about my mother or family...

A student said, "My worst experience was in standard 7th when I was been beaten by my best friends because of just not having his Tiffin, because I didn't like his breakfast, then those friends didn't use to talk to me and when one day I was going home they beat me, punched me and gave bad words about my family and I had also beaten them and gave the same bad words to their family and them. After Diwali vacation they came to me and said me to do friendship again, but I did little friendship with them". The 11.7% students in school experienced one time that someone said bad things about their mother or family. The 7.4% students experienced the same a few times. Chi-Square test reveals that significantly more boys than the girls experienced it.

47. Someone made me do something I did not want to do ...

The 12.7% students in school experienced one time that

someone made them do something they did not want to do. The 9.8% students experienced the same a few times.

48. Someone would not let me play or be with my friends ....

A student said, "My worst experience is when I was not let me play with my friends. I was not allowed to go from home and play out with my friends. I felt very bad, and cried in the heart". The 7.6% students in school reported to have experienced one time that someone would not let them play or be with their friends. The 7.5% students experienced the same a few times.

49. Someone made me miss class or school ....

The 9.0% students in school experienced one time that someone made me miss class or school. The 9.7% students experienced the same a few times. Chi-Square test reveals that significantly more boys (12.7%) than the girls (8.1%) experienced to have missed their class or school a few times.

50. Someone messed up my clothes on purpose ....

A student said, "Someone messed up my clothes during the holi". The 7.3% students in school experienced one time that someone messed up their clothes on purpose". The 4.0% students reported the same a few times. Significantly more boys (11.5%) than the girls (5.2%) experienced to have messed up their clothes one time.

51. Someone killed him or herself ....

The 5.4% students reported to have experienced one time that someone killed him or herself. A student said, "One person was killed during the time of riots because he was Hindu".

52. I saw someone be threatened with a gun, knife, or other weapon ....

A student said, "Once when I was writing my paper during my 9th standard I commented a boy on his sheer size just because I did not like his behavior (actually). So after my paper was over this boy came out and slapped me in face for teasing him mainly because I did not even know him or his name. Ever since that day whenever he saw me he threatened me either by picking me or by some violent actions". The 10.2% of boys and 5.0% of girls saw someone be threatened with a gun, knife, or other weapon one time. Chi-Square test reveals that significantly more boys than the girls experienced this.

53. Someone said there was bomb in the school and we had to leave ....

The 16.9% of students experienced one time that someone said there was bomb in the school and they had to leave. The 2.0% students experienced the same a few times. A student said, "In my school, when I am in 8th std. our mathematics teacher was taking a lecture and she was teaching about math to us. And then one peon entered the class and told teacher there was a bomb in the school. And I was very scared about the bomb and I was crying and all other children also started crying. This is my worst experience in my life; after this experience I wanted to live very lonely and I didn't want to talk with my friend and parents".

54. I was given a punishment that was not fair ....

A student said, "The worst experience in school was when I was punished for no fault of mine. Other girls were shouting and misbehaving in the class and when teacher came, they gave my name and she shouted at me and wrote a note to my parents and teacher asked me a question to be answered as a punishment. After sometime they started to tease, and harass me in the class". Another student said, "In 10th std I had an awful dictator as a principal who drove away very good and experienced teachers with whom we also had emotional attachment. We were given punishments that were not fair like our prefect's day was about to be cancelled. Due to that principal I still have a slight bad patch in my memory about school life. The 28.0% of boys and 15.1% of girls experienced a few times that they were given a punishment that was not fair. Chi-Square test reveals that significantly more boys than the girls experienced this.

55. I was in a fight ....

A student said, "The worst experience I faced was when I was slapped by my school sir as he was frustrated and of no fault of mine. It was a free lecture and I was talking and laughing with my friends and sir slapped me. It was horrible first ever slap on my cheeks. And in another incident I was involved in a fight with a friend when she talked all nonsense and made me cry in 9th std". Another student said, "We were studying in the hall and there was a fight between us and she went and told my name to teacher. Teacher came out of the room and slapped me and she did not listen to what I was saying and listen to her only. The 19.6% students in school experienced one time that they were in a fight. The 19.0% students experienced the same a few times. Chi-Square test reveals that significantly more boys (26.1%) than the girls (15.4%) experienced a fight a few times.

56. Someone made fun of me because of my race ....

A student said, "I was teased by a group of boys just for fun and enjoyment but it hurt me a lot. They used to treat me as untouchables in the classroom. In class and out of school they used to tease me 'Bakri' (Mea Mea). When the teacher used to give our notebooks back to us after checking, it used to go around whole class and then come to me". Another student said, "I was badly teased everyday by my classmates, friends and my subject teacher. Whenever I entered the class they all would laugh and make comments about my simple and honest nature. They used to think I was a fool and they also made fun about my parents by saying the son is a fool what about his parents, how much fool they must be". The 6.4% students experienced one time that someone made fun of them because of their race. The 5.9% students experienced the same a few times. Chi-Square test reveals that significantly more boys (9.0%) than the girls (4.1%) experienced this a few times.

57. I got in trouble for something I did ....

The 18.5% students in school experienced one time that got in trouble for something they did. The 19.5% students experienced the same a few times. A student said, "I had got fewer marks in my exams in the 10th std. My coaching sir used to trouble me very much". Chi-Square test reveals that significantly more boys (26.1%) than the girls (16.1%) got in trouble for something they did a few times.

Though the students experienced more than one stressor one time or a few times in school. The 966 students were asked to select one of the above 57 sources of victimization that best described their very worst experience in school. These are as follows:

VERY WORST EXPERIENCE IN SCHOOL

Sr. no. (as per tables above)	Frequency	Percent
1. I was teased.	166	17.2
2. I was yelled at.	95	9.8
3. I was embarrassed.	69	7.1
4. Someone threatened to do something bad to me or to someone I care about.	23	2.4
5. Other students were allowed to hit, push, or slap me.	2	.2
6. I was given detention.	8	.8
7. I was suspended.	12	1.2
8. I was expelled from school.	1	.1
9. I was not allowed to be part of special subjects or activities.	18	1.9
10. I was not allowed to go to the bathroom.	7	.7
11. Things like a book, eraser, or something else, were thrown at me.	8	.8
12. I was beaten up.	26	2.7
13. I was pinched or squeezed so hard that it hurt.	7	.7
14. I was slapped.	47	4.9
15. I was pushed.	11	1.1
16. I was grabbed very hard.	3	.3
17. I was shaken.	9	.9

18. I had my ear or hair pulled.	13	1.3
19. I was hit with a ruler, paddle, or something else.	19	2.0
20. I was chased.	11	1.1
21. I was picked last.	7	.7
22. Other students stopped talking to me.	11	1.1
23. Someone got others to not like me.	11	1.1
24. I was tripped.	10	1.0
25. Someone talked about sex and I didn't like it.	20	2.1
26. Someone lied about me and I got into trouble.	28	2.9
27. No one helped me when I asked for help.	14	1.4
28. I was made to stay alone, away from everybody.	6	.6
29. Sexual comments were made about me.	7	.7
30. I was touched sexually.	9	.9
31. I saw something really bad happen.	14	1.4
32. I was punched.	3	.3
33. I was forced to have sex.	2	.2
34. I was locked in a closet or small room.	1	.1
35. I was tied up.	2	.2
36. I was strip-searched.	3	.3
37. Someone stole something from me	17	1.8
38. I was left out.	10	1.0
39. Someone made fun of my clothes.	9	.9
40. Someone made up a story about me.	13	1.3
41. I wanted to be friends with someone who did not want to be friends with me.	17	1.8
42. Someone took out a gun, knife or other weapon.	2	.2
43. I saw someone get badly hurt or killed.	9	.9
44. I was hurt so badly that I had to go to the hospital.	10	1.0
45. Someone picked on me on my way to or from school.	3	.3

46. Someone said bad things about my mother or family.	9	.9
47. Someone made me do something I did not want to do.	9	.9
48. Someone would not let me play or be with my friends.	8	.8
49. Someone made me miss class or school.	5	.5
50. Someone messed up my clothes on purpose.	5	.5
51. Someone killed him or herself.	1	.1
52. I saw someone be threatened with a gun, knife, or other weapon.	3	.3
53. Someone said there was bomb in the school and we had to leave.	4	.4
54. I was given a punishment that was not fair.	59	6.1
55. I was in a fight.	27	2.8
56. Someone made fun of me because of my race.	1	.1
57. I got in trouble for something I did	28	2.9
58. others such as Emotional Harassment, Hurt by a prank etc	4	.4
Total	**956**	**99.0**
Missing	**10**	**1.00**
Total	**966**	**100.0**

Conclusion

Teachers victimize students in order to discipline their classroom, as they don't know better ways of managing the classroom. Teachers are not aware as to how they harm emotional health of children. Peers bully their friends as they seek fun and thrill, they are not aware as to how they are affecting their friends emotionally.

In schools, male students receive physical victimization (such as slapped, pushed, and shaken) significantly more than the girls.

Largely in the Indian scenario, teachers don't let children

speak out in the classroom. In the Indian society, democracy is not practiced in families or in schools. Children become the victim in such situations. The school principals are not aware of the magnitude of children being victimized in school premises and the effects of victimization on children.

Victimization of children is a crime; it needs to be curbed. Schools, and also families, need to be democratised where the children have the rights to decide over matters that concern them in learning and education. The children need democratic schools where they no longer suppress themselves but instead feel free to experience life the way they wish, and develop their natural potentials they are endowed with.

Ask any child or adult (regardless of their background), she / he would tell us as to how she / he was victimized or bullied by their teachers or peers while in school. This indicates that victimization has been there for decades and it has gone unexamined and unquestioned. If we can check and stop it, we can certainly improve the mental health of our growing-up children in our society. The above data clearly reveal how our children have been exposed to maltreatment in school. The policy makers need to take note of this phenomenon and take necessary action.

Some teachers have continued punishing or harassing children over the years, even to an extent that a father said, "this teacher has not changed, she used to ask me to stand on the bench, and now she is asking my son to do the same, isn't it disgusting".

The major factor that triggered such misbehaviors of teachers was that they were not equipped or trained with knowledge or wisdom on how to manage the class without affecting an emotional health of children. Peer education has a critical role to play in order to stop teasing or harassment among students, which has mental health implications.

Victimization in school is brewing unhealthy children and giving way to an ill society. We need to expose teachers and students to these situations as narrated above, and ask them, had they gone through such situations while in school and how did they feel? We need to also ask them what would they do or how would they intervene to correct these situations in school for creating an emotional health of children a value and concern in educational institutions.

Some positive experiences of students need to be reinforced. Beside victimization, two students expressed positive notes as follows: "I was not giving due attention to the study, so during the month of November, teacher advised me to study hard not for you but also for your parents. I did try my best and passed with good marks and I felt proud for my teacher". Another student said, "There was a boy in my class, who lied that I've an affair with him. It made me little upset, but after talking to my class teacher, I felt relaxed". Only one student out of 966 students categorically wrote, "I have good experience in school and my school is very good".

Sometimes students may also victimize teachers; as one student said, "one of my favorite teacher was made to cry just because of some of the senior students were taunting her for the way she looks.... And she literally cried for that. Hence there is need for 'total mental health programme in school system'. Teacher's mental health is equally important so that they can adequately take care of students.

This 'victimization' is in the attitudes and behaviors of teachers, peers and the school system. This scenario and situation are not going to change until we take informed steps to correct these attitudes and behaviors. The schools need to invest on teachers to upgrade their mental software to deal effectively with the emotional health concerns of children. And it may take a few years to achieve a change in this direction for improved mental health of children. We definitely need healthy minds for better economies of our nations.

Question for Readers

How are Victimization in School and Crime in Society related?

3

Educational Culture in Urban Cities

The marks-oriented educational culture in urban cities has really induced high anxieties and stress among students and parents. The merit issue has particularly bothered schools and colleges. In the globalising world, the students tend to be both confused as well as focused; the first lot who is confused because the avenues to choose for further studies are too many; and the other lot who is focused because they are highly ambitious and achievement-motivated.

This chapter is an attempt to understanding concerns and problems of our student community in the present educational scenario and suggesting ways to strengthen them through school and college programmes with a view to provide them healthy adulthood.

The Context

The students from small cities are migrating into big cities for higher studies. Private institutions and coaching classes have mushroomed in a big way. The school and college students have learned skills of Xeroxing study notes and how to look good and smart. The marks-competition has settled in resulting in increased stress among students. The anxieties for educational and career issues have mounted. Parental stress has remarkably gone up. Schools, colleges, and teachers are being examined under the microscope. The preference for accredited colleges is a major concern for students. There is not a single day when the media won't reflect issues concerning students. The institutions though have updated in technology and infrastructure, are still lagging behind in providing life skills and value education to their students. In a way, the entire process of education seems to be under transition.

It is realized that the schools make children sick, unhappy, hyperactive, and failing individuals. How to convince schools that are failing children to accept and work constructively with those children? The schools are behaving the way system desires, not as per needs of the children. Classrooms are killing creativity in children. How to stop teachers pathologizing kids? How to change the educational system?

It takes a 'movement' to change the system. Pressure to change the system has to come from all sides. A struggle to change the educational scenario is on in all the countries. And also in order to make a change, some independent initiative must be started. Another view is that we should be working more with the parents than the system.

The children are searching for baseline meaning for their life. It is observed that the children in schools do not have opportunity to share deep issues in their heart. A study in U.S. found a negative correlation between the size of the school and the adverse outcome behaviors of the children. Bigger the schools, the children tend to loose personalization. But the findings of a Ph.D. thesis in Mumbai negate the possibility of size of the school influencing the curriculum and students. It shows that the big and small school concepts, geography, or locale of the school, qualifications of the principals, teachers, or parents do not influence the performance level of the children.

How effective is our system of education?

A group of one hundred experienced teachers reported:

- 19% very effective

- 37% Needs lots of improvement
- 44% do not know what to comment

These responses clearly indicate that our system of education needs a great deal of improvement.

Worst negatives in school education

We need to understand the nature of negatives that continue in our school education and hamper the effectiveness of the very objectives of education and learning in schools. Some of these problems are mentioned below:

- Academics are viewed as more important than anything else
- Child is caught in between like a ball thrown back and forth
- Faulty examination system
- Indifference of parents and lack of teachers involvement
- Lack of a counselor whom the parents and children can talk to
- Lack of knowledge on developmental issues and theories on part of teachers.
- Lack of laboratory/audio-visual equipment
- Lack of qualified people in the system
- Lack of resources for special children
- Large numbers in classrooms
- More memory oriented, stress on rote learning
- Multiple sharing of blame between parents and teachers.
- No leisure time for students or teachers
- No respect for individuality
- Parental pressures to perform
- Parental stress
- Physical and sexual abuse of children
- Rigid and restricted school life
- Teachers burdened with large syllabus
- Teacher-student relationship is non-existent.

Since counselling takes place amidst these negativities in school, the counselor must be aware of these dynamics and prepare counselling approach and plan accordingly in order to make the effects of counselling.

Anxieties of Adolescents

A recent study of 314 girls and 93 boys between 16 to 19 years of age conducted at the University Department of Psychology at SNDT Women's University in Mumbai has shown the following trend.

Besides educational and vocational anxieties being faced by every second adolescent; the emotional problems examined are the low self-esteem, anger, and disturbing sex thoughts being experienced by every sixth adolescent.

The study broadly included the psychological and social concerns of the teenagers such as educational, vocational, life satisfaction, health, self-esteem, and anxiety.

- Educational/Study Anxiety: 49.4% of female adolescents as against 36.6% of males have perceived anxiety related to their studies in school/Junior college. One of the major anxieties of the adolescents lies in anticipating if they don't score well in the present studies, they won't get admission to the desired courses in future. The educational anxiety is rising among the teenagers due to increased competition for entry into any professional colleges.
- Vocational Ambiguity: 48.4% of male teenagers as against 40.4% of their female counterparts are bothered by lack of vocational directions. The lack of guidance and career vision drives the adolescents more anxious and confused as to what they should be heading for in coherence with their aptitudes, interests, and personality.
- Support from Parents, Teachers, Peers: 66.6% of female adolescents vis-à-vis 73.1% of males perceived social support from parents, teachers and peers. The increased awareness among parents and teachers about the future pursuits of young people helps the adolescent boys and girls.

- General Life Satisfaction: Only 38.9% of girl students are against 58.1% of boys found themselves satisfied in life. Generally the lack of direction into the future, the powered self-esteem would affect the perception of adolescent towards their life satisfaction.
- Self Esteem: 11.5% (nearly one out of every ten) of girls in comparison to only 3.5% of boys were troubled due to low sense of self-esteem. The positive and negative feedback by the parents, teachers, peers would determine the level of self-esteem among the children.
- Problems with Anger: 23.9% of female students as against 19.4% of boys had problem with managing their own anger. 20.4% of girls and 21.5% of boys stated problem of disturbing thoughts. The adolescents need to be made aware of the emotional ups and downs in their life and how they can effectively manage their anger.
- Sex thoughts: 14% of boys as against 8% of girls had trouble with sex thoughts. Whereas equal number i.e. 8.6% of the both sexes perceived pre-marital stress. Understanding the facts of child sex abuse and sex crimes in our society, the education about sexuality issues needs to be integrated into the school curriculum.
- Health: 12.9% of boys and 7% of girls expressed problems related to their general health. The health education, sports, exercise need to a regular feature of the school and college life.

The above mentioned study revealed that the adolescents in schools/junior colleges suffered from high anxiety related to their studies and lack of vocational directions and guidance. They also showed concerns related to self development such as dealing with own anger, and low self esteem.

However, in order to deal with these anxieties and stresses, the adolescents in Mumbai received support from their parents, teachers and peers. At the same time, parents emphasized heavily on self-discipline, character building, academic performance, and vocational preparation of the adolescents.

Victimization of Children

Many school children are exposed to traumatic experiences in school, which affect their psychological well being. Recently, researchers and child advocates have recognized the Post Traumatic Stress Disorder (PTSD) developing from traumatic experiences in children's daily lives, including that of school. Common traumatic events, such as spanking and verbal maltreatment by teachers and peers can cause many children to develop stress symptoms and some children to develop PTSD. One out of every five students (20%) has faced these problems in schools.

Research indicates that when the school climate fosters victimization, students may become alienated to the school as an institution and to particular individuals, including peers and educators. Peer victimization, frequently ignored and trivialized by teachers and parents alike, is another source of trauma that students experience daily in schools.

Greatest sources of student victimization came from teachers and peers at school. Many worst things that happen to students in school included the following:

- I was asked to write a lesson 50 times
- I was caned by the class teacher
- I was embarrassed
- I was expelled from school......
- I was made to stand on a bench in the class for 45 minutes
- I was teased......
- I was yelled at ......
- My hair were cut
- Other students stopped talking to me......
- Someone made me miss class or school......

How do the children feel after the one worst school experience?

- I got bad grades in school......
- I got very angry for no reason......

- I got very nervous about things......
- I hated going to school......
- I lost my appetite......
- I stopped eating......
- I thought I was not as good a kid as I used to be..
- I was more tired that I used to be ......
- I was not as happy as I used to be ......
- It was harder to make myself do things ......

The counseling centre in schools needs to identify the sources of victimization on children and take adequate measures to prevent the same.

Segregation and detention in schools

Segregation is something when children are divided in different divisions on the basis of their marks. All the high scoring and bright children are put in one class and poor or low performing students are placed in another division. This normally happens in schools when they wish to concentrate more on bright students and achieve 100 percent results in 10th standard board examination. As a result, the schools start detaining or failing underachievers in lower classes such as 8th or 9th standards. Some schools go to the extent of expelling poor performers out of the school. Segregation and detention practices are educational crimes that go on presently in schools.

Segregation and detention lead to inequality, discrimination, prejudice, and bitterness in students and parents. Most of the times, the students and parents feel helpless and don't know how to react to this agony. Segregation is like introducing caste system in schools.

We need to ask schools whether they want bitterness or betterness in children.

How do teachers behave when the bright and average students are segregated in schools?

- They pamper bright students and at the same time they

make average students feel low.

- They call bright students as scholars when they call average students as dull, duffer and nuts.
- They pay more attention to bright students whereas they don't bother about average students.
- They mark bright students high and average students low in their tests and exams.
- They don't talk properly to with average students.
- The teachers become partial and prejudiced towards poorly performing students.
- They become selective in choosing children for extracurricular activities.
- The teachers make average students feel that they are lesser in some ways.
- The teachers aren't aware to what an extent child feels bad due to their discriminating and negative behaviors.
- The teachers also get segregated in the school. The bright teachers teach bright students and average teachers teach low performing students.

How do children feel and behave when they are Segregated?

- The bright and average children also start segregating among themselves.
- The bright students feel happy, they don't make friends with average students, and they look down upon average students.
- The average students feel low, depressed and lack interest in studies.
- The average students lack confidence and feel mediocre.
- The average students feel anger and hate towards discriminating teachers.

Segregation and detention are the ills in schools, the mental health effects of which are not known to the teachers and principals. They need to be made aware about how segregation and detention adversely affect children and parents. The schools need to be equally concerned to all children with regard to academic and non-academic activities. The schools, which are the temples of learning, can't discriminate between the bright and average children.

Parents' Attitudes

A research study on young people and their families indicated that both mothers and fathers emphasize learning self-discipline, building character, academic performance. As the children grow adolescents, they are concerned about vocational choice, staying out late, untidiness, too much television, neglecting chores, health etc. Sources of conflicts between both parents, sons and daughters are in the areas of smoking, alcohol, drugs, disregard for law, religion etc. The mothers and fathers stress personal qualities and conduct, which are valued in societies confidant of future economic growth and opportunity.

Every second parent is quietly bothered about her/ his child's studies, examinations, their friends, career choice, emotional development. There is an increased emphasis by parents on self-discipline, character building, academic performance, and vocational preparations of the adolescents. As a result, they are quite tense. Parents need to react with a lot of sensitivity and understanding of their children's interests, potentials and personality. They should not react according to their whims and fancies.

Attitudes and behaviors of parents towards children may affect adversely if they are always nagging, expecting a lot especially when some subject disinterests her. Parents need to be friendly, soft, supportive, understanding, loving and caring if they want children to care for their academic interests.

Needs of Counselors

Nearly 93 counselors practicing in different areas of counselling were contacted in the city of Mumbai during a research study. They were asked to indicate their needs of counselling in order to identify the areas for their further training.

These areas/problems/issues are reflected as follows:

- Clinical (Anxiety, Depression, Epilepsy, Conduct disorder, Personality disorders, Autism, ADHD, Drug addiction, Phobias, Mental retardation, OCD, Sexual abuse, AIDS issues);
- Family and Social (Parental counseling, Single parent counseling, Sibling rivalry, Marital discord, Divorce);
- School Children (Peer relations, Vocational guidance and counseling, Academic Stress, Educational backwardness, Study habits, Memory, Concentration, Interest, Personal problems of students, Dyslexia);
- Others (Self-reflection, Conflicts with superiors and colleagues, Personality workshops, Feng-shui, Acupressure, Reiki, Counseling with the elderly). The counselors need to update themselves in order to improve their skills in different areas for serving the students in a better manner.

Students Failing in SSC

Every year after the SSC (10th std.) results are declared, there are several suicide cases. It needs a strong introspection and analysis on part of school principals, teachers, counselors, and importantly parents.

Why students think to take their life as they fail?

- They think that one year has been lost.
- They think that they will lose face in front of friends, parents and teachers.
- They feel that they do not have any career or future ahead.

The students need to keep in mind a few things:

- They have to support themselves on their own at the very first place.
- If they are very emotionally upset, they need to talk to their friends and parents openly.
- They should avoid being alone.

- They need to understand that one year is not the end of life, instead it is better to live many years ahead.
- God has blessed every one with a blend of abilities, interests, and personality suitable for some occupations.
- If she/he is extremely disturbed, must call up a counsellor, psychologist or psychiatrist.

The parents need to keep in mind the following:

- The students who fail are very sensitive.
- Parents must be emotionally supportive.
- They should not criticize, shout or punish the young children.
- They must ensure the children repeatedly that one year is not the end of life. Let us live life, not finish it.

The schools need to observe that the students who fail are given an opportunity for interaction with the counselor.

Admission Anxiety after 10th Standard

Marks are the killer and taking lives of young students. Admission anxiety is dangerous. Every year suicides among the teenagers are happening as soon as the SSC results are notified. Fear of not getting admission in the college and thinking that the future ahead is dark drive the student to think of attempting suicide.

Thousands of students do not get admission into their desired stream of arts, commerce, engineering, or science due to limited number of seats in the colleges. In fact the students do not know which of these fields they are really and objectively suitable for. Inherently every student has a blend of strong aptitudes, interests and personality, which makes them suitable for certain careers.

Why to Consider One's Aptitudes, Interests and Personality, and Not the Marks:

Why not to consider marks:

- Marks are not an indicator of one's abilities.
- Marks are based on memory tests.

- It depresses the students when they don't get college admission.
- Marks only indicate academic proficiency.
- Considering college admission only on the basis of marks is doing injustice to the student's natural capabilities.
- Seats are limited and the large numbers of students do not get admission on the basis of their marks.

Why to Consider Aptitudes:

An aptitude is an inherent psychological property of an individual to learn some trade. Every student has a set of these capabilities to learn that will predispose him/her for becoming suitable for certain careers. Similarly every student has the naturally strong interest areas and predominant personality characteristics. In case the students are considered for admission on the basis of one's Aptitudes, Interests and Personality, they are distributed to a variety of professionals and vocational courses and colleges that does not really create admission hassles and chaos among the parents, students or college authorities. It is a must for every student to get his/her aptitudes, interests, and personality assessed by a vocational counselor.

Reactions to SSC/HSC results

At the time of SSC/HSC results, there is a lot of hue and cry amongst the students and their parents, and its fall out continues till the students have settled in their admissions. As it is said, SSC/HSC is a crossroad, which shows many roads. At this stage, parents should react with a lot of sensitivity and understanding of their children's interests, potentials and personality. They should not merely react according to their whims and fancies.

In case, the students have not achieved as per the expectations of their parents, both parents and children should join hands to face the situation boldly. Parents should not become emotional and punish or scold their children. Mind it, at this time, students who could not score well, are really very sensitive about their future. They need parents who could support them to make them understand what they can do. What they are capable for?

Students need to react with a great boldness and face their results with reality and courage. They should instead call upon their friends and help those who are in need. At this stage, parents and students must take help of vocational counselors and institutions that provide vocational guidance. There are always new ways and alternatives, in case you don't feel exhausted in looking ahead. At this time, parents and students should strive to seek help from their relatives, teachers, friends, neighbors, and professionals. Seeking help is a positive behavior of human beings.

Some boys and girls feel very nervous. On the other hand, certain students feel bold but their parents react with extreme anxiety about their children's future. At this time both need to support each other attitudinally and behaviorally, and go ahead.

Some students feel fussy about seeking admission to particular colleges that are not so popular. If one does not get admission in the college of your liking, she/he must be open to look for alternatives. In fact, it depends maximum on the student's hard work and commitment to shine after entering into any college. Some colleges are lucky that they get such students. Future is bright if one can visualize alternatives according to interests, personality and abilities, not the marks alone. This is the time not to over-react, but simply focus on strengths boldly and smilingly and take action.

Social Development of Young People

The social development of young people needs extra efforts on part of the Schools/Colleges. The Programmes that need constant emphasis are:

- Academic support activities e.g. additional inputs in studies/subjects perceived difficult, in order to deal with their high educational anxiety, pressure to get more marks and examination stress.

- Sharpening vocational vision and understanding through individual aptitude assessment and guidance/counselling.
- Self-development programmes specifically life skills and coping strategies, including low self-esteem, dealing with own anger and sexuality.

The Social Development Programme (SDP) for adolescents in schools and colleges needs to be developed emphasizing skills to cope up with high educational anxiety, pressure to get more marks and examination stress. Self-development programmes must include sharpening of vocational vision (understanding of potentials through individual aptitude assessment and counseling), dealing with one's own anger, sexuality and low self esteem problems.

The SDP for schools need to follow the WHO model of school mental health. WHO recommended that all countries should develop school mental health programme as part of their current national health/mental health plans.

The aim of school mental health programme is to provide an experience that will strengthen the children's coping abilities to counter environmental stress and disadvantages with which they have had to cope in growing up.

The most significant interventions for the promotion of psychosocial competence in schools are those which enhance the child's own coping resources and competencies. These skills are decision making and problem solving, critical and creative thinking; communication and interpersonal relationship skills; self-awareness and empathy; and skills for coping with emotions and stress. Providing emotional support and guidance to children along with classroom teaching is both physically and emotionally challenging.

The comprehensive school mental health programme includes developmental plan for parents, teachers, students, non-teaching staff of the school covering mental health of all those associated with the school. In order to implement a comprehensive school mental health programme, the schools need to involve all the partners and stake holders in education i.e. parents, teachers, students, Parent Teacher Association

(PTA), the mental health professionals (psychologists, psychiatrists, counselors), the State education officers, teacher educators, principals etc.

Parenting education in Schools can prove to be very enabling and empowering for the parents while learning effective techniques about child development, and respecting the child's individuality.

It is observed that the educational, vocational and life skills training of adolescent boys and girls in schools have positive impact on their social development for preparation towards their adult Mental Health of Children roles.

The idea of celebrating world mental health day on 10th October every year is to create mental health care as a value in the society. But the mental health component in our society has not been woven. The recommendations of WHO to introduce 'mental health programme in schools' have not impacted school institutions. Whose responsibility is it? The NGO's, the educational and health institutions and the State must come together. But looking at the voluminous magnitude of the learning, emotional, behavioural and other mental health problems of the children, the major share of the responsibility has to be managed by the State. But the governments in most countries have failed to introduce mental health initiatives in schools.

Democratic Schools

Democratic school system is providing new meaning to the education system. It is going to provide a new step to the child development. Freedom schools, citizenship, free and alternate schools are some names given to democratic schools. There are democratic schools in USA, Israel, Japan, Thailand, England, Russia, Canada, and other countries.

Democratic schools believe that the teacher needs to model joy, interest, excitement, and innocence of the children. Teacher needs to be transformational in her approach rather merely transactional. It is important to respond to the emotions of children. It's more important that the teacher learns how to manage her own emotions.

Informal and formal structure of the school do impact the child's learning and the way they imbibe values, which they would unconsciously use when they grow adults.

According to a scholar, "I would be happy to see a school producing a street cleaner rather a neurotic scholar".

Conclusion

The students need a big positive change in schools and colleges. The education and the learning processes are killing the creative potentials of young people. The children are searching for baseline meaning for their life.

They need an open environment in which they can express and experiment with their original and novel ideas. The present institutions and its teachers are unable to tap and develop the scientific attitudes and creativity in students, which is in abundance in them. Schools need to be democratized where the students have the rights to decide over matters that concern them in learning and education. The world needs democratic schools where students no longer suppress themselves but instead feel free to experience life the way they wish, and develop their natural potentials they are endowed with.

Question for Readers

How are educational culture and national development connected?

4

Academic Stress

Introduction

The problem of stress has become a major issue of our time. Can it really be that life conditions in our society are more stressful, more taxing than those experienced by our ancestors? From a material standpoint the answer to this question is, no! The conditions in contemporary society are less stressful than those that have been experienced by any generation. But, our age has its own problems, many of them psychological and some social in nature. This is because, life in technologically advanced societies impose new demands that trigger stress responses in individuals that cause harm in much greater proportions than those suffered by people in earlier times.

Although this review of literature pertains to the topic of academic stress, it is first important to gain an understanding of the general concept of stress and other key factors associated with it. The first part of the literature review thus attempts to provide an overview of the important aspects of stress, with the aim of helping the reader gain a broader perspective on this topic.

The Concept of Stress

In the past, the term "stress" designated both a stimulus (a force or pressure) and a response (adversity or affliction).

However, more recently it has been used to denote a set of changes that people undergo in situations that they appraise as threatening to their well-being. These changes involve not only physiological arousal, but also subjective feelings of discomfort and overt behaviors. The term "anxiety" and "fear" are also used to indicate what people experience when they appraise circumstances as straining their ability to cope with them.

Definitions of stress

Morgan *et al.* (1997) defines stress as an internal state which can be caused by physical demands on the body (disease conditions, exercise, extremes of temperature, etc) or by environmental and social conditions which are evaluated as potentially harmful, uncontrollable or exceeding ones resources for coping.

Mc Gee & Wilson (1981) defines stress as a physical or psychological condition experienced whenever demands are placed on an organism.

Baron & Byrne (2001) defines stress as the response to events that disrupt or threaten to disrupt, our physical or psychological functioning.

Jerome (2004) defines stress as the pressure, tension or worry resulting from problems in ones life.

Stressors

To understand how stress is manifested in an individual, it is first important to define what causes them. These causal factors are generally termed stressors.

The International Encyclopedia of Psychology defines stressors as a "non-specific" condition that may harm almost any part of a person. Stressors range from the catastrophic, such as the death of a loved one, to the seemingly harmless, such as getting a parking ticket; alone or in combination, all can harm a person in a general way that may not immediately be recognized.

Stressors have a number of important temporal components. Exposure to them may be relatively brief with a clear starting and stopping point (acute stressors) or may persist for extended periods of time without clear demarcation (chronic stressors). Finally, stress may also be induced by the anticipation of harmful circumstances that one thinks one is likely to confront, by an ongoing stressor, or by the harmful effects of stressors already encountered. All these factors affect people's interpretation of stressful events, how they deal with them and how effective they are at coping with them.

Cognitive Appraisal

Another key concept in stress is cognitive appraisal. Although there are some situations to which almost everyone responds with high levels of stress, there are individual differences in how people respond to these situations. Hans Selye speaks of "conditioning factors", such as heredity, previous experiences and even diet- that influence how a particular person will react to stress. The same stressors present to the same degree may lead to arthritis in one person, high blood pressure in another and to no harm at all in the third. In short, situations become stressors for an individual only if that individual construes them as threatening or dangerous. The more the individual perceives the situation to be dangerous and beyond his or her control, the higher will be the stress experienced.

Psychologist Richard. S. Lazarus has delineated two important cognitive mechanisms that determine perceptions of stressfulness and how people alter appraisals. *Primary appraisal* refers to an assessment of whether a situation is neutral, challenging, or potentially harmful. When a situation is judged to be harmful or threatening a *secondary appraisal* is made of the coping options or maneuvers that the individual has at his or her disposal. Lazarus also defined the concept of *reappraisal,* the process by which an individual, on the basis of new information, modifies the original appraisal. Consequently, the person makes a decision that the original perception was incorrect. A somewhat different sort of reappraisal is called *defensive reappraisal*. Essentially a coping strategy, defensive reappraisal is an attempt to reinterpret events in such a way as to lessen the implications of harm and threat.

Theories of Stress

An individual's response to stressful situations maybe either behavioral, psychological or physiological in nature. Most theories of stress claim that stress involves the interaction between problems people face and their resources for dealing with them. A wide range of theories emphasizes physiological responses, environmental circumstances, cognitions, personal coping skills, personal characteristics, or some combination of these factors.

The first important theorist who attempted to account for stress was Walter. B. Cannon, who claimed that the sympathetic nervous system is activated by signals from the brain when a person is exposed to an emotionally arousing stimulus. This produces a series of physiological reactions, which includes increases in heart rate, blood pressure, and respiration. This "fight-or-flight" response prepares the person for potential vigorous physical activity. According to Cannon, the confrontation with an arousing stimulus produces both the feelings and the physiological reactions associated with stress. However Cannon's view was criticized on the grounds that it did not take into consideration the role-played by physiological and behavioral factors in the overall stress response.

The work of Cannon paved the way for the efforts of Hans Selye, who claimed that stress is nonspecifically induced and can be caused by diverse stimuli. Selye labeled the body's response to stress as the General Adaptation Syndrome (GAS). This process occurs in three stages. Stage 1 is the ***alarm reaction***, during which the body activates in order to handle the perceived danger at hand. This activation resembles Cannon's flight-or-fight. The second phase of the general adaptation syndrome is the ***resistance stage***. During this stage, the person either adapts to or resists the source of the stress. The longer this stage lasts, the greater is the danger to the person. If the person accepts the stress as a necessary part of life, the stressor may persist indefinitely. The person then gradually becomes more susceptible to a wide range of stress-related problems and diseases including fatigue, headaches, ulcers, hypertension, certain forms of cancer and cardiovascular disease. The third stage is the ***exhaustion stage.*** If the stressor is extremely intense and persists over a long period of time, the exhaustion stage sets in, and the risk of emotional and physical problems sets in.

Selye's view has been criticized by John Mason, who maintains that while the general adaptation syndrome does exist, response are different to diverse stimuli. He views stress as dependent upon emotional responses to situations. Mason believes that Selye's approach is too simplistic and does not explain why some people develop stress related disorders and others do not. The theories of Cannon and Selye emphasize biological factors, while Mason's theory may be described as more of an interaction approach.

The psychological approach to stress is best represented by the work of Richard. S. Lazarus who emphasized the role of cognitive factors in an individual's response to stress. According to him, an individual's appraisal of the stressful event as well as his or her perceived ability to cope with the situation are the most crucial aspects pertaining to stress responses.

Irrespective of whether they support a biological, interactionist or psychological approach to stress, all theorists do agree that stress has the capability of increasing the risk of suffering various forms of illnesses. In addition many theorists also believe that important relationships exist between stress, personality and susceptibility to disease. This conclusion paved the way for further researches on this topic, such as those relating stress to an increased risk of heart diseases, in individuals of Type A personality. The work of pioneers such as Cannon and Selye, has also opened up new avenues of research related to stress and stress management, which has proved to be of considerable importance in today's world.

Coping

The discussion on stress will not be complete without touching upon the important coping strategies that may be used to deal with the various stressors of life. Different individual's cope with stress in different ways. Some people handle stress very effectively while others are devastated by the slightest difficulties. Such differences may be mainly attributed to the genetics, physiologies, and life experiences of the people involved.

Lazarus and his colleagues have identified two broad dimensions of coping (Lazarus & Folkman, 1984):

1) Problem focused coping

This involves taking direct action to solve the problem or seeking information that will be relevant to the solution. A simple example of problem focused coping, is developing a study schedule to pace assignments over a semester to reduce the end-of-semester pressure.

2) Emotion focused coping

This refers to the efforts of an individual to reduce his or her negative emotional reactions to stress, for example, by distracting oneself from the problem, relaxing or seeking comfort from others.

Effective coping often varies with the situation. Distraction may be an effective way of dealing with the emotional upset produced by an impending surgery, but it would be a poor way to handle the upset caused by the discovery of a cancerous lump in the body.

Several methods of coping have been described, some of the important ones being relaxation training, biofeedback and systematic desensitization. (Cited from Morgan & King, 1997). Brief descriptions of each of these methods are given below.

Relaxation training

This refers to training in various techniques for relaxing muscle tension. The procedure is based on Jacobson's progressive relaxation method, in which the person learns how to relax muscle groups one at a time, the assumption being that muscular relaxation is effective in bringing about emotional relaxation. (Cited from Atkinson & Hilgard, 2003).

Biofeedback

In biofeedback training, individuals receive information (feedback) about the aspect of their physiological state and then attempt to alter their state. For example, in a procedure for learning to control tension headaches, electrodes are attached to the participant's forehead so that any movement in the forehead can be electronically detected, amplified and fed back to the person as an auditory signal. The signal, or tone increases in pitch when the muscle contracts and decreases when it relaxes. By learning to control the pitch of the tone, the individual learns to keep the muscles relaxed. After 4-8 weeks of biofeedback training the participant learns to recognize the onset of tension and to reduce it without feedback from the machine. (Thrope & Olson, 1997)

Systematic desensitization

A behavior therapy technique in which hierarchies of anxiety producing situations are imagined (or sometimes confronted in reality) while the person is in a state of deep relaxation. Gradually the situations become dissociated from the anxiety response.

Other researchers have described a number of different ways to counteract the harmful effects of stress. These include a proper diet, daily physical exercise, meditation etc. Researchers also emphasize the role of a psychosocial support system, which refers to the interaction of the person who is struggling with a potential stressor, with caring, supportive people who is significant to him or her. (Mehr, 1983)

The above-mentioned methods of coping are primarily

behavioral techniques. An additional approach to stress management is the Cognitive behavior therapy which attempts to help people identify the kinds of stressful situations that produce their physiological or emotional symptoms and alter the way they cope with these situations.

The reduction of stress in the human environment has been identified as a critical medical challenge, as a result of which every field including businesses and industries now reorient their priorities in an effort to reduce the stress among their employees.

Now that enough has been said on the various aspects of stress, let us now move on to the actual topic on which this literature review has been conducted on –ACADEMIC STRESS.

ACADEMIC STRESS

"...Come exams and children become overly anxious. Will I pass? Will I score above 90? These are some of the questions that nag them. Add parental pressure and expectations to this and some children panic so much, that some even suffer a temporary memory loss in an exam. A few even end their lives because they believe that they have let their ambitious parents down by not scoring well..."

"...stress starts right from pre-school, when the child cries out in anxiety from separation from his parents, till he discovers diversions in the new surroundings and makes new friends..."

"...as children grow, academic, social and parental pressures create stress. Ambitious parents who want their children to be the best, pack too many things into their lives-tutorials, art class, karate, piano lessons, drums, swimming...the list is endless! Once back home there is barely enough time for homework, a quick dinner and sleep. Soon all work and no play makes Tom a dull boy. He yearns to be with his friends and feels frustrated at his "jam packed" schedule. The scenario is worse when he doesn't want to do any of these activities but just wants to read and wander about on his own. The child becomes depressed..."('The Week'. March 6th, 2005)

All of us may identify with at least some aspects, if not all, mentioned in the above article. It is indeed sad to realize that some children even resort to extreme measures such as taking one's own life as a means of ending their ordeal once and for all. The increasing number of shootouts and cases of violence in schools are all a consequence of the pressures these children face academically, if not totally, then at least to some degree. Academic stress has thus gained in importance and has become a topic of utmost priority in today's times.

In the second part of the literature review I have attempted to touch upon every important aspect pertaining to the topic of academic stress. Apart from describing the general causes, consequences, symptoms, and methods of coping, I have also dealt with how academic pressures serve to increase the rate of suicide among children.

Definitions

According to Baumel, (2001), academic stress normally occurs at certain developmental periods in education. When the expectations for academic performance increase, children feel stressed.

Examinations can be the biggest source of stress in a child's life. It is a stressful situation and sometimes students may be unable to perform at a level matching their potential. (Carlson, 1995)

It is not surprising that taking exams is one of the most stressful times in a youngster's life, particularly as their importance is drilled into them, sometimes even months beforehand. (Eder, 1985)

Examinations are an integral part of the educational system, but that alone is not responsible for causing stress among students. What makes it stressful is the undue expectation of parents, the social pressure to perform, the connotation attached to examinations and most importantly, the system's inability to accept a poor academic performer. (Sharon, 2002)

A study by Sarasin (1984) investigated the effect of examination stress on self-reported physical symptoms and sensations. The results of this study indicated that examination stress was associated with an increase in state anxiety and self-reported physical symptoms, with the exception of heart complaints.

Stress in Adolescence

Adolescence has traditionally been viewed as a time of 'greater storm and stress' as compared to other periods of life. It is clear, however, that there are conspicuous signs of tension in adolescence. Student life coincides with adolescence and stress can manifest in children as a reaction to the changes in life, in addition to academic pressures. (Durkin, 1995). Pressures to achieve academic excellence mount up in the 9th and the 10th standards, the latter being the class at which the high school students undergo the secondary school leaving certificate examination. This happens to be the entry point into the adult world of competitors, achievement and failures. Due to all of the above reasons, the academic pressure mounts up during the period of adolescence. (Cherian, 1991).

A study conducted by Kilpatrick, Ruggiero, Acierno, Saunders, Resnick & Best (2003), bring to notice the high percentage of youth in the U.S. suffering from symptoms of Post Traumatic Stress and other disorders. The study involved 4,023 youth (ages 12-17), interviewed by telephone. "Nearly 4% of boys (3.7%) and over 6% of the girls (6.3%), reported PTSD symptoms, indicating that a high percentage of youth in the U.S. encounter traumatic events and experience significant emotional responses associated with these events."

"College students frequently have more complex problems today than they did over a decade ago, including both the typical and expected college student problems as well as the more severe problems, such as depression, sexual assault and thoughts of suicide. Some other problems including those related to educational and vocational choice issues have shown a dramatic increase in the last 13 years." (Benton & Newton, 2001)

According to a survey conducted by the National Society for Prevention of Cruelty to Children, 82% of children aged 11-16 years, worry about exams, while 73% claim that they are given too much homework to do, and around half are concerned about bullying or problems with their teachers. (Times Educational Supplement, January 23rd, 2004)

Contrary to popular belief stress is not limited to students of higher education. Children as young as pre-school students, are observed to be suffering from the symptoms of stress. "Vikram was only 3 years old when he was hospitalized for stress-related heart trouble. Tuition classes', elocution classes', music classes, gymnastic classes and dance lessons took their toll on the boy. In an increasingly competitive environment, paranoid parents, fearful that their children will not make it to pre-primary school, send them to early learning centers, playschools and activity classes at the age of one and two. Experts in childcare say "this is ridiculous" as structured learning at an early age can severely damage a child." (The Times Of India, October 1st, 2005)

According to Conger (1979) there are a number of reasons for an adolescent to feel stressed. These include problems with peers, family issues or problems with parents, school related problems or pressures, child abuse, family or community violence, child sexual abuse etc. School going children suffer from stress especially when they are forced by teachers and anxious parents to meet goals, which are too high for them. The stress factor in their lives results in poor concentration, fatigue, inability to recollect learned material and a sense of failure.

The main sources of stress reported by 423 Australian final year students using the Academic Stress Questionnaire were school related as expected. The highest sources of this stress were examinations and outcomes, too much to do, worry over future, making choices about careers, studying for exams, amount to learn, need to do well imposed by others as well as the self-imposed need to do well. (Kouzma & Kennedy, 2004)

Reactions to stress vary with the adolescent's ability to cope, how long the stress continues and the intensity of the stress. There are individual differences in how people react to stress. Some adolescents' withdraw from others; some lash out at other people, while some actively seek the comfort of others. (Hetherington & Pare, 1986). Signs of stress in adolescents may include withdrawal, anti-social behaviors such as stealing, aggressiveness and acting-out rebellion at home, as well as physical complaints such as headaches and stomachaches. Missed school or poor academic performance, changes in eating and sleeping habits, difficulty in concentrating and thoughts of death and suicide are other common signs.

Common Reactions to Stress in Adolescence

Stress occurs when the body has to perform beyond its normal range of capabilities. High demands, combined with high constraints and little support from family and friends increases the stress reaction. According to Fernald and Fernald (2001), stress in children may lead to the manifestation of lethargy and other forms of decreased responsiveness in them. These outcomes are produced by approach-avoidance conflict and by uncontrollable circumstances in which feelings of helplessness are engendered. Defense mechanisms are assumed to be the unconscious means by which an individual finds protection against anxiety. One of the most common examples of defense mechanism is *repression* in which unpleasant thoughts and feelings are excluded from awareness (Baxon, 1995). Other examples of defense mechanisms are projection, denial, regression etc.

Academic stress can cause various changes in the human body. It increases the production of certain hormones such as adrenalin and cortisol. These hormones in turn produce a noticeable change in the heart rate, blood pressure levels, metabolism and physical activity. One or two of these physical reactions under certain situations may help children function more effectively under pressure (eustress), for short periods of time, but it can also be extremely damaging to the body in the long run. (The New Indian Express, August 9th, 2005).

Anti-social behaviors may be a critical factor for understanding stress among adolescents. Tolan (1988), found that different types of stressors, such as daily hassles, and developmental transitions were related to delinquency, in a study conducted of mostly white adolescents. Other important studies were conducted to study the relation between stress and academic success in adolescents. Windle & Windle (1996), found that stressful life events predicted lower grade point averages, while positive daily events predicted higher grade point averages in their sample of white high school students.

"Children weighed down by the problem of academic pressure, often turn to drugs and alcohol in an effort to escape from it which in turn, leads to further deterioration in academic performance. Comparison to a successful sibling or relative of the same age can also lead to stress and a consequent recourse to a hallucinating medium. Such stressful conditions are often manifested in symptoms like withdrawal from social life, aggressiveness and lack of communication." (The Killer Stress, The New Indian Express, august 9th, 2005).

Presley, Meilman and Lyerla (1996) compared grade averages of students, with estimated average drinks per week and found an inverse relationship between grades and alcohol consumed. "A" students consumed an average of 3 drinks per week, "B" students drank approximately 5, "C" students drank approximately 6, and "D" students drank approximately 7 drinks per week.

Exam stress and its effects on the immune functioning

According to Bootzin *et al.* (1991), the stressful events makes ones depress their normal immune functioning and thus makes him or her more vulnerable to infectious diseases.

Initial researches on this topic measured the effects of major sources of stress, like bereavement and prolonged sleep deprivation. More recently, investigators have found that even stressors like final exams can cause a decline in immune functioning.

In one study, conducted by Kiecolt & Glaser (1986), blood samples were taken from a group of 1st year medical students a month before their examination and then again on the last day of their examination period. Analysis showed a significant decline in the number of "killer" cells that helps the body fight disease microbes. A statistical procedure was used to filter out possible effects of other variables, such as poor nutrition, sleep deprivation and caffeine intake. Results of the study indicated that the students' ability to resist infection was compromised simply because of examination stress. The subjects' did not necessarily become ill, since their immune responses were still functioning at a level lower than normal. The investigators also sought to determine whether an anti-stress intervention, in the form of relaxation training might moderate the effects of stress. For this purpose, one group of subjects were given 10 sessions of instructions in various relaxation techniques which they were encouraged to practice on their own, as well as in class. The researchers found that subjects who received this training had a significantly smaller drop in immune functioning than those who did not receive the training.

The medical students' in this experiment were comparatively healthy, symptom free people, with considerable experience in taking exams. Thus, this decline in their immune functioning during exam week - a stressful period, suggests that our immune systems are quite sensitive, even to common predictable sources of stress. Another implication of this study is that any activity, which moderates the effects of stress, seems to help the immune system continue in its normal level of functioning. Thus, students who want to reduce their levels of academic stress or get through any other stressful period in good health should schedule breaks for exercise, meditation or spending quality time with friends.

A number of experiments suggest that stress increases susceptibility to colds and other respiratory infections.

In one such study, conducted on 100 subjects, throat cultures were taken every 3 weeks, for bacteria and blood was drawn every 4 months for antibodies, to cold viruses. Results indicated that, events that cause stress were 4 times more likely to precede than follow infections. People who developed a cold or bacterial infection had often been feeling more angry and tense than usual, and these feelings were not early signs of any illness, since they appeared on an average of 4 days before the physical symptoms. The effect persisted even with controls for sex, family history of respiratory infections, family size and allergies. (Cohen & Williamson, 1991)

Another experiment (Cohen *et al.*, 1991) provides even more pervasive evidence for a connection between stress and cold. In this experiment, 420 subjects (154 men and 266 women) were exposed to 1 of 5 cold viruses after answering questionnaires on psychological stress, personality, health practices and behaviors. The following 3 measures of stress were used:

(1) Occurrence of certain events. (Job loss, death in the family, divorce etc.)
(2) Feeling frightened, upset, nervous, sad, angry or irritated
(3) Feelings of inability to cope with current demands

Results of this study indicated that greater the stress a person was under, the greater the chance of infection (as indicated by the presence of anti-bodies). Among the 25% of subjects under greater stress, 90% became infected, while among the 25% under least stress, only 74% became infected. But once they became infected, people under stress were no more likely to develop cold symptoms. In other words, stress increases the danger of infection itself and not the resulting discomfort (which is produced by the immune systems defense against the virus). While stress decreases resistance to infection, social support seems to increase it. People with diverse social networks are less likely to develop upper respiratory illnesses after viral exposures, than those with relatively restricted support networks. One of the possibilities suggested by the findings concerning the susceptibility to infection is that clinicians like physicians, might now be able to help patients resist infection or recover from them. (Cohen *et al.*, 1997, Cohen *et al.*, 1999)

Causes of Academic Stress

One of the greatest contributors to stress in children's hurry- to get ready, to go from one place to another, to do well in school and to become an all-round achiever. Stress also occurs in response to pressures such as homework, tests, over-load of non-school activities, conflict with friends and family and the physical and emotional changes that come with growing up. If children are involved in too many activities and don't have time to 'just be kids', it can be extremely stressful.

Stress is created in students when there is parental pressure to perform and to stand out among other children. When they cannot rise up to these expectations, or during the process of achieving it, children may suffer from frustration, physical stress, aggression, undesirable complexes and depression. School systems are also to blame, as it crams students with tremendous amount of school work, which students are expected to complete, sacrificing their leisure hours or vacations. Unable to find enough time for them, students lose interest in studies and under perform. Besides this, teenage depression or growing up tensions adds to the academic pressure. If children are unable to adapt to the transition or change, it may result in enormous amounts of anxiety, negative personal traits and can even lead to massive attention problems. (Hendrickson, 2001).

Some of the important causal factors in academic stress have been briefly described below.

Parental pressure

Parental pressure refers to the degree to which parents become involved in, directly guiding or shaping the behavior of their child. (Baumrind, 1971). The term parental pressurization includes parental beliefs, expectations, dispositions and behaviors causing both psychological and physical strain to the child. Parents pressurize their children by being over anxious and ambitious, controlling and rigid, and forcing the child to achieve beyond his actual capabilities. (Newman, 1986). According to Varma (1980), parents who are over ambitious, demanding and who expect too much from their children, directly lead to problem behaviors in them. Excessive academic pressurizations from parents can have adverse influence on the academic achievements of children. If parental expectations are too high, children feel frustrated, which in turn can cause a dislike for studies. (Baker & Entwisle, 1987). According to Web (1990), when parents concentrate on grades alone, they become more like a dictator. The child thus, comes to believe that the only means of gaining the love and approval of his or her parents is through academic success. As a result, the child strives to excel in his academics, failure of which, leads to extreme anxiety, depression and a sense of failure.

Stress at school

The school differs from the family as a socializing institution in several important ways. The contacts and relations made in schools are most often less impersonal than family relationships. Besides this, the relationship between students and teachers are relatively short-term. (Huston & Alvarez, 1990). The stressful situation in schools may be related to a number of factors, such as, the emotional climate of the school, teacher-student relationship, inadequate facilities, overcrowding in the classroom, examinations etc.

According to Hill (1990), the stressful situations at school may also be related to the teaching strategies, learning styles, interpersonal relationships etc.

Stress and the emotional climate in school

According to Hill (1990), present day schools are not structured to promote an individual's psychological development. Fridenberg (1999), has observed that instead of encouraging independence, creativity, responsibility and self-reliance, schools often over-emphasize obedience, discipline and conformity, thereby creating a very stressful environment. Van De Griff (1985), reported that the schools emotional climate is significantly related to the scholastic achievement of its students. Better the communication skills of the teacher and the emotional climate of the class, lesser the stress observed among students and better the academic achievement.

Stress and overcrowding in the classroom

Several studies have been conducted on this topic, but the results are often shown to contradict each other. In a study conducted by Hallman and Sage (1985), an increase in the classroom size, was seen to result in an increase in the amount of stress experienced by the students. However, the results of another study conducted by Ruthers (1983) shows that classroom sizes, ranging from 20 to 40 students was not generally stressful, nor did it influence the students scholastic achievement negatively.

Stress in teacher-student relationship

The personality of the teacher and his or her style of interaction with the students have been reported to be a very crucial variable affecting classroom stress. Sharma and Santhanam (1992) reported that students prefer non-authoritarian teachers, to strict, authoritative ones, feel more freedom in communicating their difficulties with them and are also more likely to achieve higher results in their class.

Positive evaluation of the teacher was associated with lesser degrees of stress and higher levels of academic achievement. Classes that are too task oriented and that which emphasize teacher control, tend to make students feel anxious, disinterested, unhappy and bored. (Winston, 1989)

Stress in student-student relationship

Yet another important determinant of academic stress is the classroom atmosphere. When relationships with peers are good and friendly, with no friction in the classroom, then children are found to be happier, which in turn helps them to achieve academic excellence. (Stephan, 1984)

Austin and Draper (1984) reported a significant relationship between stress and academic achievement, with sociometric status and peer acceptance among students. Results of their study indicates that, students who are well adjusted, and above average in academic achievement, are significantly more popular and amiable than those who are isolated from group activities. On the other hand, students who were below average in achievement were most often rejected and isolated and as a result were seen to experience a lot of stress.

A research was conducted on how classroom social experiences served as predictors of academic performance. (Flook, Repetti & Ullman, 2005). This 3-year, longitudinal study utilized a process model, to investigate the relationship between social acceptance in the classroom and academic performance among elementary school age children. Participants included 248 children who were followed from the 4th to the 6th grade. Annual interviews were conducted and teachers assessed their behavior, relationship with peers as well as their perceptions of themselves. Report cards of reading and mathematics from the 4th, 5th and 6th grade served as measures of academic achievement. Results of the study indicated that peer acceptance in classroom has a considerable impact on children's self-concept and psychological well being thus, influencing their academic performance. Children, who were rated by their 4th grade teachers as having social difficulties, were found to have poorer academic self-concept in the 5th grade and subsequent academic decline in the 6th grade. An important implication of this study is the need to identify and implement appropriate interventions with children who experience social difficulties. This study also brings to notice the essential role of teachers' in a student's academic performance.

Teaching strategies and stress

Teaching strategies has been shown to be an important factor in academic achievement. Research studies have concluded that extroverted students find informal, unstructured, teaching methods less stressful and more beneficial, while introverted students found the formal, structured learning environment, with the traditional teaching approach less stressful and more beneficial. (Eder, 1985). Therefore, the reported academic superiority of introverts may be due to the fact that the present educational system is highly structured, formal and geared to the needs of introverts than extroverts, who require a different teaching strategy- one which stresses more on individuality, personal interaction, flexibility and spontaneity in teaching. (Chaube, 1981).

Another teaching strategy which reduces stress and improves achievement is based on Gray's theory, which states that 'extroverts find classroom adjustment less stressful, and shows more superior learning when teachers emphasize rewards and praise. In contrast, introverts find classroom adjustment less stressful and show more superior learning when teachers relied predominantly on threats and punishment.

Signs and Symptoms of Academic Stress

It is not always easy to recognize the fact that children are stressed out. Short-term behavioral changes such as mood swing, acting out, and changes in sleep pattern or bedwetting can be indicators of stress. Some children manifest physical symptoms like stomachaches, headaches, fever etc. Still others have trouble concentrating or completing schoolwork and withdraw from others and their peer group and prefer to spend a lot of time on their own.

Some of the important signs and symptoms that indicate a child might be under stress include:

- Psychosomatic complaints like headaches, migraines, ulcers etc.
- Weight loss or gain, decreased o: increased appetite
- Increased susceptibility to illnesses

- Increased irritability, low frustration tolerance, sadness, panic and anger
- Insomnia
- Lethargy, daydreaming and withdrawal from activities
- Restlessness, depression, inability to concentrate
- Reverting to immature behavior
- Nervous habits like nail biting and thumb sucking
- Subtle reactions like a strained look or frowning
- Isolation: a lack of desire to socialize
- Lack of self-esteem, sense of despair etc
- Open hostility and defiance
- Difficulties in school, usually marked by a drop in performance.
- Dizziness, trembling and shaking, palpitations
- Cardiopulmonary problems such as increased blood pressure or heart disease
- Dyspnea, (inability to catch one's breath, feeling of suffocation)

Consequences of Academic Stress

Stress due to academics may have lasting repercussions in several areas of life. (Neumann and Reichel, 1990). Few of the important implications are listed below.

1) Quality of work affected

The quality of work produced by the child in the course of his studentship can be severely affected by poor coping strategies. First, stress may produce a focus on short-term completion versus long-term learning. For instance, a fatigued student may cram for an exam rather than master the content or he may throw together material for the paper instead of thoroughly researching the subject. The result is that his/her work suffers and as a result, the child will not be able to get the maximum value from his education. Secondly, many pressured students attempt to minimize other interests and limit their efforts to what is required solely within their field of study. This causes an unhealthy isolation.

2) Further education plans are halted

Constant tension and anxiety in one's level or chosen field of education may cause the student to succumb to overwhelming fatigue that may lead to the halt of his/her education or higher education plans. Hence, despite years of investment in academic training, the student will fall short of his/her perceived goals.

3) Interpersonal relationships are stunted

In the pursuit of academic goals, students often neglect their interpersonal relationships. The hindrances of time, commitments, lack of social involvement and hesitancy towards self-disclosure, prevents the natural development of rewarding support networks. Typical coping mechanisms tend to move students to redouble their work efforts, in an attempt to catch up and to guard their personal "academic turf", from those perceived as potential competitors within their department, thereby creating greater isolation. Thus, these students do not benefit from the close community relationships that will help them cope with the pressures of academic life. In addition, emotional exhaustion may disengage the student from family relationships. In today's world the practice spending quality time with one's family is fast disappearing, as a result of which, family members fail to meet each other's emotional needs. If the student is married or is a parent, the stress from academics may affect the relationship between the spouses and may also have a crippling impact on their children. The person's own academic pressures may leave him/her too tired to deal with the problems that may affect their spouse or children, leading to further conflict and consequently a deterioration in family relationships.

4) Future career is jeopardized.

The academic life holds pressures that remain throughout

school/college etc that may continue into a person's academic career. Students who had to face extreme pressures in their student life are more likely to carry over this stress into their workplace, as a result of which they are unable to maintain a healthy professional life. Such individuals are thus forced to give up their jobs, at least temporarily until they are able to cope with the pressures in a more effective manner.

A number of researches have been done on the effects of test anxiety and its effects on the achievement and motivation of a student. Prominent researchers in the area (Hedl, 1972; Sarason, 1975; Spielberger, 1972; Trent, 1996) viewed test anxiety as a trait - a relatively stable personality characteristic, which prompts an individual to react to threatening situations with psychological, physiological and behavioral responses. There is an extensive amount of empirical evidence of the negative effects of test anxiety on academic performance. For example, in a meta-analysis of 562 students, that related test anxiety and academic achievement, Hembree (1988) found that test anxiety routinely causes poor performance. The evaluation practices of the classroom teacher were also found to have an influence on the impact of test anxiety on students' performance. (Maehr & Midgley, 1991; Pintrich & Schrauben, 1992)

A substantial body of research has documented association between problem behaviors and academic achievement. (D'Amico and Cardaci, 2003). This topic has relevance from an educational perspective that views problem behaviors as serious impediments to optimal education. From a psychopathological perspective, low academic achievement represents a significant risk factor for poor behavioral outcomes. A systematic viewpoint posits that behavioral and academic problems exert reciprocal influences on each other, which over time can negatively affect the individuals and their environment. A wide variety of problem behaviors have been linked to academic underachievement. For example, investigators have consistently revealed that aggression and other forms of anti-social behaviors display an inverse relationship with academic achievement. (William & McGee, 1994).

Academic Stress and Suicide

Amongst the various consequences of academic stress, the most important one is the increased risk to suicidal tendencies. Therefore, the final part of the literature review focuses on how academic stress increases the risk of suicide among adolescents.

"11 year old Suraj Sahadev Muskar studying in 6th standard at National Education Society High School, Bhandup, committed suicide allegedly after failing in his unit test exam in social science. According to sources, when nobody was at home, he hung himself to the roof of the kitchen..." (Mulund Plus, October 9th, 2005)

Adolescent suicide is a worldwide problem. (Conner, Duberstein, Conwell, Seidlitz & Caine, 2001). Cole, Protinsky and Cross (1992) define suicide as "the completed process of a continuum that began with suicidal ideation, followed by an attempt at suicide, and finally completed suicide". The suicide rate in the United States has tripled since 1960, making it the third leading cause of death among adolescents and the second leading cause of death among the college-age population. (National Mental Health Association, 1997). Although it is estimated that approximately 14 adolescents in the U.S. commit suicide each day, the actual number is 2-3 times higher. (American Psychiatric Association, 1996; 1998). These alarming statistics have stimulated great concern in the public at large and have led social scientists to warn of an impending rise in the number of suicides and suicidal attempts among adolescents. (Watt & Sharp, 2002).

Psychologists are now increasingly paying attention to the antecedent behaviors of suicide. According to Bush & Pargament (1995), suicidal behavior is often preceded by thoughts, threats and unsuccessful attempts at suicide.

Stress and suicide

What exactly predisposes a child to take a severe measure such as taking ones own life? The search for identity, a natural stressful demand on youth can be overwhelming to some adolescents and predispose them to thoughts of suicide. Hence, the high incidence of adolescent suicide is assumed to be indicative of societal stress in the lives of young people. (Turner, Kaplan, Zayas & Ross, 2002). Several studies have found that suicide attempts among adolescents tend to increase as stress levels increase. This may be attributed to academic pressure, work-related problems, interpersonal difficulties, death of a loved one, etc. (Butler, Novy, Gagan & Gates, 1994). Poor or an overachieved academic performance can serve as a precursor to stress, subsequent depression and suicide. (Petzel & Riddle, 1981). Serious suicide attempts seem to be higher among students who experience considerable academic success and less serious suicide attempts more indicative of students who are failing at school. (Henry, Stephenson, Hanson & Hargett, 1993). These researches argued that academically successful students experience greater amounts of stress than do their less successful peers because the more successful students feel, the more pressure they experience, to maintain their level of performance. This pressure leads them to increase the lethality of their suicidal intent. However, students who have consistently exhibited a pattern of academic failure may simply engage in risk taking behaviors, which predispose them to suicide. Petzel and Riddle observed that the majority of the suicidal students in both high schools and college receive passing scores in their academic classes, an indication that academic stress is not the only significant factor that contributes to the occurrence of suicide.

A research was conducted by Petzel and Riddle (2005), to examine the relationships among stress, self-esteem and suicidal ideation in late adolescents. The study was carried out among a group of college students. The research findings indicated that both stress and self-esteem were significantly related to suicidal ideation; low self-esteem and stressful life events significantly predicted suicidal ideation.

Self-esteem and suicide

Self-esteem, the evaluations individuals make about the self (Harter *et al.*, 1992) is shaped by individual's appraisal of how they are perceived by significant others. (Sullivan, 1953).

Research findings have indicated an inverse correlation between life stressors and self-esteem. (Garber, Robinson & Valentiner, 1997). Specifically, a negative self-esteem predisposes adolescents to depression, psychiatric difficulty and in extreme cases, suicide.

Symptoms of suicide

- Severe depression
- Feelings of helplessness or hopelessness
- Disorientation
- Direct statements about death/suicide
- Withdrawal
- Giving away personal possessions.

Extreme social, academic and environmental pressures in the United States are leading teenagers towards drastic steps such as suicide. Statistics show that the suicide rates for teenagers have increased 3 folds since 1995. High-risk groups have been identified and schools should have a suicide prevention policy in their curriculum. Parents' awareness program becomes an essential part of schools' total suicide prevention effort. (Coy, 1995).

The harmful effects of academic stress are innumerous. Turning a blind eye towards the symptoms of stress will only lead to a worsening of the situation. Hence, it is important for people to resort to coping measures that will help them to deal with the pressures in an effective manner.

Coping with Academic Stress

Signs of stress in adolescence should be taken seriously as it can lead to depression, drug abuse, and alcoholism, but most importantly, suicide. It is thus, essential to develop coping skills, to deal with the academic pressures one faces, to succeed in a healthy manner, not only in schools and colleges but also later in life. An individuals reaction to, and the ability to cope with stress is more important than lessening the load. (Antonovsky, 1979).

Developing adequate methods of dealing with stress involves recognizing strengths as well as employing outside sources. A few practical recommendations for students in dealing with the burnout syndrome are listed below:

1) Journal one's progress

Journaling one's progress helps the student to identify the symptoms of exhaustion, the conditions that trigger the stress and also to analyze destructive "self –talk" statements that minimize ones self-worth and false statements of ones progress and accomplishment that they may be engaging in. It thus, prepares the students for future episodes of anxiety, helps them to identify their strengths and most importantly gives them the opportunity to rebuild their confidence.

2) Manage time and set personal priorities

Without good time management burnout becomes a high probability. It is important to realize one's priorities and accordingly set a schedule for the different activities throughout the day. When setting schedules, it is also important to include time for leisure activities to get away from the monotony of studies and refresh one. A well-balanced diet, appropriate sleep and adequate exercise are also essential.

3) Cultivate relationships

Social networks add a balance that is vital for alleviating stress. The support of friends and family enables an individual to cope better with the pressures of school and college. It is thus essential to develop an interaction network, by spending time with close friends and with people who share the same hobbies.

4) Seek professional help

In certain situations, the stress becomes so overwhelming that the student is unable to handle it alone. In extreme cases of anxiety, even the support of friends and family are not of any help. In such cases it is important for the individual to seek professional help such as counselors, psychologists etc.

The focus here is to prevent mental illnesses, as many forms of illnesses are known to result from "environmental stressors".

Apart from these, maintaining a healthy and positive attitude towards life in general is also an important factor in coping with stress. A student's basic outlook towards his studies, his future career and the meaning of life is fundamental to the implementation of any solution.

Research conducted by Snyder, Shorey, Cheavens, Pulvers & Wiklund (2002), focused on how hopeful thinking in college academics, helped students to overcome academic pressure and the contributions of hope theory for educational research and practice. Hope theory integrates the conceptualization of goals, along with the strategies to achieve those goals and the motivation to pursue those goals. Individual differences in hope were measured by the Hope Scale (Snyder *et al.*, 1991) of college freshmen across a number of different universities. Results of the study indicated that students who had high levels of hope were more likely to have graduated than students with relatively low levels of hope.

Another study conducted by Misra & McKean (2000), investigated the relationship between academic stress, anxiety, time management and leisure satisfaction among 249 university undergraduates by age and gender. It was hypothesized that academic stress would show a significant positive correlation with anxiety and a significant negative correlation with self-reported time management behaviors and leisure satisfaction. A second purpose of the study was to examine the differences in the study variables by gender and age. Results of the study indicated that time management behaviors had a greater buffering effect on academic stress than leisure satisfaction activities. Significant gender differences were also seen to exist among all the measures. Females had more effective time management behaviors than males, but were observed to experience higher academic stress and anxiety. Males were seen to benefit more from leisure activities than females. Freshmen and sophomore students had higher reactions to stress than juniors and seniors. Thus, anxiety, time management, and leisure satisfaction were all observed to be predictors of academic stress. An important implication of this study is that, anxiety reduction and time management in conjunction with leisure activities may be an effective strategy for reducing academic stress in colleges.

5) *Role of parents in relieving stress*

Adolescence is often a period of turmoil and children in this stage of development need support and help from their parents, though they may not directly ask for assistance. Helping adolescents realize that they are important members of society can ease a great deal of their stress. (Feldman & Elliot, 1990). Adults can help adolescents cope with their stress by encouraging them to talk openly about their emotions and feelings, reassuring them and by offering their support. The first important step for parents is to be aware of the possible stressors and to recognize the different signs of stress in their children. Parents should be realistic about their child's abilities and should take care so as not to burden them with unreasonable expectations in academic as well as extra-curricular fields. (Baker & Entewisle, 1987). Parents should keep track of their child's academic performance and watch for any sudden declines in his/her academic performance, be in constant touch with the teachers to be able to identify an problem the child may be experiencing in school and most importantly reassure the child of parental love and support. (Dorman, 1990). Parents can help their children cope with their academic pressures by discussing their expectations with their children and to lower these expectations if they seem to be unattainable by the child. Parents should take an interest in and be available, when the child needs help with his schoolwork. They should help the child develop an academic routine at home. Parents should encourage children to take up hobbies, participate in extra-curricular activities and exercise regularly, all of which are effective stress relievers. Lastly, it is essential for parents to review, evaluate and change their parenting styles if they prove to be ineffective.

6) The role of schools

Schools assume a great importance in a child's life. Interaction with teachers and peers is instrumental in shaping the child's personality. The role of school, therefore, should be to provide a more psychologically oriented, scientific approach to preparations for exams, concentrating not only on the particular subject but also on how to learn and study them. Teachers should have a supportive attitude and also identify vulnerable students and give them special attention from the very beginning.

Thus, by recognizing the role of the academic environment and its oppressive nature, by understanding the personal traits such as perfectionism and the tendency to overachieve, and by identifying physiological and cognitive symptoms that indicate emotional exhaustion, the student can learn effective coping strategies to stop the destructive cycle of burnout. (Antonovsky, 1979).

Conclusion

Education is a part and parcel of the lives of a large number of people, the importance of which is growing by leaps and bounds with each new day. Competition among students has risen over the ages and has now come to a stage, where people resort to any measures, go to any lengths, some even at the cost of their own health, to succeed in their chosen field of education. Technological advancements and other changes in the system of education have over the years made the life of students easier. In spite of this, recent years have seen a growth in stress-related disorders among students, most of which, are a consequence of the academic pressures faced by them. These may include unreasonable expectations of parents, setting of high standards that one is unable to achieve or problems with peers and teachers. Academic pressures, if left unattended to, leads to dire consequences in every aspect of the students' life- physical, mental, emotional, cognitive and social. However, the most important consequence of academic stress is its increased risk to suicide. Teenage suicide has risen in magnificent proportions over the last decade, 68% of which is attributed to the academic stress alone. (Coy, 1995).

Measures to counter academic stress have thus been given utmost priority and the role of parents', teachers, and peers have been emphasized in its conceptions. A number of researches have been conducted on the topic of academic stress, some, specifically studying the causes, consequences and the effectiveness of the different coping strategies used. Research has also been conducted on the gender differences in academic stress. However, most of the researches reviewed in this literature review, pertain mostly to studies done in the United States, and some in Australia, as data pertaining to the Indian context are virtually lacking.

The system of education in India needs introspection, and we must be prepared to question, criticize, and change ourselves. Over the years, gradual changes have been incorporated to suit the changing requirements of the students. Counseling has been made compulsory in all schools and counselors are trained experts from the field of mental health. In addition, plans are also being made to incorporate a psychiatrist on the panel of each school. However, the most important change to be made and that too with immediate effect is the change from the existing performance-oriented approach to one that is more result-oriented. (Bhat, 2002).

Question for Readers

Is there a possibility of academic stress and suicide among students and how to prevent it?

5

Learning Disorders

Reproduced below is a personal but famous letter written at 19 years of age:

Dear mother,

Started store several weeks I have growed considerably I don't look much like a boy now how's all the fold did you receive a box of books Memphis that he promised to send them languages....

Your son AL

"EXCELLENT WITH HANDS"

This son AL was THOMAS ALVA EDISON, inventor of the bulb and of 300 other patented products. But, he was a dyslexic. He excelled in skills which only needed the use of HEAD and HANDS without requiring reading or writing. But, as can be seen from his letter above, he never really mastered the basic skills of writing or spelling. This condition is called DYSLEXIA or LEARNING DISORDER [LD].

LD is a developmental disorder, present from Childs birth as a silent neurological handicap. Many LD children have overlapping behaviour or emotional problems, LD is not a mental or behavioural disease. LD children are not dull or mentally retarded either.

Defining Learning Disorders

This group manifests a significant difficulty in the acquisition and use of basic academic skills –skills of reading, writing, spelling, maths, language etc. Surveys show that about 10% of all school children are affected by this handicap. Boys are effected 3 times more than girls.

Loses the Joy of Learning

By the age of 7, the child with LD may have substantial difficulty in reading or writing. He may become de-motivated in studies. He loses the joy of learning; school becomes a burden. Older children who do not receive remedial help face repeated failure in written work, finally to be labeled as 'lazy' or plain 'stupid'! Many of these children lose their confidence, and become frustrated with life. Their internal tensions may manifest as adjustment problems at home or in school.

Becomes a 'Negative Child'

Getting addicted to TV or COMPUTER provides an easy escape for these children. Quitting or giving up in defeat is another way they cope with LD. Cheating in tests [to avoid failure] and forging progress reports, when seen in young children, should raise the suspicion of LD such an occasional misbehavior may not be treated as a moral issue.

Naughtiness, aggressive behaviour and defiance can sometimes be a cover for low self esteem in a child with LD. Refusal to do school work, truancy or other behaviour problems in a young child may also indicate an underlying LD.

Create Awareness

It is essential to mention that many teachers and parents are still reluctant to accept LD as a genius cause for poor school performance. Many seem justified to ask," when the child is good at everything else, why is he backward only with his studies"?

Or sometimes, it is perceived as a problem of pushy parents or stylish teachers! Therefore, the need of the hour is to create awareness about the various causes of poor scholastic performance among teachers, parents, school authorities, journalists and the media. Awareness of the various learning problems in school children can lead to early identification.

Identifying Learning Disorders

Identification of any disorder is based on the awareness about it. In the case of learning disorders, parents and teachers make the best diagnosticians.

Identifying LD In Small Children

- Pre-school children with delayed development of speech and language.
- Lack of clarity of speech or ideas.
- Clumsy and slow children.
- Difficulty with fine movements such as buttoning, lacing or holding a crayon.
- Children who trip and bump and fall excessively.
- Poor concentration or over-activity
- Children who enjoy being read to, but are at the same time, disinterested in looking at the letters or words in the books.
- Difficulty in narrating stories or events in sequence.
- Persistent difficulty naming colours and shapes.
- Persistent confusion between left and right.

READING AND WRITING PROBLEMS

- If the child struggles beyond the first one or two standards in school to achieve the simple skills of reading, writing etc., the cause for this struggle may be LD.
- Though they may score poor marks, LD children are generally 'smart'. On testing, they reveal normal intelligence {IQ}. And most posses rote-memory.
- They easily answer questions ORALLY, but may be

unable to WRITE the same on paper. Thus, there is a DISCREPANCY between what they know in the head, and what then appears on their answer sheets.

- Usually they are good with their hands-in sports or games, music or dance, sketching or painting, motors or machine, computers or creative thinking. They make good leaders with their people skills, or smart managers with their organizational talents.
- The young Dyslexics have difficulty to READ or WRITE.
- It is important, therefore, to spot the special skills or talents in every LD child, as given above.
- They read slowly and monotonously, word by word. With omissions or guessing of words. They miss lines in the text or read lines over again. They may read by following the text with the fingers,between the line, and may not pay attention to punctuations or intonations.
- Most dyslexics prefer being read to, than reading on their own. This is because they may not understand or register what they themselves read, but comprehend very well when you read out of them.
- LD children are slow to write, have poor handwriting. They have difficulty to complete class-notes or exam papers within the given time.
- Reversals of letters or numbers{b/d, m/w, 6/9, 15/51, saw/was}are common.
- Glaring spelling-mistakes in writing is the reason why most LD children with PSP get harassed. Dyslexic children may spell the words right orally, but make gross mistakes when they write the same.
- Indian languages like HINDI or MALYALAM seem to be more difficult than ENGLISH for many LD children. This probably is because many letters in our languages are visually similar, and sound similar.
- Profound difficulties are therefore experienced by LD children during a 'dictation'. In more severe cases,

Dyslexic children are unable to even pick out alphabets from a display, or match the same alphabets.

Arithmetic

- Arithmetic/maths is the problem for many LD children. They may have concepts, reasoning or operations.
- Many of them use fingers for calculations even after 8 years. Some get confused with signs like addition and multiplication. They may do half a problem with correct sign and other half sum with another sign.
- For some, multiplication tables may be puzzling, though they learn them easily by rote.
- Many of these unfortunate children may get the right answer in the working column, by making a mistake by transposing digits while copying {34689 may become 43689}. Some of them may also reverse numbers- 21 for 12.
- Some have difficulty with place value in arithmetic, or may not understand the concepts of 'greater than, less than'.

Left or Right???

- Many LD children may be left handed and may have confusion between left and right sides; there may be delay in deciding which hand to use for a purpose.
- The concepts of time, speed or distance may be difficult for some LD children. They find it difficult to tell the time or to read the time from the face of clock.
- Confusion about days of the week, yesterday, tomorrow etc., are also seen. Time management is also a difficult task for many.

Communication and Social Skills

- Using language for communication is difficult for some LD children. Some are unable to narrate a story or an incident in a sequence.

- Some older children may still have difficulty finding the right words to express their ideas.
- Many have difficulty with motor skills, in coordinating fine motor movements. Threading a needle, doing the buttons, gripping a pencil, writing in straight lines etc.
- Social competence is not easy for these children. Many may not have friends of their age. Their self-esteem is abysmally low because of constant poundings from their parents, peer and teachers.
- They may have difficulty giving and asking for the right information. Many may not understand indirect meanings or jokes in conversations. They may be naïve, and fail to recognize larger meanings from a little things in life.
- On the contrary, a good % of LD children does display social and interpersonal skills as their major asset and strength.

Associated Behaviour Disorders

Lack of concentration, over activity, defiance, aggression, oppositional behaviour, addiction to TV or COMPUTER etc. are some of the complaints for which LD children are taken to the specialists. Muscle tics, obsessive or compulsive disorders, anxiety, depression, headache, school phobia, examination fear etc are some of the other overlapping problems seen in children with learning disorders.

What Causes Learning Disorder???

Mind And Its Functions—New Concepts

With the exponential growth in technology today, live brain cells can be photographed while in action by using a technique called functional neuro-imaging. Thereby doctors now know that the mind is generated by the brain. Movement of a hand is carried out by orders from the specific part of the brain controlling that hand. This is a simple concept to understand. Similarly, the minds functions such as thinking, feeling, learning, speaking, writing etc. are carried out by specific biochemical systems in designated parts of the brain.

Mind, Brain And Learning Disorders

The brain has 2 halves or hemispheres, left and right. School-skills like reading, writing, spelling, language, etc. are controlled mainly from the left hemisphere. The right hemisphere controls skills like art and music, sports and games, use of motors or machines etc. - skills that do not need reading or writing. There are specific brain areas and specific brain biochemicals controlling each of these functions. Therefore any deficiency in the brain area controlling the allocated function gives rise to disability in that specific function. Mal-development of brain areas that control academic skills gives rise to LEARNING DISABILITY.

Silent Neurological Handicap

It is now clearly understood, therefore, that learning disorders are neurological in origin. An LD child's brain cells are arranged differently, or function differently that from a ordinary persons. These brain cells abnormalities may arise from genetic factors, or environmental causes{before, during or after birth}. Learning disorders are inherited the same way as our physical characteristics. It has been shown that 88% of children with LD have immediate relatives with the same disorder.

Parents may feel unduly guilty when their young children do not perform upto their expectations, but the 'fault' for dyslexia lies mostly with the wiring inside the brain.

The LD Brain

Whether due to genetic or environmental, the brain of the LD child functions differently. The LD brain functions inappropriately because of damage, malformation or inadequate maturation of the concerned brain cells. Snapshots-special photographs of these differences from an ordinary brain can now be taken using special brain scans. Dyslexic brains have differences from the normal brain, mostly in the left hemisphere and in the connecting brain pathways, which carry out the learning functions.

Diagnosing LD

A child struggling in school with his studies can be diagnosed as a case of learning disorder by a sensitized parent or teacher, merely by using the information about LD. In each child with learning disorders a different academic skill like reading, writing, spelling or arithmetic may be affected. Alongside LD in the same child, there may be overlapping language or speech or motor-coordination disorders. Emotional or behavioural disorders, or attention deficit disorders also co-exist. In short, it takes a team of different professionals to look at each child from these angles, and with the consent of the parents.

The team is multi-disciplinary, with a special educator/ teacher, psychologist, social worker etc. For assessment and accurate diagnosis a stepwise paradigm is followed:

1. Intake Interview

This is the most important step that involves the parents and if possible the teacher. The child's current problems, developmental history, home/ school environment and inputs, life events, academic progress, strengths and potential etc. are evaluated on a structured protocol.

2. Examination and Testing of the Child

A physical/ neurological examination, with tests of hearing, vision, EEG or any appropriate tests is in order.

3. Assessment of Learning Disorders

The basic tests yield skill deficits that produce poor school performance{PSP}

a. Tests to measure general intelligence{IQ} by clinical/ educational psychologist.

b. Assessment of reading skills, writing and spelling skills, maths skills, handwriting, concentration etc.
c. Tests of speech and language by the speech and language pathologist.
d. Identification of special abilities/talents.

These tests reveal the level at which the functions in each skill in each subject.

4. *Assessment of Overlapping Disorders*

This is a vitally significant aspect of assessment, done in a clinic with a Multidisciplinary Team. Disorders such as epileptic disorders, attention deficit disorder, tic disorders, emotional disorders like anxiety, school phobia or exam phobia, speech and language disorders, etc. need to be identified and diagnosed.

5. *Other Assessments*

Other areas assessed include handwriting, handedness, fine motor coordination, comprehension, concentration etc. Children below 6 years of age are assessed for pre-academic or pre-school skills. In our country, pre school children are unfortunately pushed to undertake school tasks before they are ready for them. In the KG classes, they need to possess the readiness skills to learn, which can be assessed even before the age of 6 years.

6. *Individualised Education Programme{IEP}*

All these evaluations reveal the nature of difficulties faced by the underachieving child. Based on such a document, remedial strategies for each child can be worked out by the teachers, school and parents. This is called an [IEP] for a particular child. An IEP is necessary because each child's problems are different from another. Just as each child is different from another. Different professionals are qualified to evaluate the different difficulties faced by the child. Child Guidance Clinics are set up on this Multidisciplinary model.

Emotional and Behavioural Problems with LD

Co-existing Problems

In a child with LD certain other disorders can co-exist. Many of them like LD are developmental in origin, meaning that they are present from birth. Some other co-morbid disorders like school phobia or exam fear or anxiety may arise in the child because of the learning problems. It is important to diagnose each of these disorders and manage every one of them to enable the child's optimal performance. Correction of one disorder, while leaving another unattended, may fail to produce the desired improvement in the child.

Therefore, in every child diagnosed with LD, we must consciously look for overlapping problems or disorders. Because as stated repeatedly, LD never exists in isolation.

Overlapping Disorders

Attention Deficit Disorders {ADHD}

Gaurav, a student of 5th sometimes can disrupt the entire class. Some children get bullied by him and others don't like to sit next to him. He may distract them or even nudge them. He too, gets easily distracted by everything that goes on around him. Teachers know that he is smart and quick on the uptake. But he is very inattentive, and hardly sits in his seat. He may blurt out answers in the class out of turn, and is not bothered if he is right or wrong. His parents find his behaviour embarrassing at social gatherings where he constantly moves around and even opens the food packet before being served'.

Gaurav is a child with ADHD which is distinct and different from learning disorders.

Symptoms of Adhd

A] Inattention

B] Hyperactivity

C] Impulsiveness

Now lets have a look at the EMOTIONAL DISORDERS:

ANXIETY DISORDERS

Children with learning problems may experience persistent anxiety. This in turn, affects their performance. Although anxiety is a psychological disturbance, it produces a great number of corresponding physical symptoms. The psychological component is a constant feeling of apprehension a feeling of weight on the chest.

But children mostly manifest only the physical symptoms of anxiety which are very distressing and therefore, easily recognizable. These physical symptoms are grouped under three headings:

a. Muscle Tension Increase: Trembling, feeling shaky, aches and pains{body or chest pain, body ache}, fidgetiness, restlessness, easy fatigability and tiredness.

b. Symptoms of Internal Organs: Palpitations{heart beating and hard}, breathlessness/ choking sensation in the chest, dry mouth , blurring of vision, increased sweating of palms/ soles, dizziness, sense of lump in the throat, nausea, abdominal pain, gas problems, frequent urination, tingling/numbness/ burning sensation of hands and legs, etc.

c. Symptoms of Vigilance: Feeling keyed up, wound up, loss of concentration, irritability, problems of sleep, mind going blank due to anxiety {commonly seen in exams}, etc.

SOCIAL PHOBIA, which is a fear of facing social situations such as class or the assembly, is very common among LD children. When these children have an inherent problem to read, asking them to read aloud in the class can be petrifying. Phobia of examination generates severe anxiety in the children during exam time. Anxiety is the commonest human emotion. It is abnormal only when it interferes with child's day to day functioning.

Depression

It is a mood disorder which many children, especially

those with learning problems, suffer from. Children with depression are usually withdrawn and do not undertake pleasurable activities. Games and play become limited, and are inhibited. They have poor attention and concentration and may seem to be day-dreaming. Some of them are led to tears easily. Sleep may be disturbed, and many of them may appear drowsy in class. Depressed children eat poorly and fatigue easily. Lack of confidence, feelings of guilt and sometimes suicidal thoughts are characteristic of depression. Irritability and tantrums may often be symptoms of depression in children.

Obsessive Disorders

These, in our experience in COCHIN, have a special significance in children with leaning disorders. Children with Obsessive disorders have a need for perfection. They may need to arrange and rearrange their tables, check and recheck their exam papers, or clean and wash again and again.

These children may be stubborn and excessively fussy about neatness, orderliness and sameness. If someone disturbs their stack of books they may get into rage. These children may not allow others to handle or share or touch their belongings. They may be perfectly behaved children outside their homes, but inside they may explode with unbelievable rage.

Another group of obsessive children may be afflicted by a slowness which is morbid. Starting them off to school in the morning is the main task for the mother, having to push them from one morning chore to another. The past years of our working with LD children at cochin have shown a greater number of them have disturbing obsessive behaviour. Some LD children suffer from TIC DISORDERS. These disorders in children manifest as involuntary, rapid tics, muscular or vocal. The comman tics are eye-blinking, neck jerking, shoulder shrugging or grimacing. If worse the child may hit himself.

Right and Left Hemispheres : The Other Side of LD

Schooling vs. education

"I have never let my schooling interfere with my education," said Mark Twain.

Educationists realize today that schooling does not nurture the entire potential of a child. However the goal of education is primarily to create component, confident and self-reliant citizens. A remarkable performance in school tests may not assure future success in life. Conversely, poor school performance may not predict failure in later life.

In our present system of education, school tests only a few paper pencil skills based on reading and writing. Judging a child's intelligence based on his academic performance can snuff out his dreams at an early age.

On the other hand, identifying and nurturing the real world skills in a child can make it possible for even hopeless kids to go on to be widely successful in life{as the quotation on top implies} IQ testing, in the past, reduced many children to a mere number, based on table top tests and sit-down MCQs{Multiple Choice Questions} Schools unfortunately pass or fail a child based on sit-down tests or paper-pencil tests alone. We determine that a child is dull or clever by looking at this limited performance!

Disability or ' Different ability'?

Certain faculties such as maths or chess are labeled as intelligence, whereas competences like music or cooking are alluded to as merely talents. Due to this perception, inability to write is considered a disability, whereas inability to sing is considered as a lack of talent!

Our clinic experience at Cochin compels us to take serious note of the skills which the so called LD children are endowed with. It has been consistently possible for us to recognize multiple talents in these children. Instead of a disability they have a different ability. Each child has a different gift. Each child has distinctive profile of his abilities and disabilities- skills and skill deficits.

These multiple intelligences are gifted genetically but developed by opportunity, motivation and hardwork. Each competence or intelligence is controlled by an allocated brain area on the left side or the right side. Schools depend mostly on the left brain skills- academic skills- to measure the child's competence.

However, the real world intelligences cannot be tested on table tops and are mostly controlled from the right brain. Music or dance, acting or mimicking, fantasy or imagination, crafting or designing, drawing or painting, architecture or agriculture, sculpture or horticulture, navigation or exploration, cooking or homemaking, stitching or sewing, sports or games, motors or machines, repairs or mechanisms, management or team skills, life skills or leadership skills are all dependent on competent right brain.

One can imagine the number of fulfilling vocations that can be generated out of the above competencies for a child who may be a poor school performer.

The Other Side of LD

Schools perhaps reward all roundedness, but successful people have brains that are specialized such as in dyslexics. Such dyslexics thrive after escaping school. Discovering talents in a school child through focused and deliberate observation by teachers and parents will help such children not to lose their way while in school. In fact, doing that will be throwing him a lifeline for success in future life. That must become the goal of our education systems.

Specific Culture Features: Care should be taken to ensure that intelligence testing procedures reflect adequate attention to the individuals ethnic or cultural background. This is usually accomplished by using tests in which the individuals relevant characteristics are represented in standardization sample of the test or by employing an examiner who is familiar with aspects of the individuals ethnic background. Individualized testing is always needed to make the diagnosis of the learning disorder.

Prevalence

Estimates of the prevalence of learning disorders range from 2% to 10% depending on the nature of ascertainment and the definitions applied. Approximately 5% of students in public schools in the US are identified of having a learning disorder.

Differential Diagnosis

Learning disorders must be differentiated from normal variations in academic attainment and from scholastic difficulties due to lack of opportunity, poor teaching, or cultural factors. Inadequate schooling can result in performance on standardized achievement tests. Impaired vision or hearing may affect learning ability and should be investigated through audiometric or screening tests. A learning disorder may be diagnosed in the presence of such sensory deficits only if the learning difficulties are in excess of those usually associated with these deficits.

In mental retardation, learning difficulties are commensurate with general impairment in intellectual functioning. However, in some cases of mild mental retardation, the level of achievement in reading, maths, or written expression is significantly low below the expected levels given the persons schooling or severity of mental retardation.

An additional learning disorder diagnosis should be made in context of a pervasive developmental disorder only when academic impairment is significantly below the expected levels given the individuals intellectual functioning and schooling. Mathematics disorders and disorder of written expression most commonly occur in combination reading disorder.

Question for Readers

Is it a learning difficulty of the learner or
teaching difficulty of the teacher?

6

Depression in Children

What about children and adolescents?

A lot less is known about depression in children and adolescents. Depression in children is very similar to depression in adults with a few exceptions. Rather than having a depressed mood, children are much more like to have an irritable mood. Adults often will not enjoy anything when they are depressed, but there are usually some activities children and adolescents will enjoy doing no matter how depressed they get. To say a child has clinically significant depression (Major Depressive Disorder or MDD), they must have 5 of the 9 symptoms listed below to such a degree that it significantly interferes with their functioning for at least 2 weeks straight.

- depressed or irritable mood most of the day, nearly every day
- markedly diminished interest or pleasure in all, or almost all activities most of the day, nearly every day
- significant weight loss when not dieting or failure to make appropriate weight gains
- trouble sleeping or too much sleeping nearly every day
- restlessness or really slowed down nearly every day which is obvious to others

- fatigue or loss of energy nearly every day
- feelings of worthlessness or excessive guilt nearly every day
- diminished ability to think or concentrate, or indecisiveness, nearly every day
- recurrent thoughts of death, suicidal thoughts or suicide attempts

Although it is not one of the criteria, some physical symptoms are very, very common in depression. Headaches are one of these. About 10% of children have severe headaches at least once a month. However 40% of girls with depression have severe headaches. The same does not hold true for boys.

Common clinical pictures of Depression in Children

Pure Depression (MDD)

In this type of depression a child with no other psychiatric problems suddenly becomes depressed, sometimes for little or no reason. Sometimes their sleep is disturbed. They are not hungry, have no energy, are afraid of all sorts of things, think life is hopeless, cannot concentrate at all, are less social and are very irritable.

Dysthymia

This is a milder depression that goes on for years at a time. Children and adolescents with Dysthymia often have been depressed so long that they can not recall what not being depressed is like. People think it is a part of their personality. Typically they are irritable, hard to please, unhappy with nearly everything and very trying to be around. They tend to have fewer problems with sleep and appetite than children with major depression. To have this disorder you must be depressed or irritable for at least a year straight with at least two of the following:

- poor appetite or overeating
- insomnia or excess sleeping

- low energy or fatigue
- low self-esteem
- poor concentration or difficulty making decisions
- feelings of hopelessness

Children with dysthymia often can still enjoy some activities. Children with dysthymia are at a very high risk to get MDD. Over 70% of dysthymia children will get severely depressed, and 12% will get manic depressive disorder. Rather than recover, they often go back to their dysthymic selves. A long episode of dysthymia will screw up a child's life far more than a brief episode of severe depression.

Double Depression

Many children with dysthymia will go on to develop episodes of major depressive disorder. When they do, their episodes of depression plus dysthymia are more serious. The illness lasts longer, is more severe, they are more disabled and they are more likely to kill themselves.

Psychotic Depression

Some children will develop signs of psychosis along with depression. A child might have hallucinations. The child might be very paranoid. The child might develop all sorts of bizarre and unusual ideas. This is the most serious type of depression. It is also quite uncommon.

Co-morbid Depression

Co-morbidity means that certain disorders occur more often together than one would expect by chance. For example: diabetes and obesity. The concept of co-morbidity is very important in psychiatry. It is very common that a person with depression will also have another childhood neuro-psychiatric disorder. In this situation, a child may have a preexisting chronic psychiatric illness and then becomes depressed. The episode of depression occurs with the other disorder so that the child actually shows signs of 2 or 3 psychiatric disorders at the same time. About 50% of children also have conduct disorder or oppositional defiant disorder, 40% of children with depression have anxiety disorder and 25% of children with depression have attention deficit disorder. Often the episode of depression will go away and leave the other psychiatric problem unchanged.

Bipolar Depression

In this case, children have episodes of depression, some episodes of wellness and also some episodes of mania, which is the opposite of depression. The depression looks pretty much the same as above. Sometimes children are depressed and manic at the same time. It is highly treatable. Despite the chronicity of the illness, effective drugs such as lithium have enabled persons diagnosed with bipolar illness to lead productive lives.

Seasonal Affective Disorders (SAD)

It has become clear in last few years that some children have depression only in one season, usually winter. It starts to worsen in late October and reaches its peak in January. By March things are usually on the mend. This can be extremely disabling, as this is usually when the hardest school work is. Approximately 3-4% of school-age children have SAD. There are many studies to show that light box can help adults with this condition. There are also studies in which this technique is used in children. This usually means sitting in front of a specially made light box and doing something about 30 minutes five times a week. Unfortunately, children are sometimes not complaint with them. Another technique is a dawn stimulator, which is a light which gets steady brighter, mimicking a spring or summer morning.

How common is Depression in Children?

About .3% (3 out of 1000) preschoolers, 1-2% of elementary school age children and 3-4% of Jr. high students have MDD. Another 3.3% have dysthymia. About 3-4% of children have seasonal affective disorder. Co-morbidity is a very important determining factor. In most studies, nearly all of the cases of pediatric depression also have another comorbid diagnosis. This is in the same range as adults.

What happens to Depressed Children?

In many cases, it disappears. About 90% of the time it is gone within 1 year. Sometimes it disappears without any treatment at all. That is the good news.

The bad news is that depression in children is recurrent. That is, even after a child recovers, he or she is much more likely to get depressed again. About 35% will again meet criteria for MDD within a year from recovering. By 2 years, half of the children who recovered will have had a recurrence of their depression within 4 years of their first episode. Each time depression recurs, it makes it that much more likely that it will recur again.

Children are more likely to have their depression recur if they started having depression before age 14, if there is divorce at the time of depression, or if one of the parents is also depressed at the same time. No one can predict exactly who will have another episode of depression and who will not. Some of the predictors for another episode are: one parent has been clinically depressed, one parent has another psychiatric problem other than depression, and the child has other psychiatric disorders (like attention deficit disorder, learning disabilities, or anxiety disorders). If all 3 of these are present, it is almost certain that a teenager will develop another episode of depression over the next 4 years. If a child lives in a family with a lot of conflict, they are more likely to relapse.

What causes Depression in Children?

Depression in children is caused by a combination of 3 things: genetics, what is happening in a person's life, and what is going to happen in their body. Usually, more than one is present in a child. For a child to get depressed, there must either be major things wrong with their lives, something major wrong with their body and or mind, or a strong family history of depression. Often more than one is present.

Medical problems: Children who have chronic medical problems are much more likely to get depression. Severe asthma, severe head injury, diabetes, epilepsy and many of the less common chronic childhood diseases can result in depression.

Neuropsychiatric: Children with certain disorders of the brain often get depression because the same chemicals and the same nerve pathways are involved in both. Children with following neuropsychiatric illness are more likely to get depression: Attention deficit hyperactive disorder, Learning disabilities, Anxiety disorders, Eating disorders, Obsessive-Compulsive disorder and autism and related conditions.

Environment: Some children, but not all, react to problems in their environment with depressive signs and symptoms. Common causes are abuse of all kinds, families that are in chaos, neglect, poverty, no consistent parent, school or home, and horrible thing like witnessing deaths, finding bodies, losing parents, etc. Although children who get depressed are more likely to have a stressful life event happen to them in the year before they get ill, the more important relationship is for children who have multiple stressful events. In a study, 50% of depressed children and adolescents had 2 or more major stressors in the year before getting depressed. In children without depression, no child had 2 or more major stressors in the past year. There is an interaction between environment and genes. If bad things happen to a child and there is a family history of depression, a depressed child is a very likely outcome.

Television: Children who are watching a lot of TV are more likely to have a host of different psychiatric symptoms. Recent studies have shown kids who are watching over 6 hours a day have more problems with depression, anxiety and aggression.

Drugs and Alcohol: Substance abuse is very common, especially alcohol and marijuana. About 14% of teenagers test positive for street drugs and alcohol use. However, it was found that it is more common that a child will become depressed and then start using drugs or alcohol rather than the other way around. In adults, when people stop drinking or using drugs, their depression usually clears over the next 2 or 4 weeks. In children and adolescents, this rarely happens. Even after they are clean, most depressed children and adolescents are still depressed.

Depression runs in Families: If one of the parents has depression, about 40% of the children will get depressed at sometime before their 20th birthday. The younger the parent was when he or she got depressed, the more likely the children are to become depressed. When mothers have been seriously depressed (an episode every year or so and hospitalized at least once for depression) their children are even more likely to become depressed, and when they do it is more severe, last longer and is accompanied by other psychiatric problems, too. These children also are more likely to commit suicide.

Why does Depression run in Families?

Genetics: Even if a child never has contact with a parent, if that parent was depressed, it means that the children are also more likely to get depressed, too.

Marital Difficulties: Depression in adults goes hand in hand with marital problems. The combination of divorces plus depression in parents makes it much more likely that the children will get depressed.

Parenting Problems: It is damn hard to be a good parent when you are depressed, and it can be pretty depressing trying to parent a depressed child. Parenting problems, whether they come from the parent or child, can make everyone's depression worse.

Not all children of depressed parents get depression

That's right, common as depression is, many children don't get depressed even when depression runs in families or bad things happen to them or they get sick. What helps protect these children from depression?

Diagnosing Depression

In medicine, a diagnosis is based on the history (talking with a patient and their families), a physical examination, and lab tests.

History

In adults, it is often possible to get by with only talking with the patient. This is never possible with children and adolescents. Children often will not say they are depressed. They are most likely to blame all their problems on school, friends or family. Only by talking with the family can you get an outside perspective. On the other hand, children are better reporters than their parents of their own feelings. You need to check for all sorts of other possible psychiatric disorders and other medical disorders, too.

Examination

In children and adolescents, this may mean a large variety of things, depending on the history. Besides doing parts of the physical and neurological exam, a careful assessment involves observing how the child behaves, does school work and gets along with his or her family.

Lab Tests

This depends on the history, the exam and age of the child. Sometimes, no tests are necessary. Common things that end up being checked are thyroid tests, urine drug screens, tests for medical conditions that can mimic depression (infectious mono, for example), and other routine lab tests.

Why should you treat Depression, since most people recover from it spontaneously?

If your child's depression resolves on its own, you are right. But, if it goes on very long or recurs, that means that your child is more likely to get an episode of severe depression or chronic depression. The longer depression goes on, the harder it is to treat. The longer it goes on, the more it damages the social, academic, psychological maturation of your child. Depression is a horrible problem in children and adolescents. The only thing more horrible is doing nothing about it.

What can be done to prevent the condition?

Depression may not be preventable. Some steps that may be helpful in preventing depression include the following:

- avoiding alcohol and illegal drugs
- avoiding cigarette smoking
- getting prompt treatment for other psychiatric disorders
- seeking effective treatment for chronic diseases
- talking with a counselor if the child experiences a major trauma

Depression can lead to suicide. It is important to recognize and treat the condition early. Children should be encouraged to talk to someone if they are concerned about depression. There are many people they can talk to including the following:

- a clergy member
- a family doctor
- parents or a trusted family member
- a professional at a mental health center
- a psychologist
- a school counselor

Articles

More Women Suffer Depression

By: *Hara Estroff Marano*

Summary: Females are twice as likely as males to be depressed.

For a while now, I've been thinking about some of the psychological differences between men and women. In studies conducted around the world, which is to say, in a variety of cultures other than our own, one of the differences that turn up most reliably is the preponderance of females among those with depression. Until puberty, males and females develop depression with about the same frequency. If anything, boys are a bit more likely to be depressed. Once puberty hits, everyone becomes more susceptible to depression—but females are twice as susceptible as males. What is interesting is that the gender difference in rates of depression begins to wind down among those in their 50s. Another way of looking at is that depression seems to be especially, but by no means exclusively, a disorder of women in their childbearing years. It's not clear what purpose this might serve. But there are some interesting clues about what is going on. Kenneth S. Kendler, M.D., is director of the Virginia Institute for Psychiatric and Behavioral Genetics at Virginia Commonwealth University. There he presides over "the best natural experiment that God has given us to study gender differences"—thousands of pairs of opposite-sex twins. Kendler reports that efforts he has made to explain the gender difference have been "pretty stunningly unsuccessful." No major differences have panned out so far. Except one. His studies pinpoint a significant difference between men and women in their response to adversity. "Women seem to have the capacity to be precipitated into depressive episodes at lower levels of stress." Low levels of stress are ubiquitous for both men and women, although each of the genders reacts to a somewhat different array of difficulties. Men seem to experience more stress from job loss than women do, for example, while women are more reactive to crises in their social network. But there are some stresses women experience that men don't. Exhibit A is role strain, carrying the load of housework and childcare while holding down a paying job. Kendler says his own wife, also a physician, once inadvertently supplied the most succinct definition of role strain when she declared, "I spend four hours a day with my kids and I feel guilty as hell, you spend two hours a day and feel like you're a great father. It's not fair." Adding injury to insult, recent evidence from the physiology lab shows that women's bodies respond to stress differently than men's. They pour out higher levels of stress hormones, and they fail to shut off production of the stress hormones readily. The female sex hormone progesterone blocks the normal ability of the stress hormone system to turn itself off. Sustained exposure to glucocorticoids kills brain cells, especially the hippocampus, crucial to memory. It's bad enough that, through the stress system, females are set up biologically to amplify internally their negative life experiences. They are prone to it psychologically too. Women ruminate more over upsetting situations, going over and over negative thoughts and feelings, especially if they have to do with relationships. Too often they get caught in a downward spiral of hopelessness and despair. It's entirely possible that women are primed by biology to be highly sensitive to relationships. Eons ago it might have helped alert them to the possibility of abandonment while they were busy raising the children. Today, however, there's a clear downside. Ruminators are unpleasant to be around. With their oversize need for reassurance they wind up torturing those closest to them. Of course, women have no monopoly on unpleasantness. Men fend people off, too. At least as pronounced as the female tilt to depression is the male excess of alcoholism, drug abuse and antisocial behaviors.

Prevalence of Depression and Its Treatment in an Elderly Population

The Cache County Study by: *David C. Steffens, MD; Ingmar Skoog, MD, PhD; Maria C. Norton, MS; Andrea D. Hart, MS; Joann T. Tschanz, PhD; Brenda L. Plassman, PhD; Bonita W. Wyse, PhD; Kathleen A. Welsh-Bohmer, PhD; John C. S. Breitner, MD, MPH Arch Gen Psychiatry. 2000; 57:601-607.*

Background: Previous estimates of the prevalence of geriatric depression have varied. There are few large population-based studies; most of these focused on individuals younger than 80 years. No US studies have been published since the advent of the newer antidepressant agents.

Methods: In 1995 through 1996, as part of a large population study, we examined the current and lifetime prevalence of depressive disorders in 4559 nondemented individuals aged 65 to 100 years. This sample represented 90%

of the elderly population of Cache County, Utah. Using a modified version of the Diagnostic Interview Schedule, we ascertained past and present *DSM-IV* major depression, dysthymia, and sub clinical depressive disorders. Medication use was determined through a structured interview and a "medicine chest inventory."

Results: Point prevalence of major depression was estimated at 4.4% in women and 2.7% in men (*P*=.003). Other depressive syndromes were surprisingly uncommon (combined point prevalence, 1.6%). Among subjects with current major depression, 35.7% were taking an antidepressant (mostly selective serotonin reuptake inhibitors) and 27.4% a sedative/hypnotic. The current prevalence of major depression did not change appreciably with age. Estimated lifetime prevalence of major depression was 20.4% in women and 9.6% in men (*P*<.001), decreasing with age.

Conclusions: These estimates for prevalence of major depression are higher than those reported previously in North American studies. Treatment with antidepressants was more common than reported previously, but was still lacking in most individuals with major depression. The prevalence of subsyndromal depressive symptoms was low, possibly because of unusual characteristics of the population.

Pituitary-Adrenal and Autonomic Responses to Stress in Women After Sexual and Physical Abuse in Childhood

Christine Heim, PhD; D. Jeffrey Newport, MD; Stacey Heit, MD; Yolanda P. Graham, MD; Molly Wilcox, BA; Robert Bonsall, PhD; Andrew H. Miller, MD; Charles B. Nemeroff, MD, PhD
JAMA. 2000; 284:592-597.

Context: Evidence suggests that early adverse experiences play a preeminent role in development of mood and anxiety disorders and those corticotrophin-releasing factor systems (CRF) may mediate this association.

Objective: To determine whether early-life stress results in a persistent sensitization of the hypothalamic-pituitary-adrenal axis to mild stress in adulthood, thereby contributing to vulnerability to psychopathological conditions.

Design and Setting: Prospective controlled study conducted from May 1997 to July 1999 at the General Clinical Research Center of Emory University Hospital, Atlanta, Ga.

Participants: Forty-nine healthy women aged 18 to 45 years with regular menses, with no history of mania or psychosis, with no active substance abuse or eating disorder within 6 months, and who were free of hormonal and psychotropic medications were recruited into 4 study groups (n = 12 with no history of childhood abuse or psychiatric disorder [controls]; n = 13 with diagnosis of current major depression who were sexually or physically abused as children; n = 14 without current major depression who were sexually or physically abused as children; and n = 10 with diagnosis of current major depression and no history of childhood abuse).

Main Outcome Measures: Adren corticotrophin hormone (ACTH) and cortisol levels and heart rate responses to a standardized psychosocial laboratory stressor compared among the 4 study groups.

Results: Women with a history of childhood abuse exhibited increased pituitary-adrenal and autonomic responses to stress compared with controls. This effect was particularly robust in women with current symptoms of depression and anxiety. Women with a history of childhood abuse and a current major depression diagnosis exhibited a more than 6-fold greater ACTH response to stress than age-matched controls.

Conclusions: The findings suggest that hypothalamic-pituitary-adrenal axis and autonomic nervous system hyperactivity, presumably due to CRF hyper secretion, is a persistent consequence of childhood abuse that may contribute to the diathesis for adulthood psychopathological conditions. Furthermore, these results imply a role for CRF receptor antagonists in the prevention and treatment of psychopathological conditions related to early-life stress.

Chronic stressors, social support, and depression during pregnancy

L *Seguin,* L *Potvin,* M *St-Denis, and* J *Loiselle*

Objective: To analyze the relationships between stressful life conditions, social support, and depressive symptomatology during pregnancy in women of low socioeconomic status and a comparison group of women of higher socioeconomic status.

Methods: Study participants were recruited from four hospital prenatal care clinics. Low socioeconomic status was defined as no more than 11 years of education and a household income below the poverty level. Higher socioeconomic status was defined as at least 12 years of education and a household income at least one and one-half times the poverty level. All subjects were nulliparous, over 18 years of age, and French-speaking. Questionnaires were administered verbally at the participants' homes during the 30th week of pregnancy, approximately. The Beck Depression Inventory was used to measure depressive symptomatology during the preceding 7 days.

Results: Approximately 47% of the low socioeconomic status women and 20% of the higher socioeconomic status women scored 10 or more on the Beck Depression Inventory, indicating a depressive state. Multiple regression analysis demonstrated that chronic stressors (e.g., financial and housing problems), negative life events, and inadequate social support were all linked to high depressive symptomatology during pregnancy.

Conclusion: During pregnancy, depressive symptoms are common, especially in women of low socioeconomic status, and are strongly related to socio environmental factors.

Increasing Rates of Depression

G. L. Klerman and M. M. Weissman, Department of Psychiatry, Cornell University Medical College, Payne Whitney Psychiatric Clinic, New York, NY 10021.

Several recent, large epidemiologic and family studies suggest important temporal changes in the rates of major depression: an increase in the rates in the cohorts born after World War II; a decrease in the age of onset with an increase in the late teenaged and early adult years; an increase between 1960 and 1975 in the rates of depression for all ages; a persistent gender effect, with the risk of depression consistently two to three times higher among women than men across all adult ages; a persistent family effect, with the risk about two to three times higher in first-degree relatives as compared with controls; and the suggestion of a narrowing of the differential risk to men and women due to a greater increase in risk of depression among young men. These trends, drawn from studies using comparable methods and modern diagnostic criteria, are evident in the United States, Sweden, Germany, Canada, and New Zealand, but not in comparable studies conducted in Korea and Puerto Rico and of Mexican-Americans living in the United States. These cohort changes cannot be fully attributed to artifacts of reporting, recall, mortality, or labeling and have implications for understanding the etiology of depression and for clinical practice.

Beliefs and Attitudes Associated With the Intention to Not Accept the Diagnosis of Depression Among Young Adults

Benjamin W. Van Voorhees, MD, MPH, Section of General Internal Medicine, The University of Chicago, 5841 South Maryland Avenue, MC 20007, Chicago, IL 60637

Purpose: Negative attitudes and beliefs about depression treatment may prevent many young adults from accepting a diagnosis and treatment for depression. We undertook a study to determine the association between depressive symptom severity, beliefs about and attitudes toward treatment, subjective social norms, and past behavior on the intent not to accept a physician's diagnosis of depression.

Methods: We conducted a cross-sectional study of 10,962 persons aged 16 to 29 years who participated and had positive screening results on the Center for Epidemiologic Studies Depression (CES-D) score in an Internet-based public health depression screening program. Participants reported whether they would accept their physician's diagnosis of depression. Based on the theory of reasoned action, we developed a multivariate model of the factors that predict intent not to accept a diagnosis of depression.

Results: Twenty-six percent of the participants stated their intent not to accept their physician's diagnosis of depression. Disagreeing that medications are effective in treating depression (strongly disagree, odds ratio (OR) = 6.5, 95% confidence interval (CI), 4.6–9.3), that there is a biological cause for depression (strongly disagree, OR = 1.9, 95% CI, 1.3 – 2.7), and agreeing that you would be embarrassed if your friends knew you had depression were associated with the intent not to accept a diagnosis of depression (strongly agree, OR = 2.3, 95% CI, 1.8–2.9). Beliefs and attitudes, subjective social norms, and past behavior explained most of the variance in this model (84%).

Conclusion: Negative beliefs and attitudes, subjective social norms, and lack of past helpful treatment experiences are associated with the intent to not accept the diagnosis of depression and may contribute to low rates of treatment among young adults.

Conclusion

This chapter is very useful in understanding depression and its impact on not only the sufferer but also the people around him. Depression is a widely faced problem in the world today and more than 60% of people worldwide have experienced this negative emotion at some point in their lives, in varying degrees.

Depression is a self terminating disorder. People who suffer from this disorder as victims of a grave. The disorder penetrates into human at both an internal as well as external level. Destruction of meaningfulness, no fulfillment and distrust of love are some of the many characteristics of this disorder.

Depressed people not only need to be accepting to their

state but also need to fight and overcome the depression within them. This fight is not one that is overcome by the depressed person himself but also needs co-operation from the family and friends.

Referring one's self to a psychologist or therapists for help seems to be wise act. Therapy involves not only distinguishing what kind of depression does the person suffer from but also is a form helping the person to deal with their problems.

In some cases hospitalization is also necessary. Support from family members and friends also aid the person to overcome and break the monotony of his existence.

The depressed person should not be treated as a patient as this would enhance his feeling of depression and bring bout self-pity. The people in his environment should treat him with a little bit of attention and a level of tolerance.

Quoting Mr. Arnold Ludwig:

"Without emotion man would be nothing but a biological computer. Love, joy, sorrow, fear, apprehension, anger, satisfaction and discontent provide the meaning of human existence".

Depression is an emotion characterized by sadness, crying, withdrawal from others and feelings of inadequacy.

In depressive episodes, sad feelings are accompanied by persistent problems in other areas of life problems, such as appetite change, altered sleep patterns, loss of interest or pleasure in usual activities, including sex, loss of energy, diminished ability to think and concentrate, feelings of worthlessness or self-approach or suicidal thoughts or acts.

During a depressive episode, the person's mood and thought patterns may be strikingly negative. The depressed person often appears lost, vulnerable, detached, and unable to find joy in any aspect of daily life, life seems to have lost its validity and a sort of numbness has set in. Often the person seems constantly on the verge of tears. Thoughts about the self are likely to be overwhelming negative, the person may feel unattractive, inferior to others, incompetent as a spouse or parent and unsuccessful at school or work. The future may seem almost completely hopeless and this of course, is no reason that suicide becomes a risk.

An estimated 20% of American and European women have experienced a major depressive episode at sometime, for the men the figure is about 10%. Some 6% of women and 3% of men have had episodes serious enough to require hospitalization. An estimated 46% of college students are thought to have experienced depressions serious enough at some time, to have warranted professional help. Many depressed people are treated as out patients, but many others suffer in silence and solitude.

Question for Readers

What can teachers and parents do about dealing with depression among children?

7

Eating Disorders

More than 90% of those afflicted with eating disorders are adolescent and young adult women. One reason that women in this age group are particularly vulnerable to eating disorders is their tendency to go on strict diets to achieve an "ideal" figure. Researchers have found that such stringent dieting can play a key role in triggering eating disorders. Approximately 1% of adolescent girls develop *anorexia nervosa,* a dangerous condition in which they can literally starve themselves to death. Another 2 to 3% of young women develop *bulimia nervosa,* a destructive pattern of excessive overeating followed by vomiting or other "purging" behaviors to control their weight. These eating disorders also occur in men and older women, but much less frequently.

The consequences of eating disorders can be severe. For example, one in ten cases of anorexia nervosa leads to death from starvation, cardiac arrest, other medical complications, or suicide. Fortunately, increasing awareness of the dangers of eating disorders–sparked by medical studies and extensive media coverage of the illness–has led many people to seek help. Nevertheless, some people with eating disorders refuse to admit that they have a problem and do not get treatment. Family members and friends can help recognize the problem and encourage the person to seek treatment.

The eating disorders anorexia nervosa and bulimia nervosa have assumed an increased importance over the past two decades as clinicians and investigators have recognized their prevalence and the difficulties associated with their treatment. The conditions have become more common since 1970 and are now frequently encountered in clinical practice. Moreover, cases unresponsive to therapy are associated with a significant mortality; between 5 and 20 percent of such patients die as a result of these disorders. Chronic forms of eating disorders develop in about 25 percent of patients, including patients who are habitually at low body weight or who display wide fluctuations in weight as a result of regular purging. Frequently, such patients experience a variety of metabolic complications and psychosocial sequelae, including a high prevalence of affective and anxiety disorders as well as markedly isolated life-styles. Because of these issues there has been interest in investigations directed to improving an understanding of and treatments for eating disorders. The increase in eating disorders would be puzzling enough if they were occurring across the population as a whole. What makes them even more intriguing is that they tend to be culturally specific. Until recently, eating disorders were not found in developing countries, where access to sufficient food is so often a daily struggle; only in the West, where food is generally plentiful, have they been rampant. Now this is changing; there is evidence that eating disorders are going global. Not everyone in the world is at risk. In fact, eating disorders tend to occur in a relatively small segment of the population. More than 90% of the sever cases are young females, mostly in families with upper socioeconomic status, who live in a socially competitive environment.

Eating disorders are real, complex, and devastating conditions that can have serious consequences for health, productivity, and relationships.

Eating disorders are not just a "fad" or a "phase." They are serious, potentially life-threatening conditions that affect a person's emotional and physical health.

People struggling with an eating disorder need to seek professional help. The earlier a person with an eating disorder seeks treatment, the greater the likelihood of physical and emotional recovery.

History

From its earliest description anorexia nervosa was recognized to resemble, but also to be distinct, entirely somatic disorders. In 1694 Richard Morton described two patients whom he differentiated from other tubercular patients as having nervous consumption. In 1868 Williams Gull rediscovered the syndrome and six years later began to use the term "anorexia nervosa" and to discuss factors he felt were important in the pathogenesis. At about the same time Ernest Charles, Lasegue independently described the disorder. In addition to his detailed clinical descriptions Lasegue stressed that the patient's active psychological disgust for food led to the weight loss and noted familial involvements in the disorder. Those initial descriptions of anorexia nervosa were of a psychological disturbance in which starvation was considered to be responsible for many of the prominent symptoms.

Following that period of redefinition of anorexia nervosa as a core syndrome Hilde burch, beginning in the 1950s, helped shape and understanding by highlighting psychopathological features. She was able to suggest that the determined efforts for weight loss represented a distorted attempt at mastery for persons who felt helpless in their worlds. She linked that sense of ineffectiveness with difficulties in body image and with awareness of inner feeling states in the patients. Bulimia had been long described as a symptom of voracious hunger, early descriptions exist in the Babylonian Talmud complied between the years 400 and 500 BC. As a part of the anorexia nervosa syndrome, bulimia was observed by Gull in the 1870s. Following that there is little recorded on bulimia in relation to anorexia nervosa for the next 60 years.

By 1980 over 50 percent of anorexic patients were bulimic. As attention was drawn to bulimia because of its increased frequency within the anorexia nervosa syndrome, Gerald

Rusell described a group of persons whom he felt has a variant of the syndrome and termed the condition bulimia nervosa. In the following year, 1980, the third edition of diagnostic and statistical Manual of Mental Disorders (DSM – III – R) provided diagnostic criteria for bulimia as a syndrome.

In the revised third edition of DSM (DSM – III – R) anorexia nervosa and bulimia nervosa were classified as a disorders usually first evident in infancy, childhood, or adolescence, which reflected their onset during adolescence.

Comparative Nosology

Anorexia Nervosa

Both anorexia and bulimia are characterized by a morbid fear of gaining weight and losing control over eating. The major difference seems to be that people with anorexia are proud of both their diets and their extraordinary control. People with bulimia are ashamed of both the problem itself and their lack of control.

Since 1969 a variety of operational criteria have been developed; these usually include the psychopathology, the behavior, and disturbed endocrine function. In 1970 Russell suggested three criteria for the diagnosis: (1) the behavior that is designed to produce marked weight loss: (2) the characteristic psychopathology of a morbid fear of becoming fat: and (3) evidence of an endocrine disorder, amenorrhea in women, and loss of sexual potency and interest in men.

Behaviour and Marked Weight Loss

There has been general agreement that a drive for thinness is necessary for the diagnosis. That criterion has been described in somewhat differing terms: the "relentless pursuit of thinness" (Bruch). "the deliberate wish to be slim" (Mara Selvini-Palazzoli). The DSM – III – R criteria added a degree of precision by describing "the refusal to maintain body weight over a minimal normal weight for age and height" and by including both weight loss and a failure to make expected weight.

Morbid Fear of Becoming Fat

This criterion involves both an intense fear of becoming fat and the importance of weight and shape to the person's attitudes and feelings about her body in governing her sense of self. DSM – III criteria described that feature in terms of body image disturbance. Many studies of body image in anorexia nervosa focused on a narrow definition related to visual self perception; however, data indicate that many persons with anorexia nervosa do not overestimate their size and that overestimation is not unique to persons with the disorder. Given those data, it was appropriate to change the criterion in DSM – III – R to focus on the attitudinal and affective dimensions of body image, and the condition was described as "disturbance in the way in which one's body weight, size or shape is experience.

In DSM – III – R bulimia nervosa was described as an overconcern with weight and shape, but the term "overconcern" is vague and hard to determine reliably. The person does not recognize that her changed body is no longer healthy or attractive, Because of those issues, the wording of the criterion in DSM IV emphasizes the central concern of weight and shape in the evaluation of the self, and the denial of the serious consequences of the weight loss.

Endocrine disorder in women and loss of sexual potency and interest in men

There is value in this criterion for amenorrhea, because it is seen so regularly in anorexia nervosa and emphasis is given to the hypothalamic dysfunction that occurs in the syndrome.

Many people lose weight because of a medial condition, but people with anorexia have an intense fear of obesity and relentlessly pursue thinness.

DSM-IV specifies two subtypes of anorexia nervosa. In the restricting type, individuals diet to limit calorie intake; in the binge-eating-purging type, they rely on purging.

Binge-purge anorexics engage in such impulsive behavior

as stealing, alcohol and drug use, and self-mutilation more than restricting anorexics, and their moods are more variable (labile).

A girl with anorexia is never satisfied with her weight loss. Staying the same weight from one day to the next or gaining any weight at all is likely to cause intense panic, anxiety, and depressions. Only continued weight loss every day for weeks on end is satisfactory. Another key criterion of anorexia is a marked disturbance in body image.

Medical Consequences

The most common medical complication of anorexia nervosa is cessation of menstruation (amenorrhea). This defining feature is an objective physical index of the degree of food restriction. In fact, studies have demonstrated a strong correlation between ovulation and resulting menstruation and weight (Pirke, Schweiger, & Fichter, 1987), but overwhelming evidence indicates that alterations in endocrine levels resulting in amenorrhea are a consequence of semistarvatin rather than a cause. Other medical signs and symptoms of anorexia include dry skin, brittle hair or nails, and sensitivity to or intolerance of cold temperatures. Also it is relatively common to see lanugo, downy hair on the limbs and cheeks. Cardiovascular problems, such as chronically low blood pressure and heart rate, can also result. If vomiting is part of the anorexia, electrolyte imbalance and resulting cardiac and kidney problems can result.

Health Consequences of Anorexia Nervosa in summary

In anorexia nervosa's cycle of self-starvation, the body is denied the essential nutrients it needs to function normally. Thus, the body is forced to slow down all of its processes to conserve energy, resulting in serious medical consequences.

Abnormally slow heart rate and low blood pressure, which mean that the heart muscle is changing. The risk for heart failure rises as the heart rate and blood pressure levels sink lower and lower.

- Reduction of bone density (osteoporosis), which results in dry, brittle bones.
- Muscle loss and weakness.
- Severe dehydration, which can result in kidney failure.
- Fainting, fatigue, and overall weakness.
- Dry hair and skin; hair loss is common.

Growth of a downy layer of hair called lanugo all over the body, including the face, in an effort to keep the body warm.

Associated Psychological Disorders

Anxiety disorders and mood disorders are often present individuals with anorexia. One that seems to co-occur frequently is obsessive-compulsive disorder (OCD).

Subtypes

Important and reliable differences have been described between anorexic persons who are periodically bulimic and those who are consistent dietary restrictors. In addition the group who engage in purging behaviors without binging, generally display the characteristics of the binge-eating group, Bulimic anorexics have generally weighed more before the illness and more commonly have been obese; they also come from families in which obesity is more common. They are much more likely to induce vomiting and misuse laxatives in their attempts to control their weight. They are also an impulsive group. That is evident not only in their eating behavior but in other behaviors as well they frequently have problems with alcohol or street drugs they may steal and compared with restrictors they more frequently attempt self-mutilation and suicide. The bulimic group of anorexics also differ in personality characteristics they are frequently borderline, narcissistic, or antisocial - a group that discharge impulses through action, in contrast to the far more inhibited restrictors, on all those dimensions the bulimic anorexic group resemble persons with bulimia nervosa. Therefore, some have recommended that the two groups of bulimic patients be classified together. However, there must be important differences between bulimic persons who lose large amounts of weight and meet criteria for anorexia nervosa and those who never do. For that reason and because of the important differences between the two anorexic groups, DSM-IV for the first time sub-classifies anorexia nervosa by the presence or absence of bulimia.

Differential Diagnosis

Anorexia Nervosa

The differential diagnosis of anorexia nervosa complicated by the patient's denial of the symptoms, the secrecy, surrounding the patient's bizarre eating rituals, and the patient's resistance to seeking treatment. Thus, it may be difficult to identify the mechanism of weight loss and the patient's associated ruminative thoughts regarding distortions of body image. The clinician must ascertain that the patient does not have a medical illness that can account for the weight loss because; Weight loss, Peculiar eating behaviors, and vomiting can occur in several mental disorders. Depressive disorders and anorexia nervosa have several features in common, such as depressed feeling, crying spells, sleep disturbance, obsessive ruminations, and occasional thoughts. However, the two disorders have several distinguishing features. Generally: a patient with a depressive disorder has a decreased appetite. whereas an anorexia nervosa patient claims to have a normal appetite and to feel hungry.

The hyperactivity seen in anorexia nervosa is planned and ritualistic. The preoccupation with the caloric content of food recipes, and the preparation of gourmet feasts are typical of the anorexia nervosa patient and are not present in the patient with a depressive disorder. And in depressive disorders the patient has no intense fear of obesity or disturbance of body image, as the anorexia nervosa patient has. The depressed patient displays a generalized reduction of self-esteem, whereas self-esteem in the person with anorexia nervosa is governed by the mirror and the scales. Weight fluctuations, vomiting, and peculiar food handling may occur in somatization disorder. On rare occasions a patient fulfills the diagnostic criteria for both somatization disorder and anorexia nervosa.

Generally, the Weight loss in somatization disorder is not as severe as that in anorexia nervosa, nor does the patient with somatization disorder express a morbid fear of becoming overweight, as is common in the anorexia nervosa patient. Occasionally, schizophrenic patients may lose large amounts weight because they refuse to eat. That may relate to their delusions about food (for example, fear that the food has been poisoned) or the effects of food on the body (for example, that the food will cause the intestines to rot) or rarely, may result from the negativistic behavior associated with catatonia.

People with either anorexia or certain forms of depression also tend to have higher than normal levels of cortisol, a brain hormone released in response to stress. Scientists have been able to show that the excess levels of cortisol in both anorexia and depression are caused by a problem that occurs in or near a region of the brain called the hypothalamus.

Bulimia Nervosa

When Russell first proposed diagnostic criteria for bulimia nervosa in 1979 he suggested three components: (1) the patients suffer from powerful and intractable urges to overeat; (2) they seek to avoid the fattening effects of food by inducing vomiting, abusing purgatives, or both and (3) they have a morbid fear of becoming fat.

Clinical Description

Powerful and Interactable urges to Overeat

In defining a binge some have focused on the quantity of food eaten, others on the subjective state, and others on the need for discrete episodes of overeating or on the rapid rate of eating. With regards to quantity, what is relevant is that the person is eating more than is normal.

Binge-eating episodes are characterized by a subjective sense of loss of control, which is the sense that the person cannot prevent the occurrence of the binge or terminate it once it has started. A variety of dysphonic mood states precede the binge and precipitate it; the binge itself has the immediate effect of reducing the unpleasant mood, but his is then followed by physical discomfort and fear of gaining weight. The final characteristic of the binge, that the eating occurs in a discrete period of time, is included to moreover continual snacking from qualifying as a binge.

Inducing Vomiting and Abusing Purgatives

In DSM-III-R a broader statement was included, namely, "vomiting, use of laxatives or diuretics, strict dieting or fasting or vigorous exercise in order to prevent weight gain."

There are reasons to restrict the criterion to vomiting and laxative abuse : (1) Self-induced vomiting or laxative misuse are thought to be pathological behaviors in our society and are not given the social acceptance associated with dieting and vigorous exercise : (2) there is evidence to suggest that purging bulimic persons differ from nonpurging binge eaters in terms of degree of psychopathology: (3) purging bulimic cases may have a different course because the serious physiological complications of the disorder are often related to the consequences of the weight control methods.

It is wise to subdivide bulimia nervosa into purging and nonpurging types, as in DSM-IV. The non purging group may include a number of persons with the proposed diagnosis of binge-eating disorder. That group of obese persons have many features of bulimia nervosa but lack the purging behavior and extreme concern with body weight and shape.

Morbid Fear of Becoming Fat

In DSM-III-R it was incorporated as "persistent over concern with body weight and shape".

Concerns with weight and shape are common in the

general female population, but empirical data have shown that they differ in bulimia nervosa by virtue of their intensity and, as for anorexia nervosa, by their central role in governing the person's evaluation of her self-esteem.

The hallmark of bulimia nervosa is eating a larger amount of food typically, more junk food than fruits and vegetable than most people would eat under similar circumstances (Fairburn & Cooper, 1993). Patients with bulimia readily identify with this description, even though the actual caloric intake for binges varies significantly from person to person. Just as important as the amount of food eaten is the fact that the eating is experienced as out of control a criterion that is an integral part of the definition of binge eating.

Another important criterion is that the individual attempts to compensate for the binge eating and potential weight gain, almost always by purging techniques. Techniques include self-induced vomiting immediately after eating, and using laxatives (drugs that relieve constipation) and diuretics (drugs that result in loss of fluids through greatly increased frequency of urination).

Some exercise excessively, others fast for long periods between binges. Bulimia nervosa is sub-typed in DSM-IV into purging type and nonpurging type. Approximately two-thirds of bulimics are purgers the remaining third are nonpurgers.

Medical Consequences

Chronic bulimia with purging has a number of medical consequences. One is salivary gland enlargement caused by repeated vomiting, which gives the face a chubby appearance.

Repeated vomiting also may erode the dental enamel on the inner surface of the front teeth. More important, continued vomiting may upset the chemical balance of bodily fluids, including sodium and potassium levels. This condition, called an electrolyte imbalance, can result in serious medical complications if unattended, including cardiac arrhythmia (disrupted heartbeat) and real (kindly) failure both of which can be fatal.

Intestinal problems resulting from laxative abuse are also potentially serious; they can include severe constipation or permanent colon damage. Finally, some individuals with bulimia have marked calluses on their fingers or the backs of their hands caused by the friction of contract with the teeth and throat when repeatedly sticking their fingers down their throats to stimulate- the gag reflex.

Health Consequences of Bulimia Nervosa in summary

The recurrent binge-and-purge cycles of bulimia can affect the entire digestive system and can lead to electrolyte and chemical imbalances in the body that affect the heart and other major organ functions.

Electrolyte imbalances that can lead to irregular heartbeats and possibly heart failure and death. Electrolyte imbalance is caused by dehydration and loss of potassium, sodium and chloride from the body as a result of purging behaviors.

- Potential for gastric rupture during periods of bingeing.
- Inflammation and possible rupture of the esophagus from frequent vomiting.
- Tooth decay and staining from stomach acids released during frequent vomiting.
- Chronic irregular bowel movements and constipation as a result of laxative abuse.
- Peptic ulcers and pancreatitis.

Associated Psychological Disorders

Bulimia seems strongly related to anxiety disorders, and somewhat less so to mood and substance use disorders.

Bulimia Nervosa

The diagnosis of bulimia nervosa cannot be made if the binge eating and purging behaviors occur exclusively during episodes of anorexia nervosa. In such cases the diagnosis is anorexia nervosa, binge eating/purging type. The clinician must ascertain that the patient has no neurological disease, such as epileptic-equivalent seizures, central nervous system tumors, Kluver-Bucy syndrome, or Kleine-Levin syndrome.

Binge-eating Disorder

Individuals who meet preliminary criteria for BED are often found in weight-control programs. Individuals with BED who seek treatment are typically in their 40s people with BED show an increased frequency of additional psychological disorders and more psychopathology in general than obese people who don't binge.

Individuals with binge eating disorder feel that they lose control of themselves when eating. They eat large quantities of food and do not stop until they are uncomfortably full. Usually, they have more difficulty losing weight and keeping it off than do people with other serious weight problems. Most people with the disorder are obese and have a history of weight fluctuations. Binge eating disorder is found in about 2% on the general population–more often in women than men. Recent research shows that binge eating disorder occurs in about 30% of people participating in medically supervised weight control programs.

Medical Complications

Medical complications can frequently be a result of eating disorders. Individuals with eating disorders who use drugs to stimulate vomiting, bowel movements, or urination may be in considerable danger, as this practice increases the risk of heart failure.

In patients with anorexia, starvation can damage vital organs such as the heart and brain. To protect itself, the body shifts into "slow gear": monthly menstrual periods stop, breathing, pulse and blood pressure rates drop and thyroid function slows. Nails and hair become brittle; the skin dries, yellows and becomes covered with soft hair called lanugo.

Excessive thirst and frequent urination may occur. Dehydration contributes to constipation and reduced body fat leads to lowered body temperature and the inability to withstand cold.

Mild anemia, swollen joints, reduced muscle mass and light-headedness also commonly occur in anorexia. If the disorder becomes severe, patients may lose calcium from their bones, making them brittle and prone to breakage. They may also experience irregular heart rhythms and heart failure. In some patients, the brain shrinks, causing personality changes. Fortunately, this condition can be reversed when normal weight is reestablished.

In National Institute Of Mental Health (NIMH)-supported research, scientists have found that many patients with anorexia also suffer from other psychiatric illnesses. While the majority has co-occurring clinical depression, others suffer from anxiety, personality or substance abuse disorders and many are at risk for suicide. Obsessive-compulsive disorder (OCD), an illness characterized by repetitive thoughts and behaviors, can also accompany anorexia. Individuals with anorexia are typically compliant in personality but may have sudden outbursts of hostility and anger or become socially withdrawn.

In rare instances, binge eating causes the stomach to rupture; purging may result in heart failure due to loss of vital minerals, such as potassium. Vomiting causes other less deadly, but serious, problems–the acid in vomit wears down the outer layer of the teeth and can cause scarring on the backs of hands when fingers are pushed down the throat to induce vomiting. Further, the esophagus becomes inflamed and glands near the cheeks become swollen. As in anorexia, bulimia may lead to irregular menstural periods. Interest in sex may also diminish. Some individuals with bulimia struggle with addictions, including abuse of drugs and alcohol and compulsive stealing. Like individuals with anorexia, many people with bulimia suffer from clinical depression, anxiety, OCD and other psychiatric illnesses. These problems, combined with their impulsive tendencies, place them at increased risk for suicidal behavior.

People with binge eating disorder are usually overweight, so they are prone to the serious medical problems associated with obesity, such as high cholesterol, high blood pressure and diabetes. Obese individuals also have a higher risk for gallbladder disease, heart disease and some types of cancer. Research at National Institute Of Mental Health (NIMH) and elsewhere has shown that individuals with binge eating disorder have high rates of co-occurring psychiatric illnesses–especially depression.

Health Consequences of Binge Eating Disorder in summary

Binge eating disorder often results in many of the same health risks associated with clinical obesity.

- High blood pressure.
- High cholesterol levels.
- Heart disease as a result of elevated triglyceride levels.
- Type II diabetes mellitus.
- Gallbladder disease.

Course and Prognosis

The eating disorders display an extremely varied course, ranging from a single mild illness in adolescence to a lifelong disorder with remissions and exacerbations, or at times to a persistent lifelong disorder.

Anorexia Nervosa

Studies have repeatedly shown that a younger age of onset is a good prognostic sign. Other indicators of a favorable outcome are less denial, less immaturity, and improved self-esteem. Such factors as a parental conflict, vomiting, laxative abuse, and various behavioral manifestations (such as obsessive-compulsive, hysterical, depressive, and denial symptoms) have been related to poor outcome in some studies. 30 to 50 percent of anorexia nervosa patients have the symptoms of bulimia nervosa, and usually the bulimic symptoms occur within 18 months after the beginning of anorexia nervosa. Sometimes the bulimic symptoms precede the onset of anorexia nervosa.

Bulimia Nervosa

Bulimia nervosa is a chronic disorder with a waxing and waning course. Some patients with mild courses have long-term remissions. Other patients are disabled by the disorder and have been hospitalized etc. In some cases of untreated bulima nervosa, spontaneous remission occurs in one to two years. It is likely that for many patients bulimia or mood disorders recur at times of later stress.

Epidemiology

Estimates of the incidence or prevalence of the eating disorders have varied because the findings depend on the definition of a case, the method of sampling, and the population from which the sample is obtained.

Incidence rates for anorexia nervosa have generally been about one to via cases per 100,000 population.

Eating disorders often develop in adolescence, with biomodal risk ages of onset at 14 and 18, and a usual range of 12 to 25 but about 5 percent of patients develop the disorder ark. 25. Studies of anorexia and bulimia nervosa repeatedly note that 90 to 95 percent of patients are women.

Statistics with respect to USA Findings

In the United States, as many as 10 million females and 1million males are fighting a life and death battle with an eating disorder such as anorexia or bulimia. Approximately 25 million more are struggling with binge eating disorder.

The Prevalance of Eating Disorders

Because of the secretiveness and shame associated with eating disorders, many cases are probably not reported. In addition, many individuals struggle with body dissatisfaction and sub-clinical disordered eating attitudes and behaviors.

For example, it has been shown that 80% of American women are dissatisfied with their appearance.

The drive for Thinness

- 42% of 1st-3rd grade girls want to be thinner.
- 81% of 10 year olds are afraid of being fat.
- The average American woman is 5'4" tall and weighs 140 pounds. The average American model is 5'11" tall and weighs 117 pounds.
- Most fashion models are thinner than 98% of American women.

Dieting

- 51% of 9 and 10 year-old girls feel better about themselves if they are on a diet.
- 46% of 9-11 year-olds are "sometimes" or "very often" on diets, and 82% of their families are "sometimes" or "very often" on diets.
- 91% of women recently surveyed on a college campus had attempted to control their weight through dieting, 22% dieted "often" or "always".
- 95% of all dieters will regain their lost weight in 1-5 years.
- 35% of "normal dieters" progress to pathological dieting. Of those, 20-25% progress to partial or full-syndrome eating disorders.
- 25% of American men and 45% of American women are on a diet on any given day.

Americans spend over $40 billion on dieting and diet-related products each year.

Cross Cultural Considerations

The prevalence of eating disorders among African-American and Asian-American females is low than among Caucasians, but they are equally common among Hispanic females and more frequent among Native Americans.

There is a relatively high incidence of purging behavior in some minority groups. Anorexia and bulimia are relatively homogenous and until recent, overwhelmingly associated with Western cultures.

Causes or Etiology of Eating Disorders

While eating disorders may begin with preoccupations with food and weight, they are most often about much more than food. Eating disorders are complex conditions that arise from a combination of long-standing behavioral, emotional, psychological, interpersonal, and social factors. Scientists and researchers are still learning about the underlying causes of these emotionally and physically damaging conditions. We do know, however, about some of the general issues that can contribute to the development of eating disorders.

People with eating disorders often use food and the control of food in an attempt to compensate for feelings and emotions that may otherwise seem overwhelming. For some, dieting, bingeing, and purging may begin as a way to cope with painful emotions and to feel in control of one's life, but ultimately, these behaviors will damage a person's physical and emotional health, self-esteem, and sense of competence and control.

Biological, psychological, and social factors contribute to the development of these serious eating disorders. Anorexia and bulimia nervosa can be viewed as illnesses with a variety of predispositions. Many persons in a population may have the predisposition to such an illness, but only some actually develop it. In trying to understand the causes of eating disorders, scientists have studied the personalities, genetics, environments and biochemistry of people with these illnesses. As is often the case, the more that is learned, the more complex the roots of eating disorders appear.

Personalities

Most people with eating disorders share certain personality traits: low self-esteem, feelings of helplessness and a fear of becoming fat. In anorexia, bulimia and binge eating disorder, eating behaviors seem to develop as a way of handling stress and anxieties. People with anorexia tend to be "too good to be true." They rarely disobey, keep their feelings to themselves and tend to be perfectionists, good students and excellent athletes. Some researchers believe that people with anorexia restrict food–particularly carbohydrates–to gain a sense of control in some area of their lives. Having followed the wishes of others for the most part, they have not learned how to cope with the problems typical of adolescence, growing up and becoming independent. Controlling their weight appears to offer two advantages, at least initially: they can take control of their bodies and gain approval from others. However, it eventually becomes clear to other that they are out-of-control and dangerously thin. People who develop bulimia and binge eating disorder typically consume huge amounts of food–often junk food–to reduce stress and relieve anxiety. With binge eating, however, comes guilt and depression. Purging can bring relief, but it is only temporary. Individuals with bulimia are also impulsive and more likely to engage in risky behavior such as abuse of alcohol and drugs.

Genetic and Environmental Factors

Eating disorders appear to run in families–with female relatives most often affected. This finding suggests that genetic factors may predispose some people to eating disorders; however, other influences–both behavioral and environmental–may also play a role. One recent study found that mothers who are overly concerned about their daughters' weight and physical attractiveness may put the girls at increased risk of developing an eating disorder. In addition, girls with eating disorders often have father and brothers who are overly critical of their weight.

Although most victims of anorexia and bulimia are adolescent and young adult women, these illnesses can also strike men and older women. Anorexia and bulimia are found most often in Caucasians, but these illnesses also affect African Americans and other racial ethnic groups. People pursuing professions or activities that emphasize thinness–like modeling, dancing, gymnastics, wrestling and long-distance running–are more susceptible to the problem. In contrast to other eating disorders, one-third to one-fourth of all patients with binge eating disorder are men.

Biochemistry

In an attempt to understand eating disorders, scientists have studied the biochemical on the neuroendocrine system–a combination of the central nervous and hormonal systems. Through complex but carefully balanced feedback mechanisms, the neuroendocrine system regulates sexual function, physical growth and development, appetite and digestion, sleep, heart and kidney function, emotions, thinking and memory–in other words, multiple functions of the mind and body. Many of these regulatory mechanisms are seriously disturbed in people with eating disorders.

In the central nervous system–particularly the brain–key chemical messengers known as neurotransmitters control hormone production. Scientists have found that the neurotransmitters *serotonin* and *norepinephrine* function abnormally in people affected by depression. Recently, researchers funded by NIMH have learned that these neurotransmitters are also decreased in acutely ill anorexia, bulimia patients and long-term recovered anorexia patients. Because many people with eating disorders also appear to suffer from depression, some scientists believe that there may be a link between these two disorders. In fact, new research has suggested that some patients with anorexia may respond well to the antidepressant medication fluoxetine which affects serotonin function in the body.

Social Dimensions

What drives so many young people into a punishing and life-threatening routine of semi starvation or purging? For many young women, looking good is more important than being healthy. In fact, for young females in middle- to upper-class competitive environments, self-worth, happiness, and success are determined to a large extent by body measurements and percentage of body fat, factors that have little or no correlation with personal happiness and success in the long run.

The message from the media to be thin is clearly aimed at women. There was a strong relationship between amount of media exposure and eating disorder symptomatology in college women. In adolescence, cultural standards are often experienced as peer pressure, and are much more influential than reason and fact.

Culturally, prejudice against obesity is strong and the idealization of thinness is high. Conflict between pressures on women to perform professionally and also to be nurturing may highlight concerns about personal control that are manifested in weight regulation. Further, some career choices link thinness and achievement, and those special populations- notably dancers and fashion models have been shown to be at unusually high risk for the development of eating disorders.

Social factors in summary

- Cultural pressures that glorify "thinness" and place value on obtaining the "perfect body"
- Narrow definitions of beauty that include only women and men of specific body weights and shapes
- Cultural norms that value people on the basis of physical appearance and not inner qualities and strengths

Family Influences

Much has been made of the possible significance of family interaction patterns in cases of eating disorders. Typical anorexic's family is successful, hard-driving, concerned about external appearances, and eager to maintain harmony. To accomplish these goals, family members often deny or ignore conflicts or negative feelings and tend to attribute their problems to other people at the expense of frank communication among themselves. After the onset of an eating disorder, particularly anorexia, family relationships can deteriorate quickly.

At the level of family history of depressive disorders, alcoholism, obesity, or an eating disorder increase the risk for the development of an eating disorder. For example, a recent study found that mothers of bulimic daughters and of eating – disordered adolescents differed from a nondisordered eating sample by having a greater frequency of an eating disorder or dieting behavior, greater preoccupation with their daughters dieting, and greater dissatisfaction with the general functioning of the family system. Particular family patterns in which independence is discouraged may also be a contributor.

Individual Factors

At an individual level predisposing factors for eating disorders include a sense of personal helplessness, fear of losing control, a self-esteem that is highly dependent on the options of others, and an all-or-nothing thinking style.

There is evidence to show an association between borderline personality disorder and bulimia, whether it is the bulimic form of anorexia nervosa or bulimia nervosa. That personality disturbance may present a risk for eating disorders by virtue of problems such persons have in separation and individuation, and in problems with self-esteem and linking self-esteem to external phenomena.

Interpersonal factors in summary

- Troubled family and personal relationships
- Difficulty expressing emotions and feelings
- History of being teased or ridiculed based on size or weight
- History of physical or sexual abuse

Neurohumoral Factors

For many years there has been debates as to whether some of the striking changes that occur in eating disorder patients result from a fundamental neuroendocrine abnormality or from the starvation process. Many of the abnormalities occur in starvation from other causes and are therefore likely to be the result of weight loss or reduced intake of nutrients. Starvation does produce changes in neurotransmitter levels, which in turn can be responsible from some manifestations of anorexia nervosa.

Biological Dimensions

Eating disorders run in families and thus seems to have a genetic component. A person might inherit a tendency to be emotionally responsive to stressful life events. This biological vulnerability might then interest with social and psychological factors to produce an eating disorder. Low levels of serotonergic activity are associated with impulsivity in general and binge eating specifically.

Psychological Dimensions

Many young women with eating disorders have a diminished sense of personal control and confidence in their own abilities and talents. Women with eating disorders are intensely preoccupied with how they appear to others. They also perceive themselves as frauds, considering false impressions they make of being adequate, self-sufficient, or worthwhile. In this sense they feel like impostors in their social groups and experience heightened levels of social anxiety.

Psychological factors in summary

- Low self-esteem
- Feelings of inadequacy or lack of control in life
- Depression, anxiety, anger, or loneliness

Other factors that can contribute to eating disorders

Scientists are still researching possible biochemical or biological causes of eating disorders. In some individuals with eating disorders, certain chemicals in the brain that control hunger, appetite, and digestion have been found to be imbalanced. The exact meaning and implications of these imbalances remains under investigation.

An Integrative Model of Causes

No one factor seems sufficient to cause Eos. Social and cultural pressures to be thin motivate significant restriction of eating, usually through severe dieting. The intonations in high-income, high-achieving families may well be a factor. An emphasis on looks and achievement may help establish very strong attitudes about the overriding importance of physical appearance to popularity and success.

Treatment of Eating Disorders

People with serious eating disorders may be mistrustful of physicians, whom they see as being interested only in refeeding them or making them lose their will and becoming fat. The physician must also emphasize that he or she will remain with the patient though difficult times and focus on many different issues as required. The goal is not control of anorexic patients but rather relief of suffering. It is helpful to have a firm, nonjudgmental attitude and to reinterpret patient's low body weight, which they see as a sign of their control as actually representing their loss of control.

There is a great value in education. Patients benefit from learning about body weight regulation and the effects of starvation. Dietary misconceptions can be clarified. It is important to review the effects of vomiting and laxatives on bodily functions. The physician should have a frank discussion with the patient about how easily people can be manipulated by cultural phenomena. It is also important to discuss issues of self-esteem and how a person can relate self-worth entirely to a body size and weight and in doing so is forcing herself / himself to be something that is not natural for him or her. Treatment of bulimia nervosa consist of various interventions, including individual psychotherapy with a cognitive-behavioral approach, group therapy, family therapy, and pharmacotherapy. Because of the comorbidity of mood disorders, anxiety disorders, and personality disorders with bulimia nervosa, the clinical must factor those additional disorders into the treatment plan.

Drug Treatments

At present, drug treatment have not been found to be effective in the treatment of anorexia nervosa. The drugs generally considered the most effective for bulimia are the same antidepressant medications proven effective for bulimia are the same antidepressant medications proven effective for mood disorders and anxiety disorders. In fact, the Food and Drug Administration (FDA) in 1996 approved Prozac as effective for eating disorders.

Psychosocial Treatment

Bulimia Nervosa

In the cognitive-behavioral treatment approach, the first stage is teaching the patient the physical consequences of binge eating and purging, as well as the ineffectiveness of vomiting and laxative abuse for weight control. The adverse effects of dieting are also described, and patients are scheduled to eat small, manageable amounts of foods five or six times per day with no more than a 3-hour interval between any planned meals and snacks, which eliminates the alternating periods of overeating and dietary restriction that are hallmarks of bulimic. In later stage of treatment, cognitive therapy focuses on altering dysfunctional thoughts and attitudes about body shape, weight, and eating.

Interpersonal psychotherapy (IPT) focus on improving interpersonal functioning. There is now evidence that combining drugs with psychosocial treatments might boost the overall outcome, at least in the short term.

Anorexia Nervosa

In anorexia, of course the most important initial goal is to restore the patient's weight to a point that is at least within the low-normal range. If body weight is below 70% of the average or if weight has been lost very rapidly, inpatient treatment would be recommended. Knowing they can leave the hospital when their weight gain is adequate is often sufficient to motivate young women.

Without attention to the patients underlying dysfunctional attitudes about body shape they will almost always release. For restricting anorexics, the focus of treatment must shift to their marked anxiety over becoming obese and losing control of eating, as well as to their undue emphasis on thinness as a determinant of self-worth, happiness, and success. Every effort is made to include the family in order to accomplish the goals. Attitudes towards body shape and image distortion are discussed at some length in family sessions. Unless the therapist attends to these attitudes, individuals with anorexia are likely to face a lifetime preoccupation with weight and body shape. And be subject to repeated hospitalization. Family therapy seems effective, particularly with young girls with a short history of the disorder.

Psychological Treatment

The psychological treatment has a number of components:

1) An educative role as described earlier.
2) A focus on cognitive elements to reduce the tendency of diets to help in problem solving and cognitive restructuring.
3) Reinterpretation of the patient's distortions regarding her body. That involves having the person learn to trust how others see her and to feel her body to be a source of comfort and pleasure.
4) Self-esteem has been tied to weight and to a look. The person should gradually recognize that self-esteem cap be built up by factors other than those.
5) Identifying and addressing the major interpersonal problems associated with the illness.
6) Family therapy is useful but individual therapy was superior for older patients.
7) Group therapies are generally useful, especially for bulimia nervosa. The group may take different forms including psychodynamic, behavioral, feminist, or self-help orientations.

Inpatient Treatment

Anorexia Nervosa

Most patients can be treated entirely as outpatients. A minority may require admission to hospital for different reasons. The patient who has lost a substantial amount weight (often 30 percent or more) and who has not been able to gain weight during outpatient treatment needs admission. Sometimes hospital admission and observation are necessary to confirm the diagnosis. Metabolic or suicidal crises may also require emergency admission. For the anorexic patient who has elected to come into a structured setting the following outline is widely used. It is useful to meet first with the prospective patient and her/his family so that clear goals and expectations can be agreed on from the outset. As no single treatment technique is superior, a combined multidisciplinary approach involving behavioral family interpretive, and pharmacological techniques is generally used. In setting a target weight it is important to take into account the patient's premorbid weight when menses occurred and dieting was not an issue.

Patients can be weighed three times a week and informed of the weight. Behavioral contingencies can be provided for weight gain.

In the hospital setting individual psychotherapy involves supportive. cognitive and interpretive elements. Which may vary in degree depending on the person's ego strengths. Self-reflective capacities and requirements at the particular time, recognition and appropriate expression of affect together with the development of a sense of worth distinct from weight control are common themes. Early contact with the family to enlist their support and to reassure them that they are not to blame for the illness can make a substantial difference.

Bulimia Nervosa

For bulimic patients who are unable to halt the dangerous sequence of dieting, binging, and purging, admission to the hospital may be necessary to break the cycle. A schedule can be negotiated during which a normal eating pattern, without vomiting or purgative misuse, is initiated. That can be followed by exposure of patient to so-called binge foods under supervised conditions.

Outpatient Psychotherapy

Many patients with anorexia nervosa or bulimia nervosa do not require management in a hospital, and all of those who are treated in a hospital setting require outpatient follow-up. The outpatient program involves three components: (1) monitoring eating and weight (2) monitoring appropriate biochemical indices and (3) ongoing psychotherapy, both for the person and often for family members. Family therapy is especially important for an orexic and bulimic adolescents. At present the psychotherapy generally involves cognitive, behavioral, and psychodynamic components.

Other Eating Disorders

The following eating disorders are often associated with mental retardation and involve rather bizarre eating patterns. However, as with order eating disorders, if they are not treated there is a substantially increased risk of illness or death.

Rumination Disorder

Rumination is the process of regurgitating and then reswallowing partially digested food. In the past the term mercyism (from the Greek word for abnormal regurgitation) was often used. When this process interferes with appropriate nutritional intake or weight gain, rumination disorder is present. Rumination usually seems to be an enjoyable to those engaging in it as eating the food initially. Rumination is classified as a disorder of infancy, childhood, or adolescence in DSM-IV, and it affects approximately 10 % of adults who have mental retardation. Some believe that the causes are in combination of biological and psychological variable. Rumination can also occur with bulimia.

PICA

Pica is a characterized by the repeated eating of non-nutritive substances and occurs in infants and people with mental retardation or dementia. Individuals typically eat paint, plaster, string, hair, or cloth or their children may eat animal droppings, sand, insects, leaves, or pebbles. most cases involve individuals with severe or profound intellectual abilities. Pica poses serious health problems. There is a danger of lead poisoning and roundworm infection; sometimes surgery is required to remove ingested objects. Psychosocial factors such as stress are an important contributions to this behaviors. Psychological factors are usually associated with substantial neglect or abuse. Operant conditioning procedures have been used with pica, primarily the systematic reinforcement of appropriate eating and mild punishment or withholding of reinforcement when the behavior occurs.

Feeding Disorder

Feeding disorder of infancy or early childhood, may result in a "failure to thrive syndrome"; that is failure to eat adequately results in insufficient weight gain. Older children who fail to thrive may be found in a disorganized, chaotic family, exhibit oppositional behavior, or most likely, have a conflicted relationship with a caregiver. Treatment always involved regulating eating in the hospital and attempting to improve family functioning.

Helping the Person with an Eating Disorder

Treatment can save the life of someone with an eating disorder. Friends, relatives, teachers and physicians all play an important role in helping the ill person start and stay with a treatment program. Encouragement, caring and persistence, as well as information about eating disorders and their dangers, may be needed to convince the ill person to get help, stick with treatment, or try again. Family members and friends should read as much as possible about eating disorders, so they can help the person with the illness understand his or her problem.

Preventing Eating Disorders

Attempts are being made to prevent the development of eating disorders. If successful methods are confirmed they will be very important, since many cases of eating disorders are resistant to treatment and most individuals who do not receive treatment suffer for many years, in some cases all of their lives. Before implementing a privation program, however, it is necessary to target specific behaviors to change.

Literature Reviews and Researches

Fearing Fat: A Literature Review of Family Systems Understandings and Treatments of Anorexia and Bulimia

Kyle D.killian

Definitions of Anorexia Nervosa and bulimia are given precisely in this article.

Prevalence of eating disorders is found out.

It was more among young adolescent women. Prevalence of bulimia is difficult to estimate because they do not show weight loss and are hesitant to go to the doctor.

Family factors in the etiology of Anorexia and bulimia were examined, researchers examined the influence of Psychopathological, sociological and interpersonal factors on the development of eating disorders.

Psychopathology of Family members: Here, occurrence of Anorexia in biological relatives of anorectics was found. Some cases of eating disorders stem from family vulnerability, but how genetics and environment interact to produce eating disorders still remains unclear.

Sociological factors: Influence of social class, race, birth order, etc. has been studied. Of these, only social class was found to be associated with the eating disorder especially Anorexia. Cultural expectations especially the western ones have preoccupation with food, dieting and being attractive and this in turn is connected to the incidence of eating disorders. Subordinate position of women in society is connected to eating disorders. Women's role as nurturers and care givers causes them to be self-sacrificing.

Family relationships like the psychosomatic family wherein enmeshment rigidity etc. are common and they are connected to anorexia. People with Anorexia find their fathers but not their mothers to be overprotective. Another familiar characteristics reported is the presence of parent – child coalitions and blurred generational boundaries.

Treatments

Family therapy is one of the most important ones for treating eating disorders. Structural family therapy, strategic family therapy, transgenerational therapy for Anorexia nervosa were included in this study whereas for bulimia the therapies included are - therapy for perfect overprotective and chaotic families.

Some of the models studied here in this research with respect to treatment of eating disorders were transgenerational model, object relations/family systems model and internal family systems model.

Researchers in this filed have concluded that family therapy is an important component in treating eating disorders. Also many support the use of talk therapy. More research is needed to determine which treatment or combinations are effective in treating eating disorders. Thus, use of clearly defined problem definitions, outcome criteria and follow-up over longer periods of time will improve the quality of outcome research on this topic.

Social Location, Significant Others and Body Image among Adolescents

Richand Levinson, Brian Powell, Lala Carr Steelman.

In this research using adolescence as a target group, their influence of significant others and social locations on one aspect of self evaluated attractiveness, namely body, weight is investigated. Person self-perceptions may be related to his or her actual physical qualities, but this research focuses more on subtle influences. Pressure to improve one's appearance is a common theme transmitted by the media. Thus, physical appearance is one aspect of self scrutiny, susceptible to external pressure from media and social audience.

In addition to this, the role of location in social structure also deserves examination. These feelings of maintaining the body image and good physical appearance are nurtured more by women than men. Another factor brought in the studies of physical attractive is race or ethnicity. For example Blacks assign positive qualities of well-being and power to heavy women. Socioeconomic status also plays an important role the way in which adolescents view their bodies obesity is more common among lower status people and the reverse is true for thinness.

This study investigates the impact of gender, race and significant others on how adolescents view their own weights. The study relies on information secured from a large nationally representative sample of adolescents. The data analyzed in this research was taken from Cycle III of the National Health Examination Survey collected by the division of health examination statistics, national center for health statistics (NCHS). This sample represented cross section of the civilian, non institutionalized population between the ages of 12 and 17 and was completed in 1970. Adolescents were asked to rate themselves as 1) underweight, 2) about the right weight and 3) over weight. Responses were also coded in the above same 3 categories.

The results suggested that the hypothesis, teenagers tend to derogatory body images was confirmed. They also confirmed that blacks viewed themselves thinner then their white counterparts and conversely white youths were more likely to claim that they were heavier.

Youths' evaluations were more closely aligned with the assessments of parents than those set by physicians. Parental perceptions were more strongly inked to the weight assessments of female than those of males. In closing, this study shows how social factors may be implicated in the split of opinion between individuals and others who evaluate them. First, because standards of appropriate weights fluctuate over time, contemporary data should be collected. Second, adolescents are certainly influenced by others in their inter personal networks. Status characteristics are less powerful predictors of body image than parental assessments, which have a stronger effect on females those on males. Income affects self evaluation with higher females labeling themselves as heavier and higher income males labeling themselves as thinner.

Question for Readers

How are Eating and Health related?

8

Autism

A Developmental Disorder

Autism Disorder or Autism is a severe developmental disorder characterized by abnormalities in social functioning, language and communication and unusual interests and behaviors. It affects every aspect of the child's interaction with his or her world, involves many parts of the brain and undermines the very traits that make us human- our social responsiveness, ability to communicate and feelings for other people.

Description and History

Autism is one of several and most studied *Pervasive developmental disorders (PDDs)*, all characterized by significant impairments in social and communication skills and by stereotyped patterns of interests and behaviors. Autism was formally identified in 1943 by psychiatrist Leo Kanner, who observed 11 children, who in their first few years, withdrew into a shell, disregarded people for objects, avoided eye contact, lacked social awareness, had limited or no language and displayed stereotyped motor activities. These children also exhibited Preservation of Sameness, which is an anxious and obsessive insistence on the maintenance of sameness in daily routines and activities which no one but the child may disrupt.

Kanner (1943, 1944) called this disorder Early Infantile Autism. He viewed the core feature of autism as the child's inability to relate themselves in the ordinary way to people and situations from the beginning of life. There is still another extreme Autistic Aloneness where the child disregards, ignores, shuts out anything that comes to him from the outside. The early onset of this disorder led Kanner to conclude that autism resulted from an inborn inability to form loving relationships with other people. Kanner described the parents of such children as cold, mechanical and detached in their relationships the so-called 'refrigerator parents'. Although he saw autism as an inborn deficit, he also gave the idea that autism resulted from a child's defensive withdrawal from an intellectual, cold-hearted and hostile parent, but this has found no support yet. Children with autism have not withdrawn from reality because of a mental disorder rather they failed to enter reality because of widespread and serious disturbances in their development (Rutter, 1991a). Autism is not recognized as a biologically based lifelong developmental disability that is present in the first few years of life (Rutter, 2000a).

Children with autism behave in bizarre, unusual and frequently puzzling ways. They may squeal with excitement at the sight or sound of the smallest toy yet ignore somebody's full-blown tantrum to play with them. They may scream, kick and lash out at others if even a chair was moved from its usual place. Sometimes they may look through you as if you don't exist and at other times they may stare into your face or tug on your arm to lead you to something they want. When you try to speak to them, they may act as if they are deaf but may quickly turn if they hear a faint sound of crinkling of a candy wrapper. Many autistic children displayed extreme fear or avoidance of noisy or moving objects, such as running water, elevators, etc. many others were attracted to and preoccupied with objects such as a rotating fan, a flickering light, etc. these children develop unusual attachments. Therefore, rather than seeing the big picture, autistic children are likely to fixate on a minuscule object or event.

Defining Features

DSM-IV-TR gave a description of the diagnostic criteria for the autistic disorder. According to the DSM-IV, a total of six or more items from (1), (2) and (3) with atleast two from (1) and one each from (2) and (3).

(1) qualitative impairment in social interaction, as manifested by at least two of the following:
   (a) Marked impairment in the use of multiple non-verbal behaviors such as eye-to-eye gaze, facial expression, body postures and gestures to regulate social interaction.
   (b) Failure to develop peer relationships appropriate to developmental level.
   (c) A lack of spontaneous seeking to share enjoyment, interests or achievements with other people.
   (d) Lack of social or emotional reciprocity.

(2) Qualitative impairments in communication as manifested by at least one of the following:
   (a) Delay in or total lack of, the development of spoken language.
   (b) In individuals with adequate speech, marked impairment in the ability to imitative or sustain a conversation with others.
   (c) Stereotyped and repetitive use of language or idiosyncratic language.
   (d) Lack of varied, spontaneous make-believe play or social imitative play appropriate to developmental level.

(3) Restricted repetitive and stereotyped patterns of behavior, interests and activities as manifested by at least one of the following:
   (a) Encompassing preoccupation with one or more stereotyped and restricted patterns of interest that is abnormal either in intensity or focus.

(b) Apparently inflexible adherence to specific, nonfunctional and routines or rituals.

(c) Stereotyped and repetitive motor mannerisms.

(d) Persistent preoccupation with parts or objects.

Autism was termed as a *Spectrum Disorder*, which means that its symptom patterns, range from abilities and characteristics are expressed in many different combinations and in any degree of severity. At the end of one spectrum we may find a mute child, crouched in a corner, spinning paper clips for hours; at the other, a university researcher who has held corporate jobs as long as they didn't require interacting with customers. Children with autism may possess any level of intellectual ability, from profound retardation to above-average intelligence. They also vary in the severity of their language problems. The behavior of these children changes with age. Some make little progress, whereas others develop speech or become more outgoing.

Core Characteristics of Autism

Autism is a rare disorder and affects children in vastly different ways. Autism consists of several deficits that affect the child's social-emotional, language and cognitive development.

Social Impairments

Autistic children experience difficulties in relating to other people, even when they have an average IQ (Grossman, Carter & Volkmar, 1997). From a young age, they show deficits in many of the skills that are crucial for early social development like imitating others, orienting to social stimuli, sharing a focus of alternation with others, understanding other people's emotions and engaging in make-believe play. As they grow older, they initiate few social behaviors and seem unresponsive to other people's feelings.

Social expressiveness and sensitivity to others' social cues are limited and little sharing of experiences or emotions with other people takes place. Autistic children display deficits in recognizing faces and experiences difficulty integrating social, communicative and emotional behavior. Since they lack the understanding of people as social partners, they treat them as objects. Autistic children also display impairments in *Joint Social Attention*, which is the ability to coordinate one's focus of attention on another person and an object of mutual interest. Joint social attention, which normally develops by 12-15 months of age, involves getting in the same wave length with another person by directing that person's attention to objects or people by pointing, showing and looking and communicating shared interest. Autistic children process social information in unusual ways. At a young age, they may have greater difficulties than other children with imitation of body actions versus toy actions or in orienting to social versus nonsocial stimuli. In processing information about the human face, they may focus on parts of the face such as mouth or nose rather than its overall shape. They may not show typical preferences of most children for speech and non-speech sounds (Klin, 1991).

It was thought that these children failed to form a bond with their parents or that they could not tell the difference between their parents and other adults, but research proved it wrong (Dissanayake & Sigman, 2000). Most autistic children are responsive to their care-givers than to unfamiliar adults. Also autistic children slightly lower rates of secure attachment to their mothers as normal controls. They show a preference for their mothers over a stranger. Thus, autistic children do not suffer from a global deficit in their ability to form attachments. Rather, the deficit seems to be in their ability to understand and respond to social information. They also have problems in processing emotional information contained in body language, gestures, facial expressions or the voice. Preschool-age children with autism do not look for or attend to the emotional cues provide by other people. In contrast to other children of the same mental age, they may sort pictures of people according to what they are wearing rather than their facial expression. Their own bodily expressions of emotion are very different from those of normal children often characterized by limited spontaneous use of expressions. Thus autistic children both process and express emotional information in unusual ways.

Communication Impairments

Children with autism display serious abnormalities in communication and language that appear early and persist. Before children learn to talk they have at their disposal a rich array of facial expressions, vocalizations and gestures to communicate their needs, interests and feelings to others. One of the first signs of language impairments in autistic children is their inconsistency in using this early preverbal communication. An autistic child communicates through *Protoimperative Gestures* - gestures or vocalizations that are used to express needs. However, the child fails to use *Protodeclarative Gestures* - gestures or vocalizations that direct the visual attention of other people to objects of shared interest. The use of these gestures requires shared social attention and an implicit understanding of what other people are thinking, abilities that are lacking in autistic children. Other declarative gestures are also missing in autistic children such as Showing Gesture, which young children without autism use to show someone else something of interest. A number of autistic children do not develop any useful language. Some begin to speak and then regress in their speech development between 12 and 30 months of age. These children rely on primitive forms of communication. They sometimes use Instrumental Gestures to get someone else to do something for them immediately, but they fail to use Expressive gestures to convey feelings (U. Frith, 1989).

Children with autism who develop language usually do so before age 5. Almost all children with autism show delays in their language development, it is their use of qualitatively deviant forms of communication that is most striking. Most noticeable is their lack of social chatter- their failure to use language for social communication. Their communication is described as nonsensical, silly, incoherent and irrelevant, having little meaning connection with the situation in which they occur. Other common qualitative language impairments in these children are pronoun reversals and echolalia. *Pronoun reversals* occur when the child repeats personal pronouns exactly as heard, without changing them to suit the situation. *Echolalia,* which can be either immediate or delayed, refers to the child's parrot-like repetition of words or word combinations that she or he has heard. Echolalia and other unconventional verbal behavior such as Preservative Speech (going on and on about the same topic) and incessant questioning, may serve a variety of communicative and developmental functions for children with autism. They reflect the child's desire to communicate. The primary difficulty with these children who develop language is not so much with the computational (sounds, words and grammar) or semantic (meaning) use of language. Rather, these children display profound impairments in *Pragmatics,* or appropriate use of language in social and communicative contexts. Lacking pragmatic competence, autistic children often have difficulty understanding no literal statements or adjusting their language to fit the situation. Autistic children use language in a literal fashion. Often the meaning of a word becomes inflexible and cannot be used apart from its original acquired meaning.

Repetitive Behaviors and Interests

Autistic children often display narrow patterns of interests such as fascination with arithmetic, repetitive behaviors and stereotyped movements. They may show stereotyped and repetitive behaviors when they are not explicitly directed to engage in some other activity, suggesting a possible deficit in their ability to initiate activities on their own. Other stereotyped behaviors occur in novel, unpredictable situations and may serve to provide the child with a sense of control over the environment and a way of coping with changes that are not understood. *Self-stimulatory behaviors* are repetitive behavior body movements or object movements, which are common in autistic children. There are some common forms of self-stimulation in children with autism.

(a) *Visual:* Repetitive blinking, staring at lights, hand flapping, moving fingers in front of eyes.
(b) *Auditory:* Snapping fingers, making vocal sounds, tapping ears, spinning an object on a table.
(c) *Tactile:* Scratching, rubbing the skin with the hands or with an object.
(d) *Vestibular:* rocking front to back, rocking side to side.
(e) *Taste:* Placing body parts or objects in the mouth, licking objects.
(f) *Smell:* Smelling objects, sniffing people.

Associated Characteristics of Autism

Intellectual Deficits and Strengths

Autistic children vary widely in intelligence, from profound mental retardation to superior ability. Children with mental retardation and without autism show a general delay across all areas of intelligence. In contrast, the performances of autistic children tend to score low on verbal tests and high on non-verbal tests (Bolton et al., 1994). Only those children with average or above-average intelligence are likely to achieve independent living status as adults. Despite their intellectual deficits, a small number of autistic children develop Splinter Skills or Islets of Ability. About 25% of these children display special cognitive skills. About 5% develop an isolated and remarkable talent that is superior to normal children'. These children referred to as Autistic Savants display supernormal abilities in a number of areas. It is not clear whether special talents of a small number of autistic children reflect intact abilities or are a sign of a cognitive deficit. One idea is that autistic savants have a tendency to segment information into parts rather than looking at the whole, which leads to exceptional performance in certain domains (Pring, Hermelin & Heavey, 1995). Also these children think in images rather than abstract ideas which allow them to remember material easily.

Sensory and Perceptual Impairments

Sensory abnormalities and deficits are common in autistic

children. They include oversensitiveness or undersensitivities to certain stimuli, overselective and impaired shifting of attention to sensory input and impairments in mixing across sensory modalities. They may display such sensory-perceptual deficits as sensory dominance and stimulus overselectivity. Sensory Dominance is the tendency to focus on certain types of sensory input over others. Stimulus Overselectivity is the tendency to focus on one feature of an object or event in the environment while ignoring other equally important features. They seem to have a tunnel vision.

Cognitive Deficits

There are two types of cognitive limitations proposed to underlie autism such as specific cognitive deficits in processing social-emotional information and more general cognitive deficits in information processing, planning and attention.

Deficits in Processing Social-Emotional Information

Autistic children have an unusual social behavior which suggests a significant impairment in their social sensitivies (Sigman, 1995). But it is not that the social interaction is absent or impaired, rather they have a difficulty in situations that require social understanding. At around 12 months, most normally developing infants begin to recognize that people's actions are driven by desires and directed at goals. This ability contributes to pretend play. Autistic children do not understand pretense and hence do not indulge in such activities. The absence of such play led to the hypothesis that these children would also display impairments in their understanding of mental states of themselves and others that cannot be seen directly, such as beliefs and desires. This is referred to as the *Theory of Mind (ToM)* (Baron-Cohen, 2000b). by the age of 4, most children can figure out what others might know, think and believe, something that even older individuals with autism have great difficulty doing. Although they can think about physical events and characteristics that they can see, they have great difficulty forming higher-order representations about invisible mental states. The ToM hypothesis of autism begins with the premise that the ability to read the intentions, beliefs, feelings and desires of others from their external behavior had adaptive significance in an evolutionary sense. ToM proposes that all humans are, by nature, mind readers and they spend a lot of time reading subtle cues to know others.

The development of such an awareness of others' mental states and one's own is referred to as Mentalization of theory of mind (Baron-Cohen, 1995; Morton & Frith, 1995). Children with autism suffer to varying degrees from 'mindblindness' that is they fail to develop the capacity to mindread in the normal way. A child with ToM deficits may be able to learn, remember and know things about the social world but has little understanding of their meaning. The original test used to determine children's ability to detect mental states of others was called the Sally-Anne test. This test illustrates what it means to have everyday ToM. About 15-60% of autistic children demonstrate some knowledge of ToM. They have better verbal and communication skills. Those who succeed at ToM tasks usually understand metaphors, irony and a range of speaker emotions such as the intention to lie or tell a joke. Neuroimaging studies suggest that different brain regions are activated when normal individuals are engaged in tasks requiring them to make attributions about other people's mental states and for tasks that do not require such attributions (Fletcher et al., 1995).

General Deficits

It has been suggested that autistic children display a general deficit in higher-order planning and regulatory behaviors (Pennington et al., 1997). These processes called *Executive Functions* permit us to maintain effective problem solving by inhibiting inappropriate behaviors, engaging in thoughtful actions, sustaining task performance, self-monitoring, using feedback and flexibly shifting from one task to another. The presence of a general deficit include planning and organizing; changing to a new cognitive set; disengaging from salient stimuli; processing information in novel, unpredictable environments and generalizing previously learnt information to new situations. A second deficit hypothesized to underlie autism as a weak drive for *Central Coherence,* which refers to the strong tendency of humans to interpret stimuli in a relatively global way that takes the broader context in to account (Frith, 1993). Consistent with a general deficit in central coherence, individuals with autism perform well on tasks in which a focus on parts of a stimulus rather than the overall pattern or design serves to facilitate performance. Their advantage on such tasks may be due to their spontaneous mental segmentation of the designs into unconnected and meaningless units.

Are these Cognitive Deficits Specific to Autism?

Of all the deficits described earlier, ToM deficit seems one of most specific to autistic children. However, ToM has not been studied extensively in children with other conditions. Deficits in processing socio-emotional information appear to be less specific to autism than ToM deficits, occurring in a number of other conditions including schizophrenia and mental retardation.

Are these Cognitive Deficits found in All Individuals with Autism?

It is not very clear whether normal-IQ individual with autism have developed a ToM. The fact that many of these individuals still display sever social impairments in everyday life suggests that they have not developed a ToM but rather may have learned to use an alternative strategy to solve ToM tasks. It is unlikely that a single cognitive abnormality can explain all the deficits present in autistic children (Frith, 2000). The presence of multiple cognitive deficits some specific and some general, may help explain why autism exists in so many different forms and levels of severity.

Physical Characteristics

About 25% of autistic children develop epilepsy. Unlike individuals with mental retardation, autistic individuals display epilepsy in late adolescence or early adulthood. If epilepsy occurred in early childhood, then it is associated with mental retardation. Autistic children are described as having a normal or attractive physical appearance. They may sometimes have minor physical abnormalities such as facial asymmetries, which suggest the influence of genetic or other prenatal factors. About 20% of these children have a larger-than-normal head circumference (Courty & Fremolle, 1999).

Family Stress

Life for parents with autistic children is a daily grind, relentless effort to prevent their child from harming herself, guessing their child's needs and search for ways of preventing their child from withdrawing from them forever. Parents also experience social ostracism from friends who find it difficult to be around such demanding children.

Accompanying Disorders and Symptoms

The disorders that most often accompany autism are mental retardation and epilepsy. Other psychiatric symptoms include hyperactivities, anxieties and fears and mood problems. Some children also engage in extreme and potentially life-threatening Self-injurious behaviors (SIB) that is any self-inflicted behavior that can cause tissue damage to the child's own body. The most common forms of SIB are head banging, hand or arm biting and excessive scratching and rubbing. Head-banging if not stopped can produce bleeding or brain injuries. SIB may occur for several reasons such as self-stimulation, to gain attention or to eliminate unwanted demands and sometimes for no apparent reasons.

Differential Diagnosis

The social deficits of autistic children and low IQs may be difficult to distinguish from those of children with severe retardation with autism. Children with mental retardation display simple social behaviors such as smiling and eye contact that are appropriate to their mental age. Children with mental retardation do not display the deficits in joint attention or theory of mind observed in autistic children (Charman et al., 1997). Both groups display self-stimulation and SIBs. Distinguishing between autism and developmental language disorders can sometimes be difficult in young children. Both groups show similar delays in babbling, language acquisition, length of utterance and grammatical complexity. However, autistic children use more atypical forms of language such as echolalia and pronoun reversals; display less spontaneous social conversation and show greater impairment in non-verbal communication.

Prevalence and Course of Autism

Autism is thought to affect at least 4-5 children per 10,000 (Tanguay, 2000). However, its prevalence is on the rise with current estimates being about 3 times higher than this (Fombonne, 1999). The higher estimates are related to a broadening of the criteria used to diagnose autism over the years and to the greater recognition of milder forms of autism that occur in higher-functioning individuals. Autism is found in all social classes and has been identified worldwide. Autism is 3-4 times more common in boys than girls (Fombonne, 1999). This ratio has remained fairly constant. The gender difference is most apparent among those with IQs in the normal range.

Age of Onset

The age at which symptoms of autism first appear is uncertain. It is generally after the child is 2yrs old, does his lack of progress in language, imaginative play and social relations stand up in sharp contrast to rapid developments in these areas by children about the same age. But the elements of autism are present much before the age of 2. There was several rating of specific child behaviors such as pointing, showing, failing to orient to a spoken name and especially looking at the face of another person, accurately points out an autistic child. At present, the period from 12-18 months seems to be the earliest point in development that autism can be reliably detected (Rogers, 2000a). But with systematic screening, it is possible to detect it much earlier.

Course and Outcome

The symptom patterns of autistic children change over time. Most show a gradual improvement with age. During adolescence, some symptoms such as hyperactivity, self-injury and compulsivity may worsen. In later adolescence and adulthood, abnormalities such as stereotyped motor movements, anxiety and socially inappropriate behaviors are common even in high-functioning individuals with autism. For such individuals, feelings of loneliness, social ineptness, and work of difficulties are common. Complex obsessive-compulsive rituals may develop and speech may resemble that of individuals with schizophrenia including idiosyncratic and preservative speech, monotonous tone and self-talk.

The main findings from early studies of outcomes for autistic children who received limited help are as follows (Lotter, 1978):

(a) About 1-2% became normal in the sense of being indistinguishable from others.

(b) About 10% had good outcomes, meaning that they achieved near-normal functioning in their social behaviors and language, processed in school or work but continued to display oddities of speech or personality.

(c) About 20% had fair outcomes, making social and educational gains despite significant handicaps in areas such as speech.

(d) About 70%, the overwhelming majority, showed poor outcomes with limited progress and continuing handicaps that did not permit them to lead an independent existence.

IQ and language developments are the strongest predictors of adult outcomes in autistic children. Those with IQ below 50 are likely to show the poorest levels of social judgment and those with higher IQs show better long-term adjustment. Children who display language by age 5 also show better long-term outcomes.

Causes of Autism

The specific causes of autism are still not known, but the

understanding of the disorder has increased tremendously. It is now generally accepted as a biologically based neurodevelopmental disorder with multiple causes (Trottier, Srivastava & Walker, 1999).

Problems in Early Development

Autistic children experience more health problems during pregnancy, at birth or immediately following birth than other children. Premature birth, bleeding in pregnancy, toxemia (blood poisoning), viral infection or exposure and a lack of vigor after birth have been identified in about 25% of autistic children. Although these problems during pregnancy and birth are not the primary causes of autism, they do suggest that fetal or neonatal development has been compromised in some way (Bolton et al., 1997). A recent and extremely controversial proposal is that some cases of autism in children who have a few words and other social-communicative behaviors that disappear in the second year of life may be linked to vaccinations. The most attention has been given to combination vaccines for measles, mumps and rubella. However, some studies do not support this association.

Genetic Influences

The study of specific chromosomal anomalies and gene disorders and findings from family and twin studies indicate a substantial role for genetic factors in the etiology of autism.

Chromosomal and Gene Disorders

The discovery of the fragile-X in about 2-3% of autistic children led to increased attention to this and other chromosomal defects that might be related to autism. In general, autistic individuals have an elevated risk of about 5% for chromosomal anomalies. These anomalies do not indicate the specific gene sites underlying the disorder because autism is associated with anomalies involving most chromosomes. Autism is also associated with Tuberous Sclerosis, a rare single-gene disorder. The manifestations of this disorder can vary from mild to severe and includes neural deficits, seizures and learning disabilities. Most cases are derived from new mutations with no family history of the disorder. About 25% plus children with tuberous sclerosis have autism. In addition, about 1-4% of autistic children have tuberous sclerosis, with the proportion even higher in those with epilepsy and mental retardation. This makes the association between them greater than that for any other genetically based condition. Although the underlying mechanisms are not known, autism could arise if the tuberous sclerosis gene mutations occur at critical stages of neural development in brain regions critical to the development of autism (Smalley, 1998).

Family and Twin Studies

Family studies indicate that about 3-7% of siblings and extended family members of individuals with autism have the disorder. Thus the likelihood that autism will occur twice in the same family is 50 to 100 times greater than would be expected by chance alone (Bolton et al., 1994). Twin studies have reported concordance rates for autism in identical twins ranging from 60-90%, in contrast to near zero rates for fraternal twins. Family members of autistic children also display higher than normal rates of social and language deficits and unusual personality features that are very similar to those found in autism, but less severe. Referred to as the Broader Autism Phenotype, these deficits include social oddities such as aloofness, lack of tact and rigidity; Pragmatic Language Problems such as over- or under-communicativeness; and poor verbal comprehension.

Molecular Genetics

Research using molecular genetics has identified a possible susceptibility gene for autism on chromosome 7 (International Molecular Genetic Study of Autism Consortium, 1998). Susceptibility genes are causally implicated in the liability to autism but do not on their own cause it directly. Anomalies on chromosome 15 have also been studied (Cooks et al., 1998). The identification of specific genes in autism may greatly enhance our understanding of this disorder and its specific components.

Brain Abnormalities

There is no known biological marker for autism but impressive advances have been made in documenting the biological basis of the disorder. Elevated rates of epilepsy and the occurrences of EEG abnormalities in about half of individuals with autism provide evidence of abnormal brain functioning. Neuropsychological impairments in autism occur in many domains including verbal intelligence, orienting and selective attention, memory, pragmatic language and executive functions. This widespread nature of these deficits suggests the involvement of multiple regions of the brain at both the vertical and subcortial levels. The types of neuropsychological deficits also vary as a function of the severity of the child's disorder.

Biological Findings

Brain imaging studies look for structural and functional abnormalities in brain development, or consistently localized brain lesions associated with the symptoms of autism. Abnormalities in the frontal lobe are consistently found in autistic individuals. Studies have identified structural abnormalities in the cerebellum and in the medial temporal lobe and related limbic system structures. The cerebellum is most frequently associated with motor movement. It is also partially involved in language, learning, emotion, thought and attention. Specific areas of the cerebellum have been found to be smaller than normal for autistic individuals and therefore they have rapidly shifting attention. The second localized abnormality is in the medial temporal lobe and connected limbic system structures such as the amygdala and hippocampus. The amygdala is important for recognizing emotional significance of stimuli and the relation between social behavior and rewards. It also plays a key role in orienting toward social stimuli, the perception of eye gaze direction and with the hippocampus, in long-term memory.

Neuroimaging studies of brain metabolism in autistic individuals suggest decreased blood flow in the frontal and temporal lobes. Studies have also found a decrease in the functional connections between cortical and subcortical regions and in delay in the maturation of the frontal cortex, as indicated by reduced cerebral blood flow in the frontal brain regions of preschool-age autistic children. These findings suggest a possible delay in the maturation of the frontal lobes that is consistent with clinical findings (Zilbovicius et al., 1995).

Autism as a Disorder of Brain Development

Biological findings support the presence of a pervasive abnormality in brain development in autism that produces generalized impairments in complex information-processing abilities. Several events in neuronal brain organization have been implicated including dendritic and axonal development, the establishment of synaptic contacts and programmed cell death and selective elimination of neuronal processes. Given the many difficulties that autistic children have with processing social information, it has been suggested that autism may involve dysfunction of a brain system that is specialized for social cognition, possibly the medial temporal lobe and orbital frontal lobe (Baron-Cohen et al., 1999).

Treatment of Autism

There has been limited success of current treatments in eliminating autism which makes individuals vulnerable to new claims of treatment. This is especially so for widely publicized treatments such as dietary modifications (like glucose-free diets), secretin (a hormone that controls digestion), auditory training, sensory integration and facilitated communication. These treatments have not lived up to their claims. Although behavioral, educational and medical treatments may improve learning and behavior and may even permit a small number of children to achieve near-normal function; there is no known cure for autism. Most treatments are directed at maximizing the child's potential and helping the child and family cope more effectively with the disorder. These treatments have shown significant developmental gains in the IQs.

Different Children, Different Treatments

Given the enormous variability in severity of symptoms, degree of language impairments and level of intellectual functioning found in autistic children, different treatment strategies are required.

Goals for Low-Functioning Children

Autistic children require supervised living and work arrangements throughout their lives. The prognosis is especially poor for low-functioning children who fail to develop speech by age 5yrs, display profound social impairments, show clear signs of neurological problems, have confirmed chromosomal abnormalities or delayed motor development. Treatment strategies for lower-functioning children generally emphasize the elimination of harmful behavior and efforts to teach the child self-help skills, compliance with simple requests and rules, basic social and emotional behaviors, communication of needs and appropriate play. As these children get older, an increasing emphasis is placed on teaching domestic and work-related skills to prepare them for supervised living or work settings. The emphasis is on rewarding progress, no matter how gradual and on enjoyment of the child for his or her uniqueness (Newsom, 1998).

Goals for High-Functioning Children

High-functioning children receive concentrated doses of early intervention and show rapid learning early in treatment and eventually achieve normal outcomes. Their goals also include teaching language fluency, age-appropriate social interactions with normal peers and the behaviors and skills expected in typical classrooms. Extensive parental involvement and support including the use of in-home therapy aides are common. For older children who have not received early intervention, goals include successful functioning in their special education classrooms and elaboration of their language, social, community and work skills. In general, outcomes for high-functioning children can be extremely variable depending on the child, family, quality of early treatment and education and later opportunities (Newsom, 1998).

Overview

This includes general strategies for engaging children in treatment, specific techniques to decrease disruptive behaviors and programs for teaching appropriate social behavior and communication skills. Family interventions enable parents to participate fully in their children's treatment and to cope with the autism. These treatments are often used in the context of comprehensive programs of early intervention. Treatments generally target the specific social, communication, cognitive and behavioral deficits of autistic children. These children have great difficulty making changes and generalizing previously learned skills to new environment.

Initial Stages

Initially treatment focuses on building rapport and teaching the child learning-readiness skills. A variety of procedures have been used to help the autistic child feel comfortable being physically close to the therapist and to identify possible rewards that can strengthen the child's social behavior, affection and play. These children must learn to sit on a chair, come when called and attend to their teacher if they are to progress. Some procedures involve a step-by-step approach to presenting stimulus and requiring a specific response called *Discrete Trial Training*. Other procedures attempt to strengthen behavior by capitalizing on naturally occurring opportunities, referred to as *Incidental Training*.

Reducing Disruptive Behavior

Autistic children display many disruptive and interfering behaviors such as tantrums or throwing objects as well as self-stimulation, aggression and self-injury. Such behaviors are common reactions to demands that are made of the child early in treatment and must be eliminated if the child is to learn more adaptive forms social interaction and communication. A variety of procures are effective in eliminating disruptive behavior including rewarding competing behaviors, ignoring and administering mild forms of punishment.

Teaching Appropriate Social Behavior and Communication Skills

Autistic children are taught social cues by pairing people with actions, activities and events that the children find pleasant or useful. They are also taught ways to express affection through smiling, hugging, tickling or kissing-behaviors that enable them to return affection. They may also be shown how to display verbal and facial affect. Other efforts include teaching social toy play, social pretend play and such specific social skills as initiating and maintaining interactions. Operant Speech Training is a step-by-step approach that increases the child's vocalization.

Early Intervention

The promise of early intervention derives from the plasticity of neural systems are early in development and yet to be tested hypothesis that providing young autistic children. These programs can be carried out at home and in pre-schools. Children entering this program are about 3-4yr olds and have an average IQ in the mid-50s.

Curriculum Emphasis on Core Skills

The curriculum emphasis core skills such as paying attention to people, complying with requests, imitating others and attending to elements of the environment that are essential for learning. Also emphasized are verbal and motor imitation, language, functional and symbolic play with toys and social interaction.

Supportive Teaching Environment

Core skills are first taught in a highly structured and focused one-to-one learning environment that is designed to maximize attention and reduce distractions.

Teaching Generalization

Gradual and systematic fading of the high-support environment is implemented to facilitate the spontaneous occurrence of core skills and their generalization to more natural, complex environments.

Predictability and Routine

The child is assisted with the inevitable changes in routine and activities that occur during a typical day. This is done by using visual and verbal cues and photographs, signaling the child well in advance of the changes, walking the child through transitions, providing a transitional object or carrying out a familiar ritual during the transition.

Functional Approach to Problem Behaviors

Enhancing the child's interest and engagement in preferred activities and providing a high level of structure helps to minimize problem behaviors. Any problem behavior that occurs is dealt with by analyzing the functions that the behavior serves, changing the environment to support appropriate behavior and teaching the child more appropriate ways of coping with the situation.

Transition from the Preschool Classroom

Priority is given to helping children make a successful transition from preschool to kindergarten or first grade, by teaching them the skills needed to function as independently as possible in the classroom. These include complying with adult requests, taking turns, listening to directions, sitting quietly during activities, volunteering, waiting and walking in a line, picking up toys and materials after use and communicating basic needs. Placements are sought that provide the best match for the child with respect to class size, structure and teaching style.

Family Involvement

Parent involvement is a critical component in treatment, although the nature and extent varies with the needs of individual families. To varying degrees, parents are trained in treatment methods, contribute to the development of these methods and are included in the educational process at home, at school or both. Programs are sensitive to the stresses encountered by families who have an autistic child and provide parent groups and other types of support.

Intensive Intervention

Programs average nearly 30 hours per week of school-based intervention, substantially more hours than are typically provided by most public school systems for preschoolers with disabilities. In addition, since all programs involve parent training that results in many hours of treatment in the home, the number of hours of treatment that children receive is substantially higher than that of other preschools.

Other Elements

Programs may include other treatments like speech therapy or sign language, occupational therapy, specific social skills training, peer-mediated training and the development of independent initiative and choice-making skills.

The UCLA Young Autism Project – A Landmark Research

The UCLA Young Autism Project began about 35 years ago under the direction of Ivar Lovaas. This program is the most detailed and labor intensive of the early interventions, begins the earliest and is the only program whose outcomes have been evaluated against a control group of similar age children receiving less intensive intervention. The program included many of the key elements of early intervention and is based on principles of applied behavioral analysis including the use of rewards and punishments and shaping by successive approximation. Parents are taught to be the primary therapists for their children, with direction and help from students who work with them in the home. The average age of children entering the program is 32 months.

Here autistic children were assigned to one of the three groups. The groups were comparable with respect to age, language, intellectual functioning and other measures prior to intervention. Control group 2 consisted of 21 children from a larger study who also attended special education classes but received no one-to-one instructions. Children in the experimental condition, the first year of the program emphasized reducing disruptive behaviors and teaching behaviors such as compliance, imitation and toy play. The second year emphasized expressive and abstract language and interactive play. The third year emphasized on emotions, pre-academic tasks, assertiveness and observational learning.

The first outcome data obtained when the children were 7yrs old. 47% of the children in the experimental group were found to be educationally and intellectually normal. They successfully completed a regular first-grade. The average IQ scores of these children increased by 37 points from 70 to 107. Children in the two control groups did not fare nearly as well, with only 1 of 40 children being placed in a regular first-grade; overall, these children showed only minimal increases in IQ scores. The experimental group was assessed again when their average age was 13 yrs with similar results. The nine children who were placed in regular classrooms were virtually indistinguishable from same-age normal peers. Nearly all children with autism benefit from early intervention but it remains unclear how much the rate of progress depends on the child's IQ and language ability and what the long-term outcomes will be. Several anecdotal accounts and research reports claim that some autistic children can achieve normal functioning if given intensive intervention before the age of 3 yrs. However, the question of whether they can achieve full recovery continues to be hotly debated.

Case Study

Jerry: Fear and Order

According to Jerry, his childhood experience could be summarized as consisting of two predominant experiential states: confusion and terror. The recurrent theme that ran through all of Jerry's recollections was that of living in a frightening world presenting painful stimuli that could not be mastered. Noises were unbearably loud, smells overpowering. Nothing seemed constant; everything was unpredictable and strange. Animate beings were a particular problem. Dogs were remembered as eerie and terrifying. As a child, he believed they were somehow humanoid, yet they were not really human, a puzzle that mystified him. They were especially unpredictable; they could move quickly without provocation. To this day, Jerry is phobic of dogs.

He was frightened of other children, fearing that they might hurt him in some way. He could never predict their behavior. Elementary school was remembered as a horrifying experience. The classroom was total confusion and he always felt he would 'go to pieces'.

There were also enjoyable experiences. He liked going to grocery stores with his mother so he could look at the labels of canned goods as well as the prices of the objects. He also remembered liking to spin objects but could not describe the pleasure this activity gave him. His life seemed to have changed when he discovered multiplication tables at around the age of 8 (Bemporad, 1979).

Question for Readers

How should teachers care of an autistic child?

9

Mental Retardation

Introduction

Mental retardation is one of the childhood disorders, which comes under developmental disorders. Childhood disorders are any illness, impairment, or abnormal condition that affects primarily infants and children those in the age span that begins with the fetus and extends through adolescence. Childhood is a period of change, in both the child and his environment. Changes in the child related to growth and development are so striking that it is almost as if the child were a series of distinct yet related individuals passing through infancy, childhood, and adolescence. Changes in the environment occur as the surroundings and contacts of a totally dependent infant become those of a progressively more independent child and adolescent. Health and disorders during the period from conception to adolescence must be understood against this backdrop of changes. That means childhood disorders occur in context of growing up. According to DSM-IV development disorder is that the predominant disturbance is in the acquisition of cognitive, language, motor, social skills. Moreover, the course of development tends to be chronic, with some signs of the disorder persisting in a stable forms into adult life. However in any mild cases, adoption or full recovery may occur.

Childhood is considered to be particularly important because the brain changes significantly for several years after birth; this is also when critical development occur in social, emotional, cognitive and other important competency areas. This change follows a pattern: the child develops one skill before acquiring the next skill although this pattern of change is only one aspect of development, it is important concept for us at this point because it implies that any disruption in development of early skills will, by the very nature of this sequential process, disrupt the development of latter skills. Understanding the type of developmental relationship is important for several reasons. Knowing what skills are disrupted will help us understand the disorder better. And may lead to more appropriate intervention strategies. It is also important to remember that biological and psychosocial influences continuously interact with each other. Because any disorder can have clear biological base, the presentation of disorder is different for each individual. Changes at the biological or psychosocial level may reduce the impact of the disorder. There is a real concern among developmental psychologist that some workers in the field may view aspect of normal development as symptoms of abnormality. There are some cases of children with mental retardation.

Joanna, aged 4 and 1/2, was interviewed by the director of a preschool when her parents applied to have her enrolled. Joanna smiled a great deal and was interested in the toys in the office. The director, however, was concerned about Joanna's inability to say her own name and address, to communicate basic information about her family, and to express herself verbally. After an evaluation, Joanna was diagnosed as mildly mentally retarded, and she is now enrolled in a special school where she receives individual help in language development and academics. Her teachers feel that she is benefiting from the program and will be ready to enter a mainstream kindergarten.

Michael, now 5, was diagnosed by his pediatrician shortly after his birth as having Down's Syndrome, due to certain physical characteristics such as his round face, flattened nose bridge, abnormally small head, low-set ears, short limbs, and abnormally shaped fingers. Mental retardation is inevitable in children with Down's syndrome. Michael's parents were helped to locate an appropriate early intervention program that also provides parent education.

Eddie, now in 5th grade, was always considered a little slower than his peers, but he was a likeable child who got along well with family members and friends. When academic work became demanding and he fell behind in 2nd grade, the school conducted an evaluation. He was diagnosed as having moderate mental retardation and was placed in a special education class where the material is appropriate for his cognitive ability and learning pace.,

What is Mental retardation?

Mental retardation is a term used when a child has certain limitations in mental functioning and in skills such as Communicating, taking care of him or her, and social skills. These limitations will cause a child to learn and develop more slowly than a typical child. Children with mental retardation may take longer to learn to speak, walk, and take care of their personal needs such as dressing or eating. They are likely to have trouble learning in school. They will learn, but it will take them longer. There may be some things they cannot learn. There are several definitions, which help us to understand what exactly mental retardation is all about -

1. Mental retardation means significantly subaverage general intellectual functioning, originates during the developmental period and is associated with impairment in one or more following (1) maturation, (2) learning, (3) social adjustment. (American Association Mental Deficiency)
2. Substantial limitations in present functioning. It is characterized by significantly subaverage intellectual functioning, existing concurrently with related limitations in two or more of the following applicable adaptive skill areas: communication, self-care, home living, social skills, community use, self-direction, health and safety, functional academics, leisure, and work.

"Mental retardation manifests before age eighteen"(American Association on Mental Retardation, 1992)

3. A condition of arrested or incomplete development of mind of a person which is specially characterized by subnormality of intelligence
4. "Significantly below average general intellectual functioning which originates during the developmental period and is associated with impairment in adaptive behavior. Mental retardation may be caused by genetic or metabolic defects, by problems before a child is born, by deprivation in early childhood, by a disease of the nervous system, by poisons, or by brain injury.
5. [DSM-IV], a mental disorder characterized by significantly subaverage general intellectual functioning associated with impairments in adaptive behavior and manifested during the developmental period. It is classified on the basis of severity as mild, moderate, severe, and profound; a fifth subgroup, borderline intellectual functioning, is sometimes included.
6. Mental retardation (abbreviated as MR) is a term for a pattern of persistently slow learning of basic motor and language skills ("milestones") during childhood, and a significantly below-normal intellectual capacity as an adult.

Mental retardation is disorder that afflicts three out of every hundred child, two thirds of them boys. About 1% of children ages 3-10 years had mental retardation. We also found that mental retardation was more common in older children (ages 6-10 years) than in younger children (ages 3-5 years). Mental retardation was also more common in boys than in girls, and more common in black children than in white children. Onset usually occurs in infancy or prior to birth. When onset occurs at age 18 or after, it is called dementia. Mental retardation occurs more often among children form lower socio-economic and minority groups.

Thus it is a widely prevalent disorder, often heart

breaking in its emotional costs to families and in the life long economic burdens it imposes on them and on society. For all of its prevalence however, and despite the fact that everyone feels that they know that people have about mental retardation. But in larger context, the difficulty occurs because the notion of intelligence is at the heart of mental retardation; intelligence is very difficult to define. This definition has been incorporated into DSM-V as criteria for diagnosing mental retardation. In general the diagnosis of mental retardation can only be made when low IQ is accompanied by defects in ability to cope with the demands of daily life. Adaptive behavior scales assess the degree to which an individual meets the standard of personal independence and social responsibility expected for a childs age or cultural group (Grossman, 1983). One difficulty with this type of assessment is that standards of behavior and achievement are determined by an individuals society however the skills typically assessed by adaptive behavior scales are based on standard that are relatively universal, such as toilet training control on aggression, respect for authority figure. An IQ score of less than 70 remains the long accepted criterion of mental retardation though not without its problems, the wechslers intelligences scale for children, revise (wisc-r) and other intelligence test continue to be regarded as acceptable measures to provide a meaningful criterion of mental retardation. The following ranges, based on the Wechsler Adult Intelligence Scale (WAIS), are in standard use today. The following ranges, based on the Wechsler Adult Intelligence Scale (WAIS), are in standard use today:

Class	IQ
Profound mental retardation	Below 20
Severe mental retardation	20-34
Moderate mental retardation	35-49
Mild mental retardation	50-69
Borderline deficiency	70-79

Levels of retardation

The various levels of mental retardation and their associated IQ scores :-

Mild mental retardation

The larger the group of retarded children develops social and communication skill just like all others and at quite same times. In fact their retardation is often not noticed until they are in third or fourth grade, when they begin to have academic difficulties. Without help, they can acquire academic skills through the sixth grade; with the help, they can go beyond that level, in all other respects, their needs and abilities are indistinguishable from those of other children. Special education programs often enable these children to acquire the vocational skills that are necessary for minimal self-support. When under social or economic stress, they may need guidance and supervision, but otherwise they are able to function quote adequately in unskilled and semiskilled jobs.

Moderate mental retardation

Children in this category make up 10 percent of the mentally retarded. Like other children, they learn to talk and communicate during the pre school period. But unlike other children, the moderately retarded have difficulty learning social conventions. During the school-age period, they can profit from training in social and occupational skills, but they unlikely to go beyond the second grade level in academic subjects. Physically, they may be clumsy and occasionally they may suffer from poor motor coordination. They may learn to travel alone in familiar places and can have contributed to their own support by working at semiskilled are UN skilled tasks in protected settings.

Severe mental retardation

Before they are five, the severely retarded provide considerable evidence of poor motor development, and they develop little or no communicative speech. At special schools, they may learn to talk and can be trained in elementary hygiene. Generally, they are unable to profit from vocational training, though as adult they may be able to perform simple and unskilled job task under supervision.

Profound mental retardation

Children in this category are severely handicapped in adaptive behavior and are unable to master any but the simplest motor tasks during the pre school years. During the school years, some development in motor skills may occur, and the child may respond in a limited way to training in self-care, severe physical deformity, central nervous system difficulties, and retarded growth are not uncommon. Health and resistance to disease are poor, and life expectancy is shorter than normal. These children require custodial care.

Borderline deficiency

A group of children that belongs to the lower edge of the "normal" spectrum, just below the "low average" IQ group, some children with Borderline deficiency finish high school, but most don't. Usually fit into society sufficiently well that they are not diagnosed as mentally retarded; are poor students, but frequently do well in "non intellectual" occupations; they are not normally considered "legally" retarded.

An additional method of classification has been used in education system to identify the abilities of students with mental retardation. It relies on three categories. Educable mental retardation (based on IQ of 50 to approximately 70-75), trainable mental retardation (IQ 30 to 50) and severe mental retardation (IQ below 30). (Cipiani, 1991). The assumption that students with educable mental retardation (comparable to mild mental retardation) could learn basic academic skills; students with trainable mental retardation (comparable to moderate mental retardation) could not master academic skills but could learn rudimentary vocational skills; and students with severe mental retardation (comparable to severe and profound mental retardation) would not benefit from academic and vocational instruction. Built into this categorization system is the automatic negative assumption that certain individuals cannot benefit from certain type of training. This system and potentially stigmatizing and limiting DSM-Iw categories inspired the AAMR categorization of needed support current trends are away from the educational system of classification, because it inappropriately creates negative expectations in teachers.

Historical views of mental retardation

Till 1870s, mental deficiency was regarded as homogenous category, without any distinction among forms of mental retardation. In 1877 John Down publish a monograph, called the Mongolian type of idiocy in which he describe about Down syndrome. His work suggested that mental retardation was condition that could have many causes and then Gregor Mendel and Alfred Binet took interest in mental retardation.

Mendels work on the principles of genetic inheritance in plants led to interest in the effects of genetics in human beings and the idea that mental retardation might be genetically transmitted. The Eugenics movements started which focused on improving the genetic stock of the population by sterilizing individuals who were mentally retarded in order to prevent them from passing along their genetic inheritance, they have idea that retarded persons should be institutionalized because of what was believed that tendency towards delinquency.

Binet developed psychometric tests that could select children for specialized educational programs. These tests became popular; they classify people by intelligence level. After World War II, parents groups began organizing to work toward changing this stereotype and providing adequate training for children who were mentally retarded. In 1963, President John F. Kennedy contributed to the reevaluation of attitudes toward mental retardation when he presented to congress a task force report on mental retardation for national program to help prevent mental retardation.

Until relatively recently, the term mental deficiency has been used, but this is too negative implication. DSM-IV uses mental retardation that is also some people consider too negative and prefer term as intellectual disability, but we use clinically what DSM-IV uses.

Causes of Mental retardation

There are literally hundreds of known causes of mental retardation, including following:

Environmental: deprivation, abuse, neglect, etc, **Prenatal:** for instance exposure to disease or drugs while in still womb, **Perinatal:** such as difficulties during labour and delivery, **Post natal**: head injury, infections.

Biological dimensions-Genetic influences: Sometimes disability is caused by abnormal genes inherited from parents, most researchers believe that people with mental retardation probably are affected by multiple gene disorders in addition to environmental influences. However portions of the people with more severe mental retardation have identifiable single gene disorders, involving genes that are dominant(expresses itself when paired with a normal gene), recessive(expresses itself only when paired with another copy of itself), or x-linked (presents on the X or sex chromosome) only few dominant gene result in mental retardation one example of dominant gene disorder, tuberous, is relatively rare, occuring in 1 of approximately every 30,000 births. About 60% of people with this disorder have mental retardation (Vinken and Bruyn, 1972), and most have seizures (uncontrolled electrical discharges in the brain) and characteristic bumps in their skin that during adolescence acne.

Phenylketonuria (PKU) is a rare metabolic disease, which affects 1 of every 14,000 newborns and is characterized by an inability to breakdown a chemical in our diets called phenylalanine. PKU results from the action of recessive gene that is inherited from each parents. The infant cannot metabolize phenylalanine an amino acid that is essential component of proines. As a result, phenylalanine and derivative, phenyl pyruvic acid, build up in the body and rapidly poison the central nervous system, causing irreversible brain damage, about third of children cannot walk; nearly two-thirds never learn to talk; and more than half have IQ's that are below 20. Until the mid 1960's majority of people with this disorder had mental retardation. Carriers of PKU can be identified through biochemical tests and receive genetic counseling (stren, 1981). Affected babies can be identified by simple test of their urine about three weeks after their birth, provided they are kept on diet that controls the level of phenylalanine in their system until age six, when the brain is nearly fully developed, their chances of surviving with good health and intelligence are fairly high. There are a number of metabolic disorders that are associated with mental retardation, including Tay-sachs disease, Nieman-pick disease.

Lesch–nyhan syndrome, an x-linked disorder, is characterized by mental retardation, signs of cereberal palsy (spasticity or tightening of the muscles), and self injurious behaviour, including finger and lip biting (nyhan, 1978). Only males are affected, because recessive gene is responsible; when it is on the x chromosome in males it does not have normal gene to balance it because males do not have a second chromosome. Women with this gene are carriers and do not show any symptoms.

Chromosomal influences:- 40 years ago that the number of chromosome ——46—— was correctly identified in human cells. Three years later, researchers found that people with down syndrome had an additional small chromosome. Since that time, a number of other chromosomal aberrations that result in mental retardation have been identified.

Down syndrome:- the most chromosomal from of mental retardation, was first identified by british physician langdon down in 1866. Down had tried to develop a classification system for people with mental retardation based on their resembalance to people of the other races; he describe individuals with this particular disorder as "monogloid" because they resembled people from mongolia. The term monogoloidism was used for sometime but has been replaced with the term Down Syndrome. This disorder is caused by the presence of an extra 21 chromosome and is therefore sometimes referred to as trisomy 21. During cell division of the 21st chromosomes stick together, creating one cell with one copy that dies, and one cell with three copies that divide to create a person with Down syndrome.

People with Down syndrome have characteristics facial features, including folds in the corners of their upwardly slanting eyes, a flat nose, and small mouth with the flat roof that makes the tongue to protrude. Somewhat the incidence of children born with Down syndrome has been tied to maternal age : as the age of the mother increases, so does her chance of having a child with this disorder. Down syndrome occurs at conception and immediately affects the development of the fetus. The risk for the disorder is about 1 in 1,500 for children born to mother in their 20s, it increases to 1 in 40 when mother is over 40. Many babies born with Down syndrome suffer from physical anomalies as well as cognitive delay. Fortunately due to medical advances now it is treatable. There is a case study of man with down syndrome, describes how his early development was similar to, but much slower that of his young brother.

"When I was about 3 and my sister was 5, we had a baby brother. I helped to feed him and take care of him until he was almost 3, I was 5 then and could do most of the things he could do. About that time he caught up to me. I could still do thing that he couldn't, but not many he could do some things that I had trouble with. We became good friends. Everytime he learned a new skill, I would either learn it with him, or he would teach me later. I was really little for my age, so we were pretty close in size. We share bunk bed, toys and clothes, we learnt to do lot things together. When he learned bike, I wasn't ready to learn yet, mom and dad got me a powerwheel motorized bike so I could ride a bike too. When he learned to read, he taught me to read when he played baseball, he took me with him. In those days, I still went to school in another district. So most of my friends were his friends. Now that we go to same school it is sometime hard for him to remember that I have my own friends too. I have to tell him that I am the big brother. He sometimes get teased at school because he is my brother, but he is learning to explain instead of fight. Mostly, the kids are all nice to us."

Fragile x syndrome is second common chromosomally related causes of mental retardation. As its name suggests, this disorder is caused by abnormality on x-chromosome, a maturation that makes the tip of the chromosome look as thought it were hanging from a thread, giving it appearance of fragility.The syndrome is characterized by severe mental retardation, autistic behaviours, and speech defects. Males with disorder also show hyperactivity. Short attention span, gaze avoidance, perservative speech, and physical characteristics such as large ears, testical, long faces, head circumferences are also common. Estimates 1 of every 2,000 males is born with fragile x syndrome.

It is possible to detect chromosomal problems through amniocetesis a test is administered to mother after thirteenth week of pregnancy. A small amount of amniotic fluid is drawn off and examined for the presence of abnormal chromosomes. A newer test, known as chronic virus sampling can be done earlier in a pregnancy, between eight and twelfth weeks, to test Down syndrome and other abnormalities. A sampling of cells is taken via the mother's vagina and cervix, through her abdomial wall. But amniocenttesis is more accurate.

Psychological and social dimensions

Cultural–familial retardation is presumed cause of up 75% of the cases of mental retardation. Individuals with Cultural –familial retardation tend to score in the mild mental retardation range on IQ tests and have relatively good adaptive skills. Their mental retardation is thought to result from combination of psychosocial and biological influences, although the specific mechanisms that lead to this type of mental retardation are the cultural influences that may contribute include abuse, neglect, and social deprivation. Cultural familial group have more severe form of mental retardation. Cultural –familial group of people are lower end of IQ continuum as one research shows.

Environment also appears to play an important role in the development of mental retardation the pre-natal environment to which fetus is exposed can have profound effect on development. Drugs that the mother takes while pregnant can affect fetal development. Fetal alcohol syndrome (FAS) is condition involving a variety of physical defects and deformities and mental retardation in fetuses exposed to alcohol through the mother's drinking during pregnancy. Children whose mother abused alcohol during pregnancy have an average IQ in the 60s (Grant and Barr, 1991). The emergence of crack cocain in recent decades is "crack babies" infants born to mothers who took crack while pregnant. Crack, or any form of cocain leads to reduce oxygen and blood flow to the fetus. Crack babies are born with a variety of neurological deficits, and are irritable and difficult to sooth. If mother gets an infection like rubella during pregnancy may also have a baby with mental disability. Problems at birth. If a baby has problems during labor and birth, such as not getting enough oxygen, he or she may have developmental disability. Health problems. Diseases like whooping cough, the measles, or meningitis can cause mental disability. It can also be caused by extreme malnutrition, not getting enough medical care, or by being exposed to poisons like lead or mercury. Iodine deficiency is the leading, preventable cause of mental disability in areas of the developing world where iodine deficiency is endemic. Low birth weight is a risk factor for mental retardation. Physical abuse and accidental falls and blows can cause brain damage and mental retardation

Treatment and training of the retarded

Parental counseling

Mental retardation is poorly understood and greatly feared. Parents may blame themselves for their defective children; other parents consciously or unconsciously reject them. The guilt, fear, or shame felt by parents who do not understand retardation may be the chief determinant of whether or not they decide to institutionalize their child, but far better if this decision is made on the basis of clinical advice and practical planning.

In some cases, retardation is so severe that care cannot be adequately provided in the home and institutionalization is inevitable. In case of milder retardation the question of hospitalization is more complex, and a clinical plays a valuable role in clarifying therapy issues involved. When the parents want to keep child at home and it is feasible to do so, they may benefit from counseling about special child-rearing methods, educational opportunities available to their child, and their own emotional reactions to having a retarded child at home.

Psychodynamic approach

We can apply psychodynamic and learning approaches to modify behavior of those how are mildly retarded. Psychotherapeutic and counseling procedures in cases where retardation seems to have basis in personality distortions.

The use of psychotherapy with retarded persons is typically not aimed at eliminating the retardation itself but rather at fostering maximal behavioral adequacy and personality development. Psychodynamic techniques are frequently used in-group settings, e.g., group counseling and play therapy (Clarke, 1965).

The problems of objectively evaluating the efficiency of Psychotherapeutic procedures are more formidable with retarded persons, in case of retarded person it must be judged whether or not he knew meaning of communication, while communication sessions. Systematic enquiry into psychodynamics retarded person can be attempted with detailed study of patient-therapist relationship in a significant number of cases. It can also be approached from experimental and developmental standpoints. Ziglar has surveyed literature on latter two topics and concluded that the behavior of many retarded persons is product of motivational and emotional barriers to optimal cognitive development. An anxiety and expectations of failure increase the likelihood that the retarded will fail. Research is needed to assess the joint contributions of motivational states and cognitive defects to mental retardation.

Learning approaches

Learning approaches to treatment of retarded emphasize fostering their social developmental and improved ways of teaching skills and concepts. First, the behaviorist analyzes the specific behavior that the individual needs to learn, e.g., making a phone call. He identifies the kind of number of discrete responses that make up the tasks, and then he demonstrates each response (Crossen, 1999; Peterson, C. M., 1969). Verbal praise and tokens or perhaps tangible reinforcers might then be used to facilitate acquisition of the needed responses (Ellis, 1963)

Conditioning techniques have been used with mental retarded persons in a variety of ways. In one investigation a group of children were studied in an experimental classroom (Birnbrauer, Wolf, Kedder, & Tauge, 1965). Emphasis was placed on giving the child verbal approval (praise from the teacher), knowledge of how well he performed, and tokens as rewards. Noticeable improvement in school learning was achieved through use of this regimen. In another study an operant conditioning format was followed in toilet training of severely retarded boys (Hundziak, Maurer, & Watsone, 1965). A reinforcement device issued candy for each successful defection and urination. The boys' elimination habits rapidly improved and their improvement extended outside the laboratory situation.

There is recognized need to develop efficient group techniques for strengthening the response repertories of retarded. Meeting this need, from a learning point of view, require the behavior of each individual in the group be monitored and responded to with appropriate reinforcing conditions. One study used reinforcement techniques to deal with the problem of the retarded person's inability to attend to cues in his environment and follow instructions (Zimmerman & Russell, 1986). Token reinforcement was given to subject when they follow directions in classroom. First researchers had to make tokens meaningful to the subject. Then the effect of reinforcement on their behavior was assessed. The results showed that ability to pay attention and follow directions increased as a function of reinforcement. Teachers, parents, and other skilled in use of reinforcers can help retarded persons to acquire personally and socially significant responses with carefully planned behavior management techniques.

Learning approaches have focused on training parents and teachers of the retarded as well as retarded themselves. If parents and teachers could learn to be more effective in applying techniques of behavior management techniques such as reinforcement (Lazere, Mash, Tredal, & Garner, 1969). These mothers, when compared with matched controls, improved their ability to respond consistently and effectively to both appropriate and inappropriate behavior in their retarded children. There is great need not only for practical application of learning principles in remedial programs for retarded, but also for basic studies on mental development of retarded.

Pharmacotherapy

The frequency of drug use in children with mental retardation is rare. Hill *et al.* (1984) found that 19% of group of 35,751 children with mental retardation in community residential centers received psychotropic medication. Prescribing psychotropic drugs for mental retardation children remains a controversial issue, the concern being occasional abuse, limitation in effectiveness, poor research methodology, and unpredictability of response, particularly in children with organic dysfunctions. Psychostimulant like methylphenidate are commonly prescribed for mental retardation children especially for mild retardation. The dose of methylphenidate usually vary between 0.3 and 1 mg/kg/day. Children with severe mental retardation may respond negatively & having chances of side effects. Antidepressants like Monoamine oxides inhibitors and tri-cyclic antidepressant are the oldest type of Antidepressents used for children with mental retardation.

Also tryophein has been also used along or combination with other drugs. Anticonvulsants may be rationale for use of these drugs on severely and profoundly retarded children. Narcoleptics drugs most often used with mentally retarded children are thioridazine.

Investigators are in agreement that the most commonly used psychotropic drugs tend to have general rather than specific effects on behavior. A detailed knowledge of the underlying biological causes of mental retardation is necessary for establishing need for drug therapy. Psychotropic medication should be administered on the basis of through psychiatric diagnosis and should only be used to normalize or optimize some aspects of therapy child's CNS physiology and conditions. Once this has been attained, therapeutic efforts can shift towards behavioral, educational, and psychotherapeutic paths and interventions. And main thing is that medication should be used as long as it serves purpose.

Training very much important because...

Matt is 15 years old. Because Matt has mental retardation, he has been receiving special education services since elementary school. These services have helped him tremendously, because they are designed to fit his special learning needs. Last year he started high school. He, his family, and the school took a good hard look at what he wants to do when secondary school is over. Does he want more education? A job? Does he have the skills he needs to live on his own? Answering these questions has helped Matt and the schools plan for the future. He's always been interested in the outdoors, in plants, and especially in trees. He knows all the tree names and can recognize them by their leaves and bark. So this year he is learning about jobs like forestry, landscaping, and grounds maintenance. Next year he hopes to get a part-time job. He's learning to use public transportation, so he'll be able to get to and from the job. Having mental retardation makes it harder for Matt to learn new things. He needs things to be very concrete. But he is determined. He wants to work outside, maybe in the park service or in a greenhouse, and he's getting ready!

Story of matt suggests that training and special programs for mental retardation children are very important building their own identity...

Psychosocial treatments

The first psychosocial treatment involves intensive, broad-ranging early-intervention services for families with young children that are designed to reduce risk factors and to promote healthy child development. This is easy to deliver and beneficial for long-term. Psychosocial treatments: acknowledge the important to community based activities that offer people with disabilities a choice of ways to develop their interpersonal and practical skills and self-confidence.

Early interventions: One of the most promising methods for enhancing the intellectual and social skills of young children with development disabilities, and lack of environmental stimulation, has been involvement of caregivers and other adults in intensive, child focuses activities from an early point in time for 35 years. Early education intervention consists of systematic efforts to provide high-risk children with supplemental educational experience before they enter school and frequently other family and child services.

The optimal timing for intervention appears to be during pre-school years. C.T. Ramey (1992) offer a set of practical recommendations for enhancing children' lives through early intervention.

- Encouragement of exploration. Children are encouraged by adults to explore and gather information about their environments.
- Mentoring the basic skills. A trusted, familiar adult teaches children basic cognitive skill such as labeling, sorting, sequencing, and comparing.
- Celebration of developmental advances. Family and others

who knows the child celebrates and reinforces each of the child's accomplishments.

- Guided rehearsals and extension of new skills. Responsible others assist the child in rehearsing and extending newly acquired skills.
- Protection from harmful displays of disapproval, teasing, or punishment. Constructive criticism and negative consequences for unacceptable behaviors are used.
- A rich and responsive language environment for communication. Spoken and written language is used to convey information, provide social awards, and encourage the learning new material and skills.

Recent research studies on mental retardation

All this controversy over diagnosing and treating the mentally retarded has produced a number of studies but also as they relate to their parents. Among the more significant findings are as follows:

- Mental health professional have tendency to ignore the feelings of the parents. They tend to take granted that the parents understand what is going and thus do damage to both parent and child (Murphy and Pounds, 1972)
- Life satisfaction is basically similar in most retarded children and so-called in normal. Clinical observation of retarded behavior suggests that it is not possible to say that they are unhappy children. For instance, but normal and retarded are happier in recess than in class. The key ingredients in feeling happy seem to be involvement with other people, whether one is retarded or not. (Cameron *et al.*, 1973)
- Motivation for seeking stimulation, reward, and praise goes up in direct proportion to therapy amount of deprivation; and tends to decrease with maturation. In other words, as one's inner resources increase, the need for direct stimulation decreases. This means that the slowly maturing child or the retarded child requires more attention (Ziglar and Balla, 1972)

- Training of workers with the retarded is often deficient. Careful procedures are mapped out of for behavior modification, but institutional staff members, as well as parents, need special training to understand that the child eventually has to be taught self–reinforcing behavior in which activities become rewarding for him in and of themselves, and this take considerable training of teachers, whoever they are (Kazdin, 1973)
- Even in case of institutionalized, severely retarded individuals, concentrated periods of social interactions with normal children or adults (game plying, coloring, reading, putting together puzzle) is instrumental in raising intelligence test scores (Jacobson *et al.,* 1978).

Conclusion

To conclude, childhood is often thought of as being one of the happiest times in a person's life. A time where a carefree attitude and a worryless life provide the environment in which a child grows and develops. For many children, however, this isn't always the case, especially those who are having disorder like mental retardation. As we know that precaution is better than cure, so efforts were made to prevent mental retardation and help those affected by it, and live up to their full potential. These include primary prevention, secondary prevention, and tertiary. Primary prevention: some types of mental retardation can be prevented from occurring. One outstanding example of such primary prevention program is the campaign to inform women that using alcohol in pregnancy is potentially harmful to the developing child. Public health campaigns and warning sign on alcoholic beverages and in places where alcohol is served help to accomplish this. Another type of public health effort is aimed at reducing the chances of brain damage to children after birth. The effort to reduce children's exposure lead, which may have a negative effect on their intellectual functioning by requiring the use of unleaded gasoline and by removing lead as an ingredient of most paints, as well as by making parents aware of the dangers to children of chipping paint in older house.

For the prevention of mental retardation is educating people about the importance of prenatal care for pregnant woman. Now we can use amniocentesis and ultrasound scanning. New techniques in generic reserch have been able to identify gene location related to a variety disorders. Secondary prevention: it efforts to focus on providing the treatment when children are born with disorder may cause mental retardation. PKU screening is now done routinely for newborn infants so that if the problem exits, dietary control can begin at once to prevent damage to the central nervous system. Tertiary prevention: Is aimed at improving an already existing situation. There are interventions programs have been developed for specific disorders, particular Down syndrome, as way of increasing children's skills early in developmental cycle. Others are school-based educational programs, community living programs, vocational and social skills training programs. Also treatment for psychosocial and family relationship problems for people who are mentally retarded.

Question for Readers

Do we require a support group for parents of mentally retarded children? what can we do about it?

10

Resilience in Children

An objective of this chapter is to learn about resilience in the face of family trauma, and the factors contributing to differences (if any) in the levels of resilience in children and adolescents from individualist versus collectivist cultures.

Resilience "generally means the ability to recover from some shock, insult, or disturbance. However, it is used quite differently in different fields" (Wikipedia.org). Resilience is also commonly used in psychology and child development to describe the ability of people to cope with stress and catastrophe (Wikipedia.org). Resilience is defined as "the development of competence despite adversity" (Egeland *et al.*, 1993). It reflects the ability to successfully adapt and function despite prolonged and severe trauma.

A resilient child or adolescent will generally be performing at a level that is normal for his or her age. The standards used by parents and teachers to judge how well a child is performing may vary. Still, there is some agreement about the standards for performing well, even across different cultures (Masten, 2000). A child is said to be resilient when he or she is performing well on developmental tasks considered important to that age and culture, even when the child has been subject to extreme adversity (Masten, Hubbard, Gest, Tellegen, Garmaezy & Ramirez, 1999). Developmental tasks are the "broad expectations" for children of different age groups (Masten, 2000). Developmental tasks in young children may include learning speech and movement and following simple instructions from parents. When the child enters school at a young age, we expect him or her to get along with other children and follow teacher's instructions. When an individual is in his youth, we expect him or her to go to school, abide by the law, have both platonic and romantic relationships and begin to work on financial independence from their parents (Masten, 2000). This was, of course written in the context of American society and some of the expectations may change when we apply it to the Indian model. For instance, in India, adolescents are not given as much freedom to be in romantic relationships as in the West. At the same time, they are not expected to start fending for themselves and may be able (and in some cases even encouraged) to live of their parents well into the late teens or even twenties. Though expectations may differ slightly as a function of culture, across cultures we expect children and youth to grow as per the expectations of their age, even though they may face some obstacles along the way (Masten, 2000). Broadly speaking then, resilience in children and youth is understood in terms of 3 types of phenomena; good development despite high risk, maintained competence under stress, and recovery from trauma (Werner, 1995). "Resilience is not something we're born with-it's a set of learned behaviors, and it takes strategizing to build" (Murray, 2003).

Resilience, however, is different from recovery (Bonanno, 2004). Resilience is discussed in terms of protective factors that facilitate positive outcomes for children that are faced with adverse life events. These risk and protective factors are often an interplay between genetic, personal and environmental factors (Rutter, 1999; Werner, 1995)

Internal individual factors include giving self in service to others or a cause, flexibility, autonomy, good sense of humor, internal locus of control (making life choices based on self rather than external influences), perceptiveness, creativity, self-motivation, and good decision making skills (Henderson, Bernard, Sharplight, 1999). Other than the internal factors, there are a number of protective factors and systems that foster the development of resilience. The protective factors include "good parents, faith and religious affiliations, talents valued by society and self, a sense of meaning in life, socio-economic advantages, good schools, good intellectual skills, and community resources" (Masten, 2000). Protective systems for human development include "attachment systems, family systems, community organizational systems, spirituality and religious systems" (Masten, 2000). Other environmental characteristics operating in families, schools, and other organizations include those that encourage close bonds, value and promote education, set and enforce clear rules, and establish high, but realistic standards for development (Henderson & Milstein, 1999). Research in this field suggests that children who are resilient despite obstacles have these protective factors operating to their advantage.

Of the factors that contribute to the development of resilience, environmental factors can play a crucial role in fostering and maintaining resilience. One of the most important environmental factors is the family. Sensitive and supportive parents foster the development of resilience in children, and secure attachment relationships built in infancy provide an important protective function later on in life (Egeland *et al.*, 1993). In the face of debilitating adversity, a child is more likely to be resilient if he or she has had the chance to establish a strong bond with one emotionally stable person that is concerned for the child's welfare (Werner, 1995). Another important contributor to resilience is the individual's cognitive capacity. Still, the quality of family (especially parent-child) relationships continue to play the most crucial role in the development of competence in adolescents, even when other factors like IQ and socio-economic status are controlled for (Masten *et al.*, 1999). This nurturing may come from the parents or from substitute parents such as grandparents and older siblings. Studies like the Kauai longitudinal study have shed light on this phenomenon. I have discussed the study at length later in my paper.

The research on resilience outlined above lends support to the idea that family is extremely important as a protective mechanism for children or adolescents that are growing up under adverse conditions. This has implications for the understanding of resilience in a cross-cultural setting. Individualist cultures emphasize independence, autonomy and hedonism, while collectivist cultures focus on interdependence, harmony (as opposed to autonomy) and relationships with others (Gohm, Oishi, Darlington, Duner, 1998). Triandis (1995) suggests that levels of individualism are negatively correlated with levels of support available from members of in-groups. Collectivists are more likely to offer social support in times of adversity (Villareal, Asai & Lucca, 1998). Individualist cultures emphasize a "rights based moral code" in which there is little or no obligation to help others while collectivist cultures value a "duty based moral code" in which helping members of the community is very important (Gohm *et al.*, 1998).

Miller (1994) compared American (individualistic) and Hindu Indian (collectivist) populations. He found that among Americans, the interpersonal moral code that develops in individually inclined and focuses on personal freedom, and individual responsibility. That is, when making decisions, Americans tend to weigh responsibility toward others with responsibility toward self. On the other hand, the duty-based moral code among Hindu-Indians emphasizes interpersonal obligations that are socially enforceable. The differences between rights-based and duty-based approaches have been clearly illustrated in studies examining cultural variations in the display of altruistic behaviours. Miller and colleagues (1990) presented American and Hindu Indian participants with supposed scenarios in which people did not help an individual to whom the need was a matter of life and death (the need for mouth-to-mouth resuscitation), the need was serious, but not life-threatening (aspirin for a migraine) or the need was minor, not at all serious or life-threatening (money to buy a movie ticket). The needy persons were either presented as members of the in-group (family) or as members of the out-group (strangers). The researchers found that in the case of Hindu-Indians, except when the need was minor and the needy person was a stranger, they held a moral view of the incident and displayed no variation based on need or role. On the other hand, Americans only held a moral view when the need was a matter of life and death and their responses were largely influenced by both need and role. They felt that helping behavior was a matter of personal choice and did not find it valid to regulate others behaviour. These findings support the theory that the level of moral obligation is greater in duty-based versus need-based moral codes.

Miller and Bersoff (1998) also studied the extent to which personal preferences (liking the other) influenced individual's moral responsibility toward them. The researchers manipulated the affinity of agents and asked both Americans and Indians whether they felt an interpersonal responsibility towards the person. For Indians, personal affinity did not influence moral judgments and vice-versa in the case of Americans. This suggests that for Americans, interpersonal responsibility is contingent of their personal preferences and likings of the needy person and this is not the case for Indians. This lends support to the hypothesis that individualist cultures (rights based) look at responsibility in terms of personal choices whereas collectivist cultures (duty based) look at responsibility in terms of moral obligation.

In Individualist cultures like the U.S., very early on, individuals learn to make a distinction between the self and others (Iyenger & DeVoe, 2001). In collectivist cultures, like India individuals may vary in identities of self i.e. may not make a distinction between the self and others, but make distinctions instead based on in-groups and out-groups. Thus, people from individualist cultures regard choices as either being made by themselves or by others whereas individuals from collectivist cultures find the distinction between self-made and others-made choices harder to make (Iyengar, Ross, & Lepper, 1999; Triandis, Bontempo, Villareal, Asai, & Lucca, 1988). People from individualist cultures are therefore independent- seeing themselves as unique and distinct from others, striving for autonomy and remain uninfluenced by others and outside pressures (Geertz, 1975). People from collectivist cultures, on the other hand are interdependent, less focused on themselves and more on the relationships they share with other members of the in-group. They focus not on autonomy and independence, but on fitting in and adjusting with the demands of the in-groups (Kitayama, Suzuki, Conner, & Markus, 2001).

"In individualist cultures when a conflict arises between personal and group goals, it is considered acceptable for the individual to place personal goals ahead of collective goals. By contrast, in collectivist cultures social behavior is determined largely by goals shared with some collective, and if there is a conflict between personal and group goals, it is considered socially desirable to place collective goals ahead of personal goals" (Triandis, 1989).

These findings would lead us to predict that in cultures where emphasis is placed on family, and where family members share strong bonds with one another, children and youth are more likely to be resilient when faced with adversity. Let us take the example of India (collectivist culture) and the United States (individualist culture).

As mentioned earlier, in Collectivist cultures like in India, family plays a crucial role in the life of the individual. Individuals tend to define themselves in terms of their family and community. The individual and his family are in a mutually interdependent relationship and this usually continues throughout the life of the individual. India today is undergoing a lot of changes; urbanization, industrialization, increasing divorce rates and inter-generational conflicts. Still, most Indian families are able to adjust and adapt to changing norms and values and demonstrate unique strength in keeping together despite stress and strain. The family continues to play a major role in the lives of people (Sonawat, 2001).

On the other hand, individualist cultures like in the United States value individuals, independence and autonomy. Individuals in such cultures usually do not define themselves in terms of their family and community.

Research on the United States reveals the deteriorating

mental and behavioral health of its children (Brazelton, T.B., Coles, R., Comer, J.P., Insel, T., Kline, K.K., Poussaint, A., Schore, A.N., Spear, L., Suomi, S.J., Wallerstein, J., 2003). Why is it that even in the midst of affluence, America's children often fail to flourish? The answer lies in the lack of connectedness that America's children are facing today; connectedness to people and connectedness to spiritual meaning. An astonishing finding is that the children of immigrant families' experience better mental health than children of U.S. born parents. This advantage declines with increased time spent in the United States and from one generation to the next. This implies that there is something missing in the nurturing of America's children that hinders their development and has a deleterious impact on their mental health. The most effective way of dealing with this problem is the development of authoritative communities. Authoritative communities consist of close knit groups of people that are committed to each others well being and who can provide a model for what it means to be a good person. To improve the lives of children and adolescents in the U.S., the renewal of authoritative communities is imperative.

Family is an important example of an authoritative community. It fosters in individuals a sense of morality and sets standards for appropriate personal conduct- honesty, loyalty, co-operation, personal responsibility and respect. As a culture, America has shifted emphasis away from the family and towards values such as individualism and consumerism. Over the course of 30 years from the 60's to the 90's, the strength of U.S. families was on a decline. High divorce rates, childbearing out of wedlock, and co-habitation (without marriage) (Arendell, 1997) have led to a decline in the presence of biological two parent families, where the parents are married. Parenthood is less securely connected with marriage where America's children are increasingly living in a non-traditional family set up. These include blended families, gay and lesbian parents, single parent families and para-parenting arrangements in which a friend or another unrelated adult takes care of and supervises the child either on a temporary or permanent basis (Arendell, 1997).

Since the late 90's, however, the situation has improved slightly. The percentage of children living in two parent families has increased and U.S. divorce rates are on the decline. It remains to be seen, however if family fragmentation established over so many decades will be able to be replaced by reintegration (Brazelton *et al.*, 2003). It is important to make efforts to support and strengthen the family, especially with an increasing number of alternate family forms. This may involve redefining family and parenthood (Arendell, 1997).

Despite material satisfaction, some of America's children experience deteriorating mental and behavioral health and low levels of well being. In some cases, the reverse might occur. Even in the midst of poverty and minimal wealth, some children show remarkable levels of well being. In most cases, the families of these children serve as a mediating factor and buffer the children in the face of trauma, thus allowing them to develop into resilient individuals, despite their circumstances.

Werner and Smith (1982) studied children and grandchildren of Asian and European immigrants who worked on the island of Kauai. These children were at high risk- most of their mothers had not graduated from high school, their fathers worked in semi-skilled or unskilled jobs and were born and raised in poverty. Approximately one of the ten children they studied developed into competent adults despite their circumstances thereby meeting the criteria for resilient individuals. The researchers compared the care giving environment of these children to other high risk children who showed maladaptive behaviour. They identified a number of important factors that contributed to the resilience of these children; attention provided to the child by his or her primary caregiver(s), the presence of a sibling as a caretaker and friend, cohesiveness of the family, the number of caretakers other than the mother present in the house and the availability of an extended network of supportive people (family, friends). The families of these children were poor, but the children established a strong bond with their primary caregivers in the first year of their life. The researchers concluded that this secure attachment provided a strong base for the development of the child in the second year of his or her life. Many of these children also grew up in extended family set ups that included three generations living under one roof. The children thus established strong bonds with their alternate caregivers like their grandmother or older sibling while their mothers were out working. These strong social bonds were lacking in families whose children displayed maladaptive behavior.

The absence of family support was most detrimental when the children's constitutional make up and environment (tendency toward passivity, parental psychoses) rendered them even more vulnerable. During childhood and adolescence, these youth experienced higher levels of sickness and changed schools more often. They were also subject to increasing effects of family trauma; absence of father and mental illness of mother. These youngsters developed an "external locus of control" and "learned helplessness" whereby they attributed their experiences to luck or fate. And that believed that they had nothing to do with their own success or failure. On the other hand, the resilient children developed ways of coping and managing stressful situations, which buffered them against "learned helplessness" and built in them a sense of "hopefulness" despite adversity. Based on these findings, the researchers concluded that although the parent-child relationship is crucial, other ties within the family (like grandparents, siblings etc) also plays an important role in the development of resilience in children. Grandparents play an especially valuable role as "resistance resources" (Werner & Smith, 1982) because they provide support and care in unstable conditions and can ameliorate the negative effects of family trauma and marital discord and or dissolution. These systems are often in place in developing parts of the world and sometimes neglected in western society in the pursuit of economic and technological progress.

There is also a strong association between parental marital status, marital conflict and subjective well being- the two are negatively correlated. This association differs as a function of culture, individualism and collectivism ((Gohm, Oishi,

Darlington, Duner, 1998). In cultures where divorce is common and acceptable, the negative impacts are less than in cultures where it is not as common and unacceptable. Also, when marital conflict is high, it is to the child's advantage that his or her parents get divorced, rather than stay married. The advantage of divorced, single parent households versus high conflict marriages is higher in collectivist cultures than it is in individualist cultures. One possible reason for this is that in collectivist cultures where divorce is frowned upon, and divorce only occurs where there is intense conflict. The children will experience higher levels of well being as a result of divorce rather than living in a high conflict household. Another reason for this could be the level of support available to children of divorced parents, influenced by whether the culture tends towards individualism or collectivism. As mentioned earlier people in, individualist societies have a minimum moral obligation to help others, "rights based moral code" while collectivist cultures emphasize helping others, "duty based moral code". Thus, children of divorced parents are more likely to receive help and support in collectivist cultures than they are in individualist cultures. This has important implications for the children's well being. The researchers concluded that collectivism lessens the impact of parental divorce and conflict. The extended networks of social support available in collectivist cultures provide their children with psychological and emotional support in times of trauma.

Based on the research, I hypothesize that U.S. children are less likely to be resilient in the face of family trauma than are their Indian counterparts. India has a collectivist culture and Indians place a lot of emphasis on family, relationships with others and interdependence. Most people in India live in a joint family system, where there are three generations under one roof. Even when not physically living together, there is close interaction between family members, especially grand parents. When the child is born, the grand parents play an active role in nurturing the child and this usually continues throughout the child's life. Thus, the levels of social support available to Indian children are usually very high which suggests that are likely to be resilient in the face of adversity.

On the other hand, in many industrialized and developed countries like the United States, a lot of value is placed in independence and autonomy. With family fragmentation, there are an increasing number of non-traditional families, which reduces the number of children living in two parent families, where the parents are married. The mental and behavioral health of U.S. children has been on the decline and this may be due to a lack of connectedness that they experience-connectedness to other people and spiritual meaning (Brazelton *et al.*, 2003). In addition, America, as an individualist culture follows a right based moral code, where there is minimum obligation to help others, thus, children from broken families or families where there is discord will be less likely to receive high levels of social support, thus rendering them more vulnerable.

"Promoting healthy development and competence is as important, if not more important, than preventing problems, and will serve the same end" (Masten, 2000).

It is thus possible to develop resilience irrespective of the culture an individual grows up in. The strategies targeted at the development of resilience include risk-focused, asset-focused, and process-focused strategies. Risk-focused strategies try to prevent children's exposure to hazardous situations and may include efforts such as proper prenatal care and school reforms. Asset focused strategies include working on increasing the amount and quality of resources available to children. Resources that have direct effect may include tutoring the child or making extra-curricular activities available and those that have an indirect effect may include literacy and jobs for parents, programs to teach parenting skills, training for teachers (Benson *et al.*, 1995, 1999). Lastly, process-focused strategies attempt at the development of protective factors that foster resilience. These include mentoring programs designed to ensure that every child has a responsible and caring adult looking out for them and varied efforts to make sure children have adequate opportunities to develop talents (Masten, 2000).

Henderson & Milstein (1999) identified four crucial steps for the development of resilience in children. The first is that parents or other adults should always communicate a resiliency attitude. The resiliency attitude means that care and support should be provided to the child, no matter what he or she has done in the past or what situation he or she is in at present. The second is to focus on the child's strengths as much or more than focusing on weaknesses, thereby creating culture than reinforces the child's strengths. The third is to build a "resiliency wheel" (Henderson & Milstein, 1999) or an environment conducive to the development of resilience. This resiliency wheel includes providing opportunities for meaningful participation wherein children should be encourage to make decisions and goal setting and developing a curriculum and teaching that is more suitable to learning to cope in the real world; increasing bonding with peers and other activities like sports and drama; setting boundaries that are clear and consistent and crossed, met with appropriate consequences; providing caring and support, not only from parents but teachers and other adults in creating a supportive environment for the child; teaching life skills- co-operation, assertiveness, problem solving, and decision making; and communicating high, but realistic expectations (Henderson & Milstein, 1999). Lastly, children should be taught to not give up despite adverse situations. Here it helps to have people who care about the child, believe in the child, and are willing to strive for the child's betterment.

Question for Readers

Is Resilience a personality factor or it can be taught or learned?

11

Juvenile Delinquency

Juvenile delinquency is both social and personal problem. For teenage group it draws more attention than any other social problem. The problem of delinquency and youth crime is not new to mankind. According to Ohio code, "a delinquent child is defined as one who violates a law, is habitually disobedient or truant, or who behaves in a way that endangers the health or morals of himself or others, or who attempts to enter the marriage relation without consent of parents or guardian." Legally, a delinquent is a teenage who has been brought to court, not as a criminal who is mature enough to recognize his offence, but as a maturing person who needs to be taught responsibilities of an adjusted person.

Almost all adolescent boys and large proportion of adolescent girls have at same time committed offences that, by strict legal interpretation are delinquent acts. However, only a small proportion of delinquent is officially recorded. Hence, the juvenile delinquency means crime committed by an individual below 18 years of age in females and below 16 years of age in males. Behaviourly, adolescent can be considered as delinquent, if they act in a way that is discordant with norms of society. However, most of adolescents are guilty of delinquent acts, but either is not detected or is protected from any court action by their parents or others.

Characteristics

Findings regarding the characteristics of delinquents, or causes of delinquency are based mainly on limited sampling persons who commit delinquent acts. The main finding about characteristics of delinquent is having friends who are delinquents is closely associated with ones own tendency to engage in delinquency. Delinquents have lower average intelligence. Although many delinquents have low IQ there are also many socially acceptable adolescent of the same intellectual level. Physical abnormalities can act indirectly to cause such behaviours. A delinquent differs from a normal individual mainly in emotional reactions. He is emotionally unstable and unsatisfied with the society. He resents discipline and is egoistic and immature in his view of right or wrong. They are found to be associated with poorer school performances. Other behaviours studied among delinquents are physical aggression, crimes against property, reckless driving, using hard drugs etc. Due to scholastic failure they experience low-self esteem. As children, more of them were impulsive, restless and had a history of being adventures, extroverted and stubborn. Delinquent girls tend to be more external in their orientation. Most delinquents have a history of difficulties in early childhood, but it is not necessary that early childhood difficulties necessarily must lead to juveniles. It would be necessary to study a group of children from time of birth to get authentic information about the genesis of delinquent behaviour and how it differs from genesis of non-delinquents. If researchers know in advance who is delinquent and then can easily apply wisdom of hindsight to find all sorts of reasons to explain why one child became a serious and persistent lawbreaker. Therefore, juvenile delinquency now seems to involve the type of adolescent behaviours that no longer can be classified as adolescent pranks.

Sex and Ethnic Difference

Only a small proportion of adolescent belongs to the delinquent group. Even though the group is small, it is large in actual numbers. The particular types of such behaviour items include running away from home, stealing, assaults etc. A major finding of Gold and Reimer study stated that boys higher on larceny, gang fighting and use of illicit drugs was much higher. The fact that sex difference in delinquent activities appears to be lessening is based on official statistics. According to Davis (1976) crime among black occurs most often within the black community and is directed at blacks. With increased age there is an increase in percentage of adolescent who could be classified as juveniles. However, number of adolescent who use illegal drugs rises steadily with age. Hence, sex and ethnic differences influences a lot in delinquency. Compared to female delinquency, male delinquency is most commonly being observed.

Parent – Adolescent Relations: Researchers have found that adolescent from broken homes are more likely to be delinquent than adolescents from intact homes. Parental factors also contribute to delinquency in adolescent. The nature of discipline between parent and their offspring and type of parental discipline are two parental factors on development of child. There are many who believe that juvenile delinquency should be referred as "juvenile parental delinquency". Parents have carried the burnt of the blame for the spread of delinquency. It should be noted that parents are victims of unwholesome social circumstances, frequently unable to control demoralizing conditions to which their children are exposed. For parents there is knowledge of greater importance than self-knowledge. Parents must begin here because they cannot expect to understand children unless they have understood themselves. They simply do not know how to express their love towards their children. Parents can help guard their children from juvenile delinquency by being reasonable. Unreasonableness is always an open door to irresponsibility. Also, Parents handle the task of discipline differently. Parent's first obligation is to understand child's misbehaviour and accept it without alarm and severity. Discipline should be considered as a stepping-stone to self-discipline and it should fit the child. Punishment without understanding increases child's conflict and confusion. It is duty of parents to help child discover religion as something alive and meaningful. There are some goals that parents will strive for better family life as well as protect their child from ravages of juvenile delinquency. Sincerity, honest and faith will compensate for man limitations, but serious dedication to improvement of parenthood skills will always be rewarding.

Lester D. Crow, in his version "who's to blame?"(Vol. 33, no 2, pp.20-21) asks the question that who is ultimately blamed to such delinquency. During the past several years the blame for the rapid increase in delinquency has been attributed largely to parental mistakes in child development. Parents alone cannot solve the problem. It has been argued that parents and teachers should avoid any practice that might frustrate children. They have been encouraged to stimulate the child's initiative and to permit him to do what he wants to do, with as little adult interference as possible. Over aggressive children are often permitted to behave in ways that develop habits, which interfere with their present and later interpersonal relationships. However parents are torn between what they believe is their duty and what they believe educators expect of them in the matter of child rearing.

Classification of Delinquency

A few psychiatric classification of delinquency have gained some prominence in literature. All psychiatric classifications separate delinquency, which appears to be socially, learned behaviour from delinquency, which is believed to be related to individual psychopathology. Psychoanalytic classifications are dependent upon interference as to personality structure of child. Usually, there are three categories of delinquency:

1. Environmental delinquency based on social factors.
2. Neurotic delinquency.
3. Characterological delinquency based on presence of traits as neurotic character.

According to David Abrahamsen, there are six types of 'delinquency':

1. Environmental or learned delinquency.
2. Neurotic delinquency arising from intra-psychic conflict.
3. Character disorder delinquency.
4. Genuine psychopaths.
5. Delinquents who are disturbed enough to be considered as psychotics.
6. Lastly, originally impaired delinquents those with history of encephalitis.

However, socialized or environmental delinquents are described as behaving in more reasonable manner than unsocialized delinquents.

Female Delinquency

Delinquency is not only seen in males but also in females in large extent. The two commonest forms of female delinquency are sexual promiscuity and running away from home, frequently offend our sense of property. These activities may cause great harm to the female herself. Promiscuity leads to degradation self image, guilt remorse. Running away can lead to seduction, hunger or abuse. In practice, the decision to label female misbehaviour as delinquency or illness is largely determined by social class. Middle class girls are more careful about the limits of inappropriate behaviours. They know it pays to be respectful and obedient since they have more often been rewarded for such behaviours. It is also true that stealing among upper and middle class girls has a more apparently unreasonable quality since it is less likely to be governed by economic needs. Punishment is mainly imposed upon those girls who don't have "respectable" homes or access to sufficient resources to protect against institutionalization. Many girls who end up in a training school are sent there simply because their families are unwilling or unable to care for them. A sizable number of females who regularly participate in rule breaking behaviour demonstrate, a collection of character traits that define what psychiatrists refer to as hysterical personality. Hysterical personality is typically a girl or women who is seductive and flirtatious, and often promiscuity. She is prone to periods of deep depression and anxiety. Her sense of self is poorly developed. She is illness prone and will develop a bewildering variety of physical and emotional complaints whenever the sick role is available and serves her needs. It should be apparent that the hysterical personality describes a person who is prone to impulsive actions, a person who easily become involved in sexual misconduct and delinquency. Some of characteristics of hysterical personality bear close resemblance to traits of psychopath, pranoia, and maschoism. The oppressed girl limited in physical strength, immobility and in access to socially acceptable aggression, fights back by using her best weapons, exaggerated feminity and controlling passivity. Society has to be deeply troubled with hysterical women before it causes them criminals. In female delinquency, parental deprivation and abuse seem to occur even greater frequency than among males. Though there is self-defeating quality of female delinquency, it must be admitted that some female delinquency is also damaging others. Recently youth workers have noted that female delinquency is becoming a little more like male delinquency. More and more girls form gangs, steal and drink.

As social roles of boys and girls become more alike, their delinquent activities become less distinguishable from one another.

Maintenance of Delinquency

Although adaptive advantages of initial criminal act are apparent, it is more difficult to understand the value of repetitive unsuccessful criminality. Once a person is defined as a delinquent, certain social and psychological factors intervene and tend to make criminal adaptation as self perpetuating and autonomous. To begin with a child who is termed as delinquent is exposed to social milieu in which peers are constantly enjoying him to continue an antisocial way of life. If he is jailed or institutionalized, he is required to cope with changed attitudes on part of his parents, friends, authorities etc. Being under increased surveillance and living with constant reminders of his misbehaviour can be a stress itself. Once the child begins to identify himself with the delinquent role, his learning experiences bind him more firmly to that adaptation. Sociologists have focused upon career aspects of delinquency and have described how certain criminal skills are developed in some manner as socially adjusted person develops academic and other skills. Psychiatrists are mainly interested in manner by which alterations in personality allow child to sustain a delinquent orientation. The most obvious defense mechanisms which delinquent employs are projection. The delinquent also learns to deny unacceptable feelings and behaviours both to him and others.

According to the law, parents are primarily responsible for their children's welfare. Yet in order for them to fulfill their parental obligations adequately, they need the cooperation of other community agencies such as school, the church, the courts and the other youth serving agencies. Through its leaders each of this community organizations and institutions is giving voice to an increasing awareness of its particular area of responsibility. Moreover, the fact that many attempts to prevent delinquency have been ineffective has motivate youth leaders toward more intensive and extensive study of causes of child and adolescent asocial behaviours, better preventive approaches and improved remedial techniques. Therefore, youthful misconduct or immorality appears to be a concomitant of local, national or world crises.

Causes of Delinquency

1) **Environmental, genetic and existential factors**: Delinquent conduct is obviously influenced by environmental factors and is a response to it. An adolescent would not become a thief if the environment did not provide something for him

to steal and strong enticements to do so. Moreover, many youngsters who do not live in a delinquency sub-culture become delinquent. At present, most authors place their emphasis on environmental causes of delinquency with little or no mention of heredity. Actually, no delinquent has a gene that produce in him a motive to steal a TV or a car. Their way of life is therefore shaped by their interaction by environment. In a study, newborns of normal mothers and newborns of felons (criminal) mothers were separated minimizing the environmental factors. Later on it was found that, children's of felons had greater number of arrests due criminal acts as compared to children of normal mothers. Hence, genetical factors also contribute to development of delinquency.

2) **Gang delinquency**: - According to Miller (1958, 1969), gang delinquency of adolescent street corner groups in lower class communities differ from delinquent subcultures that has arisen in areas where the lower class members deliberately violate middle class norms. The gang delinquency culture has emphasis on toughness, smartness i.e., ability to outsmart, outthink fate. Hence, many lower class individuals think that their lives are subject to set of forces over which they have relatively little control. Miller (1958) points that there are large variations in ways in which individuals respond to these standards. But from this account it is easy to see those people who have once moved into it, face difficulty in getting out of it.

3) **Delinquency as form of problem solving and emotional maladjustment:** Delinquency is a form of problem solving behaviour, a symptom of emotional maladjustment, or a response to cumulative frustrations. Seen from delinquent point of view, their acts may be means of meeting a need or solving a problem. The need may range from momentary desire to the need to fit in with his group. Similarly, delinquent acts may spring from different motives. So it is necessary to help adolescent to cope with their personal problem in a socially acceptable manner. Many delinquents are emotionally disturbed or have personality disorders that would make life

a burden to them and to others even they did not violate the law. According to Redl and Wineman, small amounts of frustration can disturb the equilibrium of delinquent. Some delinquent may experience feelings of guilt following their deviant behaviours. Some delinquents seem to work out their problems quit sufficiently well to settle as law-abiding citizen in later years. Miller states that middle class offender is most likely to be depressed than the lower class offender.

4) **Public response to delinquent:** During 1960's public distress about crime and drug abuse resulted into an increased demand for law and order. However, it seems that attitudes towards delinquents are sometimes more severe among those who have not been victims of delinquent acts. There are many people who want delinquents to be treated harshly, whereas others who have actually suffered from such acts feel compassion for them. According to Kvaraceus (1958), there is considerable evidence that public and even some professionals workers are less intrested in attacking problem of delinquency than in attacking delinquents themselves.

Theories of Causes Delinquency

Several theories with varying degree of plausibility have been proposed in an attempt to explain causes of delinquency. Prior to the turn of century many criminologists believed that causes are located in psychology of offender, and most recently it has been located in socio-cultural aspects of individuals environment. One of the major theories of delinquency, is "differential association" that has been stated by Sutherland. According to him, they learn to value delinquent acts through the influence of delinquent sub culture to which they are exposed. According to Merton, because many individuals from lower socio economic groups are unable to attain success through legal means, they are more likely to engage in delinquent acts as a way of attaining it. According to Matza, delinquency is an act that is given up with considerable ease. A study of 1,313 gangs in Chicago by Thrasher similarly shows that in parts of city where adolescents lack direction, the juvenile gang graduates into criminal gang. The White House Conference report dealing with delinquency among adolescents shows that, although rates were slightly higher among the poor, economic factors were not primarily responsible. It was clearly indicated that the type of community in which the family lived was the significant factor. The White House Conference report also showed that one half to two-thirds of all homes where delinquency was present has been broken by death of one or both parents, or by separations or divorce. The careful study of Sheldon & Eleanor Glueck matches delinquent and non-delinquent boys for socioeconomic characteristics, studying their home background and facts of their personality and experiences. This study found that delinquents had homes where families had been more mobile and had greater dearth of sanitary facilities, had been kept less tidy. The families of delinquent group had more often been dependent on relief agencies for support, and their standard of living and income were lower. The Gluecks also found that truancy was the first and most frequent manifestation of maladjustment among some 708 delinquents who misbehaved in school. Misbehaviour in school usually started earlier among the delinquent than among non-delinquent and was much more frequent. Hence, truancy has been called the kindergarten of delinquency. (P H Landis "Adolescent & Youth" 2nd Ed, pp-205:06). Lovis Bovet in his report to world health organization in 1951 stated that insecurity which gives rise to anxiety was at root of most delinquents. His view was "imperfect adaptation" to the necessity of external social world resulted in objective and subjective insecurity (W L Herbert, F V Jarvis). D H Scott states that emotional difficulties and behaviours troubles of young people arise from their being starved of the primary human needs.

Symbolic Aspects of Delinquency

The selection of criminal act is often dependent upon symbolic and unconscious meaning of that act to offender. The crime itself may be of substitute gratification, which is more acceptable to criminal than his original conscious wish. There is a tendency to assume that the cause of a crime is understood once the symbolic meaning of that crime is known. Understanding the symbolic nature of crime doesn't help very much in treating offender. Psychiatrists and other professionals become prematurely disillusioned when they discover that their arduously gained dynamic insights may not be helpful to criminals. Many types of adolescent crimes have a symbolic unconsciousness meaning to offender. Through the mechanisms of displacement, unacceptable behaviours and attitudes are transferred to substitute objects and lead to substitute actions, which may violate the law. The character trait of delinquents has its failure to evolve from pleasure principle to reality principle. Not all delinquent desires are antisocial. Some normal desires become antisocial only by their urgency, leading child to satisfy them at wrong time and in wrong place. Many delinquent impulses are antisocial in themselves. The instinctive urges of delinquent behave no differently in respect from impulses of law-abiding citizen. It is the ego, which decides which of impulses, can find their way into action and is guided in this decision of demands of reality and by voice of super ego. Three factors contribute to this character formation which manifests itself in the inability to withstand a desire regardless of results i.e. strength of unmodified instinctive urges, weakness of ego, lack of independent of super ego.

Although destructive behaviours has adaptive function of its own; the choice of property to be attacked may have symbolic meaning. The adolescent may steal an object which to him symbolizes affection or erotic love. An equation of stealing and love seeking is obviously over simplified. The problem is that such a proposition might be quite relevant for individual patient but may not be susceptible to generalization.

Psychiatry and Juvenile Courts

All psychiatric classification separate delinquency, which appears to be socially, learned behaviour, from that which is believed to be related to individual's psychopathology. Psychiatrists concede that a child who has a stable home life and a relatively integrated personality can become a delinquent if he is exposed to antisocialism.

Juvenile cases are mostly handled by juvenile court. Some practices of juvenile courts and professional youth workers, which although based on medical models seems to encourage new maladaptive responses. Juvenile courts were initially developed to protect the child from exposure to harsh punishment found in traditional institutions. They were oriented towards individual needs. One judge has expressed the juvenile court philosophy, as "The court is more like a hospital or clinic than anything else". If person's bodily functions deviate so far than normal that he cannot be successfully corrected at home, he is ordered to a hospital. If a child's conduct deviates so far from normal than he is sent to juvenile court. Studies of urban sociologists show clearly that social factors have bearing on delinquency. In slum areas of large city where social disorganization is reflected in suicide, poverty, and criminal gang activities of adults, children absorb the social climate of community, and the majority of them appear before juvenile courts before they reach the years of criminal accountability. In parts of the city where the community structure is more integrated, delinquency rates are low. The courtroom proceedings are often conducted in secrecy, with the hope that child will be protected from publicity. Juvenile courts philosophy is humane and non punitive. The delinquent is seen as an individual who needs the service of community. An obvious problem is that suspected delinquent is not offered due process; he can be arrested and institutionalized without any proof of crime. They do not have opportunities to defend themselves in the courtroom. Some institutions don't make sincere attempt to offer best kind of individualized treatments.

A professional worker who confronts adolescents in the courtroom or institutions serves a dual role, as an agent of community and as helping person. Close relationship is important for any therapy and this leads to possibility of examining ones behaviour in such a way that unfavorable personality defenses can be modified. If a worker realizes this he can tactfully, gently gradually allow a meaningful relation to develop between him and child. The delinquent knows that the person pleading with him to expose his desires, views etc may be a person with whom he or she will have only limited future contacts and whom he can trust a little. He is further aware that the helper may not be offering a true intimacy between equals. (P H Landis "Adolescent & Youth" 2nd ed pp:204)

Hostility towards those who desire to help

One of several obstacles in efforts to help delinquency is their hostility. Most of them have felt the lash of punishment, disapproval and rejection. Even when not physically punished they sense anger directed against them. More ever juveniles as well as non-juveniles often face an unequal struggle with hostile adults. Whatever their role in providing hostility of other might be, there are likely to encounter many situations where they feel helpless rage. It is often directed against persons who are eager to help the delinquent. The helpers get nothing but a sullen response. One of the most demanding aspects of working with delinquent is to appreciate the hurt and tragedy that often lie hidden behind the sullen mask. Concern about the problem of "delinquency" obviously extends beyond the plight of delinquents themselves. It should include concern about those who bear burnt of delinquency.

Interviewing Delinquents

The interview is the chief tool of social worker in his approach to any client. In interview anything that is brought forward is discussed and there is a talk between the social worker and client. In early interview, social worker needs to make some assessment of the client and situation. This should not be done too early nor the social worker gets involved into too deeply in any way at an early stage. It should be specific for instance to get information for a report. The report must be as objective as possible from the viewpoint of the social worker. It is usually carried out in office of the social worker. The advantages of interview in office are: 1) Apart from privacy and freedom from interruptions, there will be normally be practical matters to be considered. 2) Most social workers will feel more at ease in surroundings to which they are accustomed.

The first interview with the delinquent may be of more importance. If delinquent decides that social worker is not really interested in him or is prejudiced against him, help given would be made more difficult. Experience will teach the social worker that many clients, if encouraged by suitable opening remarks will begin at point where they feel their problems are centered. Any forced interview may be uncomfortable for the delinquent.

To summarize, in this kind of interview the social worker is trying to establish with client a relationship within which they can together look at problems of delinquency. Through interview some assessment of delinquents and his needs must also be sought as well as some possible line of treatment to be put into operation either in practical way or by form of approach in subsequent interviews. It is of great importance to be implicit in a relationship between social worker and the client as it is in any other professional relationship.

Case Studies

Case studies help us to understand the causes of behaviour and relationship between situations that are related to delinquent attitude. It is most widely used in connection with the treatment of individual. The following is one of the important case studies studied by Shaw (1931) titled as " The natural history of delinquent career". It is a case regarding Sidney who was eventually rehabilitated. Sidney Blotzman who was 16 yrs of age had been arrested and sent to institution a number of times. He was leader of notorious gang named as "Moron"gang by newspaper. Their major offence was of rape. These boys lived in a delinquent area. Sidney's family background was marked by poverty, drunkenness, domestic discord etc. His father had served a year in jail for nonsupport and worked infrequently. He took rather hostile attitude towards Sidney. Sidney's life, he confessed, was pointless and misunderstood. His emotions were largely those of hate and bitterness. Not having money to spend he began to take things from stores. He was given institutional treatment. When he received his final sentence, he was in a trance. Death was preferable to a life sentence in an institution. He hoped for a miracle to happen, but it didn't. The only hopeful sign in the prison was that the new commanding officer and his assistant were beginning to introduce humane methods of treatment.

Another similar case is regarding five brothers i.e., John, Edward, James, Michael and Carl Martin all of whom had criminal records. John (35) was a friendly, sociable, carefree and has been committing crimes for last 11 years; Edward (33) was industrious, ambitious and had been apprehended and arrested for 20 times; James (29) was shrewd, aggressive and had been committing crimes for last 8 years; Michael (26) was full of energy started his crimes from 4 years of his age and lastly was Carl (25) who was very reserved, stolid than his older brothers and started crimes from age of 3 years. The delinquency careers of 5 brothers started in about the same manner. The family resided in a slum and crime zone where there was great deal of unemployment, poverty etc. Neither the family nor the community exercised much positive control. The social isolation of the brothers added to the difficulties. With each of 5 brothers the social factors were more important than the personality traits in influencing their behaviour. These cases give a more complete picture of the influences that shape behaviour, including the inner life of the delinquents as revealed by their own stories. ('Brothers in crime' by Shaw *et. al.* 1938).

Hence, case analysis is an indispensable method for the study of causation. This enables others to use the same or similar research techniques and compare their findings with the original study.

Constructive Approach

Juvenile behaviour problems reflect maladjustments of the child in his social relationships rather than innate meanness. The cure lies primarily not in punishing the child for his failure but in a complete analysis and understanding of the social forces that operate to make him at odds with life. This leads to an attempt to rearrange these social forces as a means to changing his reaction to his environment. So the problems of delinquency should be approached not by clipping ears of the delinquent youth but by tearing down slums and destroying disintegrated communities. The child who obviously suffers in his social relationships becomes the subject for a mental hygiene approach rather than for punishment or further torture by group isolation produced by ridicule or criticism. Few individuals are made better by punishment, group isolation, or public exposure. The logic of these devices is to warn others. The only way an individual is better is by acquiring new behaviour patterns, by reorganizing of his values and goals, by substituting new incentives for the old incentives, which were responsible for his going in the wrong direction in the first place. Prior to days of germ theory, when it was supposed that everything that was wrong with the individual originated in his inward parts. Perhaps not fully but certainly more than ever before, that the germs of delinquency and other forms of social pathology among adolescent and youth are in the environment, not in the blood stream, in the social structure. Numerous case studies show clearly that the difficulty is with the inelastic and arbitrary authority pattern in the home or school to which no healthy vigorous individual could be expected to conform. Revolt is his only alternative, as unsatisfactory as this is likely to be. A proper balance between forces of social regulation and individuals desire for freedom and expression is rarely achieved to perfection. Social institutions tend to become static, social regulations fixed and inelastic. Adolescents and youth, on the other hand, crave excitement, adventure and new experience. In nations where the ancient regime has been perpetuated too long and gives too little room for youths to express themselves and make their voices heard, youth movements have been characteristic. Revolt can, under such circumstances, be stimulating and vitalizing. It is important that a progressive democratic society be willing to listen to the voice of youth. The older generation can sit by and allow youth to debunk the old order or can listen sympathetically to their criticisms and take reasonable steps toward progress. But whether right or wrong, the importance of home, school system, or society giving their views consideration cannot be reasonably challenged. ("Adolescent and Youth" by P H Landis 2ed pp=218-19)

There are two major approaches to prevention. The first involves the strengthening of all community forces that enables and sustain healthy growth and development. The second approach involves the early identification and detection of the "predelinquent" or the youngster who through culture influences and personal make up becomes vulnerable, exposed to norm violating behaviour. There are three levels of readiness for delinquent behaviour on basis of which forecasts of future delinquency can be done: -

LEVEL ONE: At this stage youngster has not yet engaged in any illegal behaviour, but certain modes relating to his personal adjustments, social milieu point towards eventual violation of legal norms.

LEVEL TWO: This level includes those youngsters who are beginning to engage in series of behaviour, which in them are, not specific and are norm-violating behaviour that represent minor offences.

LEVEL THREE: This level involves difference between officially noted and unofficially noted illegal conduct. One can infer that who will become an officially delinquent. Prediction at this level though not certain is more reliable than the other two levels. The pre-delinquent at his level may be defined as a norm violator who has not been caught or who has not been adjusted a delinquent. Prediction and early identification assume that past and present behaviour are linked in a cause-effect sequence. No attempt will be made here to measure the effectiveness of the various existing tools and devices for differential prediction. Nor have the predictors attempted to prove their instruments against behavioural criteria weighted on a scale of severity of norm violating acts. Whatever technique is developed and used to predict delinquency potential, the forecasting process will always be carried out on a contingency basis. ("Delinquent Behaviour" by 'W Kvaraceus and W B Miller' pp=122-24).

Suggested Therapeutic Approach

The are different kinds of treatments suggested for juvenile delinquents. Some are based on changing social conditions of delinquent whereas some are based on psychoanalytic and psychotherapeutic aspects.

Attempt at an adjustment of attitudes may include use of normal social controls. Social worker may also attempt to work with delinquent in meeting a need, which the delinquent is unable to meet on his own. EX: Bedding, Clothing or Employment. Even reeducation is given to improve condition of the adolescent. Even sometimes reeducation may be impossible in some cases, especially when the criminal is too old or his innate endowments are too poor. The question then will arise how best to protect the society against such an individual and segregation may be only possible method, which makes little difference to prisoners. Also careful investigation into causes of delinquent behaviour in any given case may be helpful.

Psychoanalytic treatment is mostly done for neurotic patients. A psychotherapeutic treatment for offenders is of still more recent date, and it will take many years of research to assess its full value. Psychoanalytic treatments of offenders of all ages offer a unique opportunity of studying in detail psychological foundations of anti social behaviour and the interaction of environmental factors in bringing about the typical character formation. In order to use this method, not only as a means of research but for purpose of cure, cases have to be carefully selected. Psychotherapy's aim is to bring about the disappearance of symptoms by pushing conflict back into unconscious. As psychotherapy and psychoanalysis have different aims, they handle the transference situation in different ways. Transference of former emotional attitudes is more evident in neurotic people. The mental disturbance, which results in antisocial behaviour, is different from disturbance, which causes neurotic illness. Psychotherapeutic methods are also used for delinquent treatment.

The juvenile court is of course responsible to the whole community and is guided by an ethic that allows him to subordinate the delinquent's interests to community stability. There are several aspects suggested for approaching the client:

1) The professional worker should be wary of expressing a moralistic attitude towards the adolescents anti social behaviour.
2) The professional might at times wish to communicate his own moral standards, which could be more or less stringent than those of his patient.
3) The professional who is in position in evaluating a patient must always explain his obligation as precisely during initial interview.
4) He must have a deep and through understanding of role of antisocial behaviour in maintaining adolescent equilibrium.
5) The professional must carefully avoid any communication that clients have same potential as him, unless this is actually the case.
6) All efforts should be done to let the adolescent develop a relationship with professional at his own pace and without extravagant promise of its value.

This code of therapeutic conduct does not affords a magical system for gaining rapport with the adolescent patient. It does however suggest an attitudinal set, which allows one to approach an extremely distrustful client. ("Psychology of adolescent" by 'A T Jersald, J S and D W Brook 3rd Ed)

As a cause of delinquency and crime became known,

society will not only be in a better position to cope with their problems, but it will also have guidelines along which preventive action can be planned. Preventive programmes might range from improved housing and income maintenance to efforts at providing children in unstable homes with community based interpersonal support. Societies response to crime and delinquency is a product of its values and priorities. An example of a promising preventive approach is a study aimed at rehabilitant predelinquent boys in a homelike setting (Philips, E. L; 1968). Community and educational faculties designed to aid the development of delinquency-prone youngsters have been devised and in some instances shown to be promising (Grosser, 1968). For example, recreational facilities for young people staffed by appealing prosocial models might be highly effective in acquainting the youngsters with desirable and effective social behaviour. Imaginative community programs based on sound psychological and sociological knowledge may help significantly to prevent juvenile delinquency.

Conclusion

Society's reactions toward those who commit crimes are a mixture of fears and conflicting feelings such as desire for retribution and mercy. Reactions also vary according to the type of crime committed. While criminals continue to be punished for their offences, society has expressed a growing desire to help them become productive law abiding citizens.

The genesis and etiology of delinquency is complex, frequently well hidden and always intricately involved with larger social forces, many of which are beyond the school's orbit of influence. The schools alone will not solve the problem of juvenile delinquency, but they are in a strategic position to render help and assistance to the delinquent, his parents, and other professional worker in the community who are also concerned with the prevention and control of norm- violating behaviour. Therefore, to some extent medical model of treatment has had a broad influence in shaping the entire system of correctional justice for juveniles. Hence, delinquency is a serious issue, extremely costly in personal happiness and social resources, and appears to be increasing in incidence and gravity in society at an alarming rate. There are some goals that will allow parents to strive for a better family life as well as protect their children from the ravages of juvenile delinquency.

Constant revision of the treatment and re-estimations of its results at a particular interval will gradually increase our knowledge about the prevention and the treatment procedure of delinquency.

Question for Readers

How schools can best deal with delinquent acts?

12

Parenting, Family Relationships and Child Development

Family is the basic unit of society. How a family member behaves and functions is an adequate reflection of his upbringing. Parenting in today's world can be a daunting task. With increasing pressures of society, peers and parents children are always at risk of developing maladaptive behaviours and disorders. In such a situation the task of a parent becomes even more challenging. The right kind of parenting and help in form of family counseling or therapy can go a long way in treating maladaptive behaviours and correcting ineffective parenting.

Parenting Styles

Parenting is a complex process. Books, theories and old wives' tales make the matter more complex. There is no single right or wrong way of bringing up your little one. In pursuit of the right kind of parenting many parenting styles have been developed. The most popular of them are as follows:

Authoritative/Autocratic: In this kind of parenting the parents are very strict and rigid, it is a very disciplined kind of parenting with no room for children's views and expressions. Punishment in the form of physical and verbal abuse is thought to be the best of bringing children up.

Democratic: This kind of parenting takes into view children's needs and expressions. Communication is the key of handling any kind of situation. Parents and children are actively involved in decision-making processes. Reinforcements are used instead of punishments.

Laissez-faire: In this kind of parenting the parents are least involved in their children's lives. The children are given a free reign over everything. It is a free parenting style.

Permissive/submissive: In this kind of parenting the parents' bow down to every wish of their children. Parents tend to grant every wish because they want to please their children and do not want to be labeled as bad parents by their children.

The most suitable among these is, of course, the Democratic parenting style, but in spite of that it cannot be said for sure which parenting will yield the best results. A short history of family therapy highlighting the kinds of families, effective and ineffective parenting, interventions to treat maladaptive behaviours and processes to make a family function to its optimum capacity will be able to provide us with a better understanding of the nature of parenting and family therapy.

Brief History of Family Therapy

The official history of family therapy describes its beginnings as a daring technical and philosophical departure from traditional individual treatment in the 1960s, inspired especially by the "system thinking" of Gregory Bateson. This celebrated origin story needs to be supplemented with a longer and larger history of both practice and thought about the family. The longer history goes back to the founding of social work by Mary Richmond, of pragmatism by William James, and of the organic view of social systems intervention by John Dewey. Seen against this background, family therapy is, among other things, a consequence of the development of persistent elements of American professional culture, experience, and philosophy. The taking of this historical-anthropological view discloses also the origins of two other histories that have made their contribution to the development of family therapy: a science of observing communication processes that starts with Edward Sapir and leads to contemporary conversation analysis, and a history of mesmerism in the United States that culminates in Milton Erickson and his followers.

There are three independent stories of invention referred to frequently in these pages, all involving psychiatrists. In one, Nathan Ackerman, a child psychoanalyst, began seeing the families of children in his New York practice in the late 1930s, and taught it at Jewish Family Service beginning in the early 1940s. In another, Murray Bowen had a ward at the NIMH in Maryland, where the families of schizophrenic research subjects lived under the observation of the staff, in 1956.

But most important, and most emblematic of the "invention" theme, is the story of the "double blind." The British anthropologist, Gregory Bateson, had a grant to investigate the communication of the families of schizophrenic patients at The Palo Alto Veterans Administration Hospital, and he recruited a psychoanalyst, Don Jackson, who had just completed a fellowship at Chestnut Lodge, to be the psychiatric member of his team. The others were Jay Haley, an expert in communication, and John Weakland, an engineer turned anthropologist. The "Theory of Schizophrenia" this group proposed in 1956 (Bateson, Jackson, Haley, and Weakland, 1956) described the form of communication exchanged between family members as the source of the thought disorder in the patient. This was the prototype for papers about the new science of cybernetics—self-regulation in a social or biological system—and its novel use in the description of family pathology, and, later on, methods of treatment.

Jackson, Haley, and Weakland went on to found the Mental Research Institute (MRI) at Palo Alto, and their work over the years perpetuated the ethos of scientific invention. Their development of strategic brief therapy was an application of systems discoveries to the technical problem of creating change efficiently, in a single intervention if possible. This efficiency was contrasted with the much longer time taken by psychoanalysis to deal with supposedly similar problems, and was evidence that the family therapists had discovered or invented something new and better. Although no well-designed study ever actually compared the effectiveness of psychoanalysis and family therapy in well-matched cases with measured outcomes, the myth persisted among family therapists, who derided analysts for using up patients' time and money, and often making matters worse. We may never know the justice of this claim for the technical superiority of family therapy (see Pinsof and Wynne, 1995, for a review of current effectiveness research).

Psychoanalysis, which was undergoing its parallel and independent development from 1910 to 1950, actually fitted this image of a scientific invention. It was presented as such by Freud in his famous Clark University lectures in 1909. Psychoanalysis was a medical response to the welter of competing therapies available at the time, and as such was especially distinguished by the Boston neurologists, who had started its propagation in America, as their professional property (Hale, 1971). They were an influential medical elite, and they sponsored not only the technique of analysis but also the whole theoretical scheme of child development and normal and abnormal psychology that it entailed. By the early 1940s, because of these special claims, it had captured the attention and control of the entire establishment of medical psychiatry, both research and practice, not to mention areas of social science, philosophy, and the arts.

Thus, to most who were learning psychotherapy of any kind in the middle of the century, psychoanalysis was the force to be reckoned with—the argument to be answered, the invention to be improved upon. We inherited from the example of psychoanalysis, as well as from the general ethos of medicine and psychology, a glorification of the image of the great medical innovator. Pasteur, Ehrlich, Koch, and others besides Freud were culture heroes, and provided a model for how great healing inventions came about.

The founders of family therapy were psychiatrists who had been trained as (or by) psychoanalysts, and they had inherited an expectation for that standard of theory. If their inventions were to hold up, they needed theories of their own, derived from a new epistemology, with enough sweep and novelty to put them on a par with Freud's revelations. Batesonian systems theory, Bowenian intergenerational theory (1966), structural theories of Minuchin (1974) and of Selvini-Palazzoli and her colleagues (1978) all were grand enough to calm the anxieties of the academic disciplines that came to sponsor family work. They spoke of social systems and their laws of operation in the same high scientific way Freud had spoken of the operation of the unconscious.

Recently, there has been an increased recognition of the importance of collaboration between the Family Medical and Family Therapy fields. In many cases, Family Therapists and Family Physicians are part of the same treatment team. However, this innovative treatment approach is still relatively rare and much more collaboration is needed.

The kinds of family therapy, which are in vogue today, are:

1. Psychodynamic
2. Behavioural
3. Experiential
4. Communications
5. Structural
6. Strategic

Now we will discuss the importance of parenting, the consequences of ineffective parenting and how family therapy can help in overcoming maladaptive behaviours and correct ineffective parenting.

Family Therapy

Family therapy is a great way to improve your parenting skills and increase your communication with your children. Parenting can be a challenge. Family therapy can help to define parenting and children needs. Family therapy can be addressed in many different ways. Sessions with a family therapist can be attended by just the parents, just the child or children, or any combination of family members. When all family members are committed to increased communication and happiness family therapy can be a huge benefit. Parenting skills do not suddenly get introduced into a parent when a child is born. The adventure of parenting can be daunting especially when there are multiple children in a household. Just when you think you have parenting figured out you find out your next child needs a whole new set of parenting skills. Family therapy is a great way to have an outside facilitator involved to increase communication. Having support in family therapy is a way to communicate to our children and spouse in a way they will understand.

Family therapy has a lot of intuitive appeal. It makes sense that if you don't deal with a person's context then it will be difficult for them to achieve or maintain change. It also makes sense to harness and coordinate the strength of a family to overcome its members' problems. The clinical effectiveness of family therapy has been a major focus of the research conducted in the field over the last two decades. A number of review articles have been published in an attempt to summarize the large number of outcome studies completed during this time (Gurman and Kniskern, 1978; Dewitt, 1978; Borduin, Henggeler, Hanson, and Harbin, 1982; Ulrici, 1983; Gurman, Kniskern, and Pinsof, 1986; Hazelrigg, Cooper, and Borduin, 1987; Bednar, Burlingame, and Masters, 1988; and Piercy and Sprenkle, in press). Juvenile delinquency, conduct disorders, psychosomatic disorders, schizophrenia and addictions have successfully been treated by family therapy.

Ineffective Parenting and Interventions Based on Models of Family Therapy

Cognitive Model

Parents' childrearing behaviours are guided by schemas of the caregiving role, their functioning in that role, what children need in general, and what their own children are like in particular. Sometimes, however, parenting schemas can be maladaptive because they are too rigid or simple, involve inappropriate content, or are dominated by negative affect. Theories of social cognition (Fiske and Taylor, 1991; Kahneman and Tversky, 1973) delineate how people process information in interpersonal interactions. These broad theories have spawned research on how relational schemas operate in parenting and other intimate relationships (Azar, 1989; Azar, Robinson, Hekimian, and Twentyman, 1984; Baldwin, 1992; Bowlby, 1969; Epstein and Eidleson, 1981). Schemas are networked, such that parenting schemas are related to other schemas about oneself, one's partner, and one's friends. Because parenting is a socially constructed role, the society within which mothers and fathers live most likely exerts the strongest influence on parenting schemas. Culturally regulated customs and practices of childrearing (i.e., role demands set by racial, ethnic, or social class groups) are internalized as ethno-theories (Harkness and Super, 1993). These become the standards against which acceptable parenting practices are judged (Azar and Cote, 2002).

Parenting schemas also are shaped by individual experiences parents have as children in their own families and by on-going experiences parents have with spouses, partners, friends, and other important people in their lives (i.e., parents learn some aspects of their role by talking to and imitating other parents).

Adaptive and problematic parenting schemas

Adaptive parenting requires schemas about children and childrearing that are flexible and differentiated enough to help mothers and fathers identify problems when they occur and not perceive problems when they do not exist. Such schemas also trigger parents' generation of a variety of potential responses to childrearing challenges and to enact those responses competently. In addition, adaptive parenting schemas enable parents to evaluate how particular childrearing responses worked so that future responses can be even more effective. Adaptive parenting schemas cannot be dominated by negative affect, such as fear, anger or suspicion, but rather should be characterized predominately by feelings such as concern, pride, and love.

Problematic schemas are often overly simplistic and rigid, or they are dominated by negative affect. Problematic schemas involving conceptions of the caregiving role can place too much or too little emphasis on the importance of control and structure in competently rearing children. For example, when parents believe too strongly that they should exercise absolute control over children's behaviour, they are more likely to use harsh discipline and are at risk of abusing their children (Peterson, Gable, Doyle, and Ewigman, 1997). They may try to exert control even when control is not appropriate or possible (e.g., to stop an ill infant's crying). Abusive parents are more likely to define punishment as a central feature of what they should do in childrearing and less likely to see inductive reasoning strategies as effective (Caselles and Milner, 2000).

Communication Model

Most of the research on *family communication* was done with disturbed families, and only recently have researchers begun to pay attention to healthy family communication and interaction.Researchers studying children at "high risk " for psychiatric disorders have begun to examine elements of family interaction and communication that provide high-risk children with resources that promote healthy functioning. These researchers have concluded that clear and logical communication on the part of the parents is most important in promoting healthy adjustment in children, providing them with with a model for developing cognitive capacities of attending, focusing, remaining task-oriented, and communicating ideas and feelings clearly and directly (Wynne, Jones, and Al-Khayyal, 1982). Lyman Wynne and his colleagues have found that mothers' healthy communication predicted successful school adjustment. The same was true for fathers' communication, but the effect was less powerful. When parents communicate clearly in a focused,well-structured, flexible manner, their children are regarded as competent academically and socially by their teachers and peers.

Psychoanalytic Model

Recent descriptions of family pathology by psychoanalytic clinicians either suggest or are explicitly based on arrested ego development and pathological early object relations. *From an object relations point of view, inadequate separation and individuation as well as introjection of pathological objects are critical determinants of poor adult adjustment.* Whether premature or delayed , difficulty in separating creates lasting problems. Guntrip (1969, p.128) described hoe separation anxiety weakens the ego, as follows:

"However caused, the danger of separation, whether by desertion or withdrawal, is that the infant, starting life with a primitive and quite undeveloped psyche, just cannot stand the loss of his object. He cannot retain his primitive wholeness for more than a short period in absence of mother and cannot go on to develop a strong sense of identity and selfhood without an object-relation. Separation-anxiety then is a pointer to the last and worst fear, fear of the loss of ego itself, of depersonalization and the sense of unreality."

Failure to develop a cohesive sense of self and adifferentiated identity causes a prolonged and intensely emotional attachment to the family.This dependent attachment to parents handicaps a persons' ability to develop a social and family life of her own. This, in object relations terms, explains the enmeshment that characterizes so many symptomatic families (Minuchin, 1974).

The parents own failure to accept the fact that their children are separate beings can take extreme forms, leading to the most severe types of psychopathology. Several investigators have remarked that anorexia nervosa is a problem that results from inadequate separation and individuation (Bruch, 1978; Masterton, 1977). Often the parents' own serious personality disorders prevent them from understanding and accepting their childrens' need for independence. Such parents cannot tolerate separation or deviation from their rules, and respond to independent overtures with extreme over-control. The result is that the children do not differentiate their own needs from those of their parents; and they become overly compliant,"perfect" children. Lidz (Lidz, Cornelison, and Fleck, 1965) described a mother of identical twins who, when she was constipated, would give her two sons an enema or laxative.

Much of the current psychoanalytic thinking about the effects of pathological object relations have come from Otto Kernberg's and Heinz Kohut's studies of borderline character disorders and narcissistic personalities. The essence of kernberg's position is that borderline pathology is an object relations disorder. Excessive rage is its cause,and splitting is the defense against it. Borderline patients are liable to sudden outbursts of anger, then equally suddenly will change to warm, friendly, and dependent behaviour. When provoked to rage, their image of the hated person corresponds to an early image of mother;their self-image as a rejected or attacked little child corresponds to an image internalized from early interactions.

The cause of pathological introjection is maternal overprotection or rejection, or both. The child who is exposed to inadequate parenting takes in narcissistic grandiosity, or devaluation and narcissistic rage.Moreover, failure to develop positive forms of identification impairs the child's ability to establish a cohesive self is organised around pathological introjects; this results in a sense of inadequacy and an inability to tolerate frustration or criticism without feeling rejected to the point of threatened destruction.

Kohut (1971, 1977) described the development of narcissistic pathology, which can take extreme forms as in narcissistic personality disorders, but in less severe forms is one of the most significant and widespread problems in human nature. The child whose needs for mirroring and idealisation are not adequately met goes through life forever hungering to be admired. This hunger may be manifest in the showy exhibitionism most people associate with the term "narcissistic", but it is equally likely to be seen as a childlike craving for dependency and appreciation. The child who hungered in vain for praise becomes an adult who alternately suppresses the craving for attention, then lets it break through in an all-or-none form in the presence of anyone who seems to be responsive.If selfishness means unconcern with others, narcissistic personalities are just the opposite. They are obsessed with the opinion of others and have an inordinate need to be loved and admired.

The more starved for appreciation as the child, the less likely the adult will ever be satisfied. The reason is that the under-responded-to child does not modify the grandiose self into realistic goals and ambitions,but represses it, where it remains as an impossible standard of unconscious ambition.

When psychoanalytic family therapists opt for crisis resolution with symptom reduction as the only goal, they function much like other therapists. Family therapists, on the other hand, believe that emotional growth and autonomy are best achieved by working through the emotional bonds within the family. Rather than remove individuals from their families, psychoanalytic family therapists convene families to help them learn how to let go off one another in a way that allows each individual to be independent as well as related. *Psychoanalytic family therapists are aware that their influence is not confined to rational analysis, but also includes a kind of reparenting.*

Behaviourist Model

The basic tenets of the behaviour therapy were not developed specifically in relation to family problems,but are assumed to be directly applicable to them. Behavioural strategies relate more to how behaviour is changed than to how families function, and therefore the theoretical foundations of behavioural family therapy are those of behavioural therapy in general.

The central premise of behaviour therapy is that *"behaviour is maintained by its consequences"*. A variety of unpleasant behaviours, including whining, nagging and temper tantrums are reinforced by attention. Even though the attention may be unpleasant- yelling it may be the most social interaction that the nagging spouse or tantruming child receives.Thus, responses are often maintained under conditions that are counterintuitive. Reinforcements are consequences that affect the rate of behaviour, either accelerating or decelarating it. Consequences which accelerate behaviour are called reinforcers, while those that decelerate behaviour are known as punishers. Within the class of reinforcers there are: (a) *positive reinforcers,* positive or rewarding consequences; and (b) *negative reinforcers,* aversive consequences terminated by a response. Thus, parents can positively reinforce their child's cleaning her room by rewarding her after she does it, or negatively reinforce her by nagging until she does it. Punishment can take the form of (a) *aversive contol,* such as yelling or spanking, or (b) *withdrawal of positive consequences,* such as having to sit in the corner or being "grounded" for a week. Because attention has such a powerful influence on behaviour, focusing attention on undesirable behaviour often provides unintended social reinforcement.

Shaping is yet another way of learning.Parents can shape a childs learning to play soccer by paying attention to and praising the childs' gradual development of the component skills game. Negative behaviour can also be shaped, as in those families where children only get attention for progressively more angry and destructive behaviour.

Behaviourists view symptoms as learned responses, involuntarily acquired or reinforced. Parents usually respond to problem behaviour in their children by yelling at them or spanking them. These reactions may seem like punishment, but they are reinforcements. In addition to countless behaviour problems unwittingly maintained by parental attention, others persist because many parents are unaware of how to make effective use of punishment. *The treatment of children and adolescents with a conduct disorder, both aggressive (e.g., physical violence against another person) and nonaggressive behaviour (e.g., lying, stealing, truancy), has been evaluated in hundreds of studies. The interventions most often used with this population can be classified as "parent management training"(Patterson, Chamberlain, and Reid, 1982; Kazdin,1984).* Parent training involves a variety of treatment procedures including didactic instruction of the parents in social learning principles. Patterson and his colleagues at the Oregon Social Learning Center have conducted the most research in this area. Treatment outcome is based on parent and teacher ratings of the child's behaviour, as well as observation of parent-child interaction in the home. Patterson and colleagues have found parent management training to be more effective than no treatment (Patterson, 1974; Patterson, Chamberlain, and Reid, 1982).

Asked to treat children, behaviourists initially began seeing them individually. The parents' behaviour is seen as *causing* the childrens' behaviour. The focus is on changing interactions between a parent (usually the mother) and a child, or between one spouse and another. The early work of Patterson, Risely, Wolf and others working with disturbed children was packaged in a diverse array of educationally oriented programs to train parents in the application of behavioural skills. With the aid of instruction and programmed workbooks, parents were taught the application of social learning principles to temper tantrums, bed-wetting, autistic behaviour, doing homework, hyperactivity, toilet training, disobedience, phobias, and aggressive behaviour. In fact behavioural parent training has been successfully applied to almost every type of behavioural problem in children (Graziano, 1977; O'Dell, 1974; McCauley, 1988).

Bowenian Family Systems Therapy

Differentiation of self, the cornerstone of Bowen's theory is both an intrapsychic and interpersonal concept. Intrapsychic differentiation is the ability to separate feeling from thinking. Lack of differentiation between thinking and feeling occurs in concert with lack of differentiation between oneself and others. Bowen originally used the term "undifferentiated family ego mass" to describe emotinal oneness or fusion in families. Since the fusion is unstable, it tends to produce one or more of the following:

1. Reactive emotional distance between the spouses
2. Physical or emotional dysfunction in one spouse
3. Overt marital conflict
4. Projection of the problem onto one or more children

Projection is the process by which parents transmit their immaturity and lack of differentiation to their children. The child who is the object of the projection process becomes the one most attached to the parents (positively or negatively) and the one with the least differentiation of self. The emotional fusion between mother and child may take the form of a warm, dependent bond, or an angry, conflictual struggle. As the mother focuses her anxiety on the child, the child's functioning is stunted. This underdevelopment enables the mother to overcontrol the child, distracting her from her own anxieties but crippling the child emotionally. Thus infantilized, the child eventually develops symptoms of psychological impairment, necessitating further parental concern and solidifying the family pattern. *Behaviour disorders in adults- such as repeated job loss, uncontrollable anger, and compulsions of substance, sex, or acquisition-are viewed in the context of either dysfunctional spouse-or adult-child triangles, and clinical interventions are planned accordingly. The goal of Bowenian therapy is to decrease anxiety and increase differentiation of self. He uses individual therapy, couples therapy and family therapy to prevent or modify pathology.*

Conclusion

Child rearing in today's times is a challenging task. To bring out the best in your child, develop him to his optimum potential, and, make him a priceless asset to the society is the dream of every parent and aim of every society. But a lot of obstacles and hurdles are placed in the path of child development.

As discussed in the above, parenting and the importance of healthy family relationships and functioning is a very important aspect in any individual's personality development. The various models of family therapy have provided us an insight on how parent-child relationship affects a child's development and how if maladaptive behaviour occurs interventions can be used to guide the child and the parents back on the right path.

All the models of family therapy have one thing in common that is rigid, abusive, restrictive, overinvolvement, binding, unhealthy communication patterns can only lead the child to grow into a maladjusted behaviour pattern. Following the dictum of psychoanalyst family therapists it is only right that parents also need "reparenting".

Parenting is a multi-faceted function and it requires a lot of investment on the part of parents in terms of emotional support, warmth, patience, sensitivity and a positive attitude. The Indian Academy of Paediatrics emphasizes that there is a need to create awareness amongst modern day parents about child health, growth and development, education and creativity requirements. Parents should take the initiative and form local cooperatives for parents. Schools should make it absolutely compulsory to have regular and active parent-teacher's associations. The local family welfare centers should organise parenting workshops andfamily workshops for overall development of the family and community. Apart from these measures there is an increasing need for family therapists and family medical fields to cooperate and collaborate for the betterment of the families.

Though a lot has been done on the area of parenting and family, there's still miles to go. At the rapid pace at which society is changing and children are being exposed to more at early ages and expected to achieve much at a tender age, it is has become very necessary for parents to be constantly upgraded with everything that is happening around and be there for their children. Parents should not hesitate in seeking help from family therapists. It is essential that the two collaborate together for producing a better and valuable generation of citizens.

Question for Readers

How are family health and social health related with each other?

13

Strategies to Deal with Victimization on School Children

"I was given a punishment, which was not fair. The teacher said a lot to me (abused) about my work (homework) despite completing my homework. She was actually getting someone else's anger on me. I told this incident to mamma and papa and they consoled me that it was not my fault. From that time onwards I stand up to support what I think is right, it has given me one lesson that speak whatever you feel and be candid" . . . A student.

I hated school... sexual experience, the children were teased, had painful experience, faced problems from friends and teachers. Teacher slapped one of my friends for small reason. When I was in 8th grade, my teacher slapped me. I just hated that teacher. Same teacher discouraged me. The teacher gave me punishment.

On reviewing school mental health researches, it is observed that a number of issues that need attention are: school climate and frustration of children, school fright and phobias, academic burden on school students, PTSD in children, segregation and school violence, psychological disturbances in school-going adolescents, peer abuse, alienation among adolescents. There is strong need to understanding the stress of overburdened child, child emotional and behavioural problems, segregation and detention in schools, heavy school bags on their backs. Some schools go as far as expelling poor performers from school. There is an urgent need of providing mental health services in schools, reducing academic burden on school students, waging peace in schools, and creating safe and caring school communities. The schools need to invest on teachers to upgrade their mental software to deal effectively with the emotional health concerns of children.

The schools are painting dark future of India by victimizing children and killing creativity in them. We can promote bright economy of India, if we promote creativity in children. Japanese economy is going down due to decreased creativity in children in schools. Ninety eight percent of children in Indian schools feel victimized by one way or another. We must stop it at the earliest, and allow children to raise their voice by democratizing schools.

Strategies to deal with victimization on children in school

School governance needs a radical change: the classrooms are highly undemocratic; children have no voice in school. School governance should not only begin and end with the principal; this must also involve children, teachers and parents. Power in Indian schools rest with the school principals and teachers in the classroom. Parents and children feel alienated and powerless.

Project "Happy Child" needs to be introduced in every school: we all are hoping to see a happy child in the school having an experience of learning filled with joy and excitement. The objectives of such a "Happy Child" project are identified below:

- To ensure continuous education of the teachers in the areas of skill development as well as attitudinal changes in order to keep themselves updated on the latest trends in the field of education with the objective of making teaching and class room learning for the child a pleasant experience.

- To provide counselling services to teachers, parents and students on a regular full time basis to achieve the objective of Happy Child on sustainable basis.
- To promote and achieve excellence in teaching and to build excellent teachers with focus on a Happy Child.
- To develop a forum for the continuous education of teachers.
- To develop a reservoir of counsellors to facilitate the counselling of teachers, parents and students on a regular need based basis.
- To undertake activities that would lead to development of a bank of teaching aids in different subjects that would be available to different schools on a shared basis.
- To undertake special projects involving adoption of schools for the underprivileged so that the objectives and benefits stated above are reached out to such schools too.

Creative Child

Most children are born right hemisphere dominant. This right side dominance is more useful as they shape events into patterns during their discovery of the world. As they grow and the connection between the two hemispheres of the brain develops, they begin to demonstrate stronger cognitive skills as right hemisphere functions of the brain move to the left. Children have much greater mental elasticity for movement between hemispheres if needed than do adults. As we age, our mental functions tend to become more localized into specific areas and relocating them becomes increasingly difficult, if not impossible.

Maximizing our creativity comes from the ability to move from left to right dominance when the need arises. This ability is not normally a routine practice of most people, and success requires specific cross-training skills and some practice. Initially, these techniques may seem difficult or unusual but with experience and time you will discover that your thinking approach is beginning to change and you are finding more creative ideas faster and with greater predictability.

The education and the learning processes in school are killing the creative potential of young people, in other words the schools are destroying the children's right brain. Children need a positive change and experience at school to evolve their inner creativity.

Qualities Needed for Successful Teachers

Since the beginning of civilization the place and importance of teacher in the school and society has always been described in the high term. In present competitive age, when teaching is widely being influenced by psychology and technology, in the system of education, the teacher acts as a crucial input, processor, evaluator and remediator. In India and abroad various studies have been carried out. Meriam (1906), Reudiger *et. al.* (1910), Knight (1922), Guthrie (1927) in their investigation found some common characteristics among effective teachers i.e. sympathetic, sense of humor, patience, impartial, pleasing manners, polite, broad-minded, intelligent and strong character besides the knowledge subject matter and teaching skills. The object of the present study was –to investigate the qualities of successful teachers. The study was conducted in Garwal region in U.P. hills. Secondary school teachers consisted the population of the study. The sample consisted of 300 teachers (178 male and 122 female; 202 rural and 98 urban) selected from different schools. Tools used were: The Teaching Efficiency Scale (TES) standardized by Chauhan and Jain (1976) and Teacher's Quality Description Questionnaire (TQDQ) prepared by the investigator himself.

Computing the data, it was found out that in the present study 62 qualities of successful teachers were identified by the teachers themselves and by their students, principal and colleagues. Out of the 62 qualities only 30 were found significantly correlated with teaching efficiency. In the present investigation, according to the nature of different qualities, these can be classified in 4 categories viz. cognitive qualities, personal qualities, social qualities and professional qualities respectively. (1) In respect cognitive characteristics the successful teachers were found to be creative, innovative, intelligent and they had originally in thought and good academic career. (2) Regarding to the personal qualities it was found that successful teachers were confident, impartial, honest, disciplined, polite, sympathetic, enthusiastic, having good habits of daily life, strong character, normal health and interest in academic achievement. (3) In terms of professional qualities, the successful teachers were found to have interest in teaching profession, subject mastery, knowledge of teaching skills, communicating ability, quality to reinforce good work and good results of students.

Further, they were found able to initiate pupil's participation in teaching process and create interest among students, along with these qualities teachers training and teaching experience were also found significantly positively correlated with teaching success. (4) In term of social characteristics the successful teachers were found to exhibit democratic behaviour in classroom, good relation with colleagues, co-operative in nature and they were usually willing to help the students.

Mental health of children is a State responsibility

The idea of celebrating world mental health day on 10th October is to create 'mental health care as a value' in the society. The mental health component in our society has not been woven. Whose responsibility is it? The NGO's, the educational and health institutions and the State must come together. But looking at the voluminous magnitude of the learning, emotional, behavioural and other mental health problems of the children in the country, the major share of the responsibility has to be managed by the State. In this regard, the State has the following tasks to perform:

a. To allocate the mental health budget separately;
b. To make appointment of counsellor compulsory in all

the schools of the state;

c. To organize refresher courses for the mental health professionals in order to update them on newer advances in the mental health field;
d. To orient the school principals over mental health issues of the children as majority of the schools have no counsellor on their roll;
e. The State education officers are not aware of the mental health significance of the children, they need to be sensitized through orientation courses;
f. To organize annual meet on the world mental health day for the mental health community; and
g. As we seriously lack indigenous research data on the learning, emotional, behavioural and other mental health problems of the children, there is a need for 'State mental health institution' that will exclusively address the research, education and advocacy aspects of the mental health of our children. Every time we refer to WHO data on these issues, why?

The National and the State Human Rights Commissions need to take up these tasks with the State authorities towards better mental health of the children in the country.

We need Democratic schools in India and everywhere in the world

Democratic school system is providing new meaning to the education system. It is going to provide a new step to the child development. Freedom schools, citizenship, free and alternate schools are some names given to democratic schools. There are democratic schools in USA, Israel, Japan, Thailand, England, Russia, Canada, and other countries.

The core aspect of the democratic school is the 'council meeting'. The child can call for council 'governed by the children' if any wrong behaviour is taking place in school. The corrective step is taken democratically. The council meeting can be called at any time during the working of the school. It calls for real personalization in the child. It is important to emphasize that the democratic meeting gives control to every one on all aspects of the school governance.

Some Features of a democratic school:

- Students are free to follow their passions;
- The school involves the supportive and interested people from the community in the schoolwork;
- Communication between children and teachers is free and continuous;
- Students enjoy personal and collective responsibility;
- Students learn to take control of their lives;
- Students of all ages mix freely and respect each other;

Democratic schools believe that the teacher needs to model joy, interest, excitement, and innocence of the children. Teacher needs to be transformational in her approach rather merely transactional. It is important to respond to the emotions of children. It's more important that the teacher learns how to manage her own emotions.

International Democratic Education Conference 2004

Central Indiana Democratic Education Consortium presented this Report. This year's themes promoted a new definition of education—one that would empower children to understand their situation, intervene, and change it. IDEC 2004 www.idec2004.com emphasized the right of children to interfere in the policy and program decisions of the classroom, school, and community that oppose children's rights.

IDEC believes children are naturally curious, and that all children are naturally creative and intelligent and want to learn. The conference suggested free schools, democratic schools, or alternative schools of choice can be a more viable alternative for many students undeserved by the conventional schooling climate.

This questioned this traditional system's beliefs about the nature of children, its approach to learning and assessment, its narrow definition of what it means to be smart, and its ideas about the role of public schools in a democracy. This also challenged traditional policy definitions of special education; its over-representation of certain groups especially males, and the use of medication for ADHD.

These themes were presented as an antidote to the problems many public schools around the world now face with respect to school violence, school disaffection, and low graduation rates.

IDEC 2004: Shanti in Education until the children are happy, there will be no peace in education

The 10-day 12th International Democratic Education Conference was held in Bhubaneshwar, India with a view to strengthen a movement that aims to make both teacher and child participants in the process of learning through democratic ideals. Around 400 delegates, including children, youth, and adults from 19 nations, attended. Various workshops about free schools, alternative schools of choice, and democratic schools were held. There was a special effort to bring awareness of learning alternatives in marginalized communities especially groups working with poor children in Asia, Africa, and South America.

Education, traditionally, has been one-sided—teachers delivering lectures and the pupil being expected to understand all that is said. Democracy in education aims at involving both the teachers and child as participants in the process of learning and making necessary amendments in the learning process within the curriculum framework. The conference was organized by School Scape Center for Educators www.schoolscape.info of Bhubaneshwar, and in cooperation with UNICEF.

The theme of the event was Shanti (Peace) in Education. According to *The International Journal of School Disaffection*, public schools around the globe are unable to meet the needs of all families and students. Experiencing school violence, disruptive and troublesome students, high expulsion, suspension and dropout rates, thus low graduation rates, are now the norm. These circumstances encouraged the conference participants to talk about and critique contemporary schooling practices. Pointing out that the classroom is the most undemocratic place in society, the conclusion of the discussion was: Until the children are happy, there will be no peace in education. In light of this summary, the conference began. Some of the more prominent workshops concerned presentations by the following international presenters and organizations.

If civic life is eroding, reinvigorating traditional civic education is not enough. We need to make education itself more democratic by involving students in meaningful deliberation of the purposes and goals of our public schools.

The Institute for Democracy in Education

Israel: Democratic Education

The keynote speaker was Yaacov Hecht, President of the Institute for Democratic Education (IDE) www.democratic-edu.org located in Tel Aviv. His theme was: *What is the purpose of education in a democratic society?* He discussed the international growth of democratic schools. Presently there are 500 democratic schools worldwide, with 25 in Israel. The IDE now has the Democratic Academy to train teachers for democratic education. There are 200 Israeli state schools involved. Historically, he argued, there have been 3 movements in education. In the 1920s, it was the progressive era, the 1960s reflected open schools and the free school/alternative education movement, and during the 1990s democratic education was discussed and practiced.

The IDE believes this decade represents the *progressive democratic education* movement. He noted that in the future it will be easy to have the structure of democratic schools, but difficult to have the culture (human rights, freedom to think and talk, equality, and respect for individuality). To encourage this culture, Hecht introduced his concept of *Pluralistic Learning,* which describes what the learning process would be like. To begin, schools must have a renewed respect for the uniqueness of an individual. Schools must be a place that discovers, emphasizes, and develops the strength(s) of each student. Every individual on earth is unique. Human diversity is the fuel that runs the world. Thus, it should be the basis for all schools and places of learning. Human diversity means that the learning framework must acknowledge the fact that, "I am different and unique." If it does not, then it is not acknowledging the individual. This learning framework is founded on the idea that each person is unique and that each one makes a unique contribution to the world. This school atmosphere will help each student acknowledge, accept, and express her/his own uniqueness.

Viewing students as a uniform audience leads to the creation of curricula that are dependent on age and content rather than on the unique individual. Pluralistic learning challenges the traditional system's narrow definition of intelligence or school success: students are tested and classified in terms of 2 kinds of abilities— their ability to memorize information, and to a lesser degree, their ability to analyze it. And this closed system has a cost because it limits the value we place on diversity. In the traditional schools, a student's uniqueness is not relevant to life. What is more important is how close one gets to the norm: if you have high grades and are excellent. Thus, students continually check to see where they are compared to the average.

The educational system must make it possible for all students to discover their individual area of strength: the areas in which each person's individual nature excels relative to others. It is paramount importance that at the beginning of our lives we are allowed to grow in those areas in which we have the interest and capability to learn on a high level and the ability to experience success.

The result of pluralistic learning is a democratic culture. In such a school, different voices are heard—the school is not concerned with marketing success, but rather with encouraging the different voices within it as an opportunity for growth of the school as a whole. Different voices are not hidden or pushed aside; they are moved to the front of the learning community. In such a school, about every subject is open to debate: the building, organization of classes, school climate, lunch menus, the curriculum, or school governance.

A democratic culture advances every individual to the place where they can discover and express the unique individual inside and become aware of the enormous importance discovering and expressing the uniqueness inside every other individual and collaborating with him/her to foster school success.

To complement this pluralism, Hecht suggests schools/ communities create *Excellent Centers* where students can be around experts who will help develop their unique individual interests and strengths. Students would spend 3 days in school and 2 in the centers.

To close his presentation, Hecht made the following points:

Democratic education views the purpose of learning as creating a developmental process, which accompanies people throughout their lifetime. Such a process promotes the multi-facet development of one's personality, encourages independence and authenticity, fosters respect to human rights and increases social and environmental responsibility.

Democratic education views the declaration of human rights, and its pertinence to individual, social and environmental rights as the basis for the development of a true democratic culture.

Democratic education views life in a democratic community culture within the school system as the basis for promoting a global democratic culture.

Democratic education views the right of every human being to be recognized as a unique individual, and to express his uniqueness, as the basis for educational interaction centered on respect, tolerance, and love.

Democratic education views the right of every human being to direct his life in general, and his life within the school system in particular, as a preliminary condition for the promotion of independent, responsible, creative, and authentic individuals.

Democratic education views the educational field as comprised of all aspects of life, such as family, play, work, school, culture, and the environment.

Democratic education views every democratic educational system as a "laboratory" and every person involved in implementing democratic education as an "education researcher" who aims at creating new methods and breakthroughs in the fields of learning and education.

"If we are to reach real peace in this world, we shall have to begin with the children." Gandhi, **India**

Democratic programs with (not for) working and street children

Some of the more exciting and impressive presentations were those by the adults and children associated with programs that were democratic.

The Concerned for Working Children

In the mid-1970s, 40% of industrial accidents involved working children. Realizing these children did not have the tools to protect themselves on the job, Ms. Nandana Reddy began organizing them. She promoted a new definition of education—one that would empower children to understand their situation, intervene, and change it. She believed children had a right to interfere in policy and program decisions that opposed children's rights. Working with 9-15 year olds, the children decided not to join the adult union, but to create their own union. The group grew into The Concerned for Working Children (CWC) www.workingchild.org and is located in Bangalore. It is a secular, democratic, national, private development agency that works exclusively on the issue of child labor and children's rights. CWC recognizes working children as the primary stakeholders in the organization.

Two other groups came out of the CWC initiative: The National Movement of Working Children (NMWC) in 1993 and the International Movement of Working Children's Organizations (IMWC) in 1996. The IMWC estimates there are presently 120 million working children in the world.

The children's participation in developing strategies is critical to the effectiveness of the CWC programs. CWC enables the children to access appropriate information, skills, and tools in order to realize their rights. CWC children have made presentations to the UN's Committee on the Rights of the Child, taken on the liquor lobby, have influenced the India's child marriage tradition, environmental and children's health issues, and have formed special groups for children with disabilities.

The Bhima Sangha, a union of, by and for working children resulted from this process. It has membership of thousands of working children in the state of Karnataka and is a powerful advocate for the rights of working children. Along with the union, CWC facilitates Makkala Panchayats (Children's Village Councils) that enable all children of an area to participate in local governance.

School children's organizations have also been formed. Realizing the classroom is the most undemocratic place in society, in October of 2003, the NMWC submitted,

"Education-related Problems Faced by Working Children and Their Recommendations" to the UN. This year CWC published, *A Unique Revolution: Children lead the way to decentralization and civil society participation*, which defends the rights of children to participate in decisions that affect them. Made with substantial contributions from working children, this informative rationale and how to book— for both adults and children—uses education related issues and examples to illustrate working children's exceptional ability to be involved classroom, school, and district shared decision-making that have real-world outcomes.

Concerned that globalization will endanger democracy, Ms Reddy concluded her workshop by re-stressing that children must practice/experience democracy in order to understand it. She encouraged schools, religious organization, and civil organizations to create ways children can intervene. Thus, she demanded children must be taught:

How to have power:

— How to intervene in decision-making processes
— How to negotiate and advocate

Information is power:

— How to collect, analyze their own information, not the data of others
— How to use democratic means to make change

"Globalization will remove democracy in 25 years." Nandana Reddy, CWC

Don Bosco Ashalayam: A movement with children in need of care and protection

Don Bosco Ashalayam is a part of a global network running educational, technical, and community programs for street children and youth at-risk. Drawing inspiration from the 19th Century educator Don Bosco, the organization started in West Delhi in 1997. The word "with" is underlined because the organization's mission is to empower the young at-risk to be agents of personal and social transformation through a participatory approach.

Ashalayam runs drop-in centers, youth homes, night shelter homes, training and development centers, employment placement agencies, and outreach programs for homeless children. The "Childline" project is a national help line for children in distress.

A Youth Bank initiated by street children supports other children in need. A board consisting of 8 street children as members manage the bank.

Butterflies Organization

In existence since January 1988 Butterflies Organization

in Delhi has a democratic program through which street children and working children can get schooling. The emphasis is on children organizing and deciding what is important for them, and on developing pride and character.

With the help of adults, the children have organized a union of factory workers, shoeshine boys, rag pickers, flower vendors, tea shop attendants, bus and train station coolies, and set up their own restaurant for other street children.

"Children are the most learning-hungry beings in the world." Ashley Montague

Montessori done the Indian way

The Abacus Montessori School is located in Chennai and was founded in 1987. Abacus believes that the child's inner needs and interests should guide a child's education. Dr. Maria developed this system of education in the early part of the last century. Montessori, initially for 3 to 6 year olds who need to touch and feel, and then gradually for higher age groups up to 12 who need to use their legs and work in groups.

Abacus makes extensive use of the learning materials of the Montessori method, but also draws the methodology from the work done over the years in the field of education in India. Abacus was set up to bring new thinking into the life of a school, to try out new ideas in education, and to evolve an intensely child focused school. Children need to learn with spontaneity, rather than be taught. And, they need space, and the right learning environment for spontaneity to flourish. At Abacus, students are provided with an environment that is just right for their specific age group. They have the opportunity to choose their work and whether to work individually or in small groups. In a mixed age group, children not only share their talent and skills with others, but more importantly, direct their own learning.

"The classroom is the most undemocratic place in society" Nandana Reddy, CWC

New Zealand: The Tamariki Democratic School

Tamariki www.tamariki.school.nz is the oldest "free

school" in New Zealand and one of the oldest in the world. It was founded in 1966 by a group of parents, teachers and people interested in preventative mental health and in supporting each child's own developmental pattern. It was loosely modeled on Summerhill.

The mission of Tamariki is to equip each child according to its nature and talents, to lead a personally satisfying life, and to be an effective and contributing member of a democratic society. To help insure the mission will be met, students direct their own learning and participate in school governance.

Tamariki stand as the antithesis of the current New Zealand public schools, a system it sees as primarily passing on only the academic part of the culture with its hidden curriculum of unquestioning obedience.

If the street children and the working children of Calcutta and New Delhi and Bombay can make important school and organizational decisions that affect them, so can urban students in America. **IDEC 2004**

England: The Sands School

A unique and innovative alternative of choice for 11-16 years olds, the Sands School www.sands-school.co.uk is located in Ashburton, Devon, UK. In a democratic climate, students have a strong say in running the school. Thus, they are free to be themselves and enjoy their school life. Students are also free to work at their own pace, and so to explore how to learn effectively.

"Peace and democracy go hand in hand." Nelson Mandela

Brazil: Lumiar School: Where students can be responsible in a democratic space

Lumiar www.lumiar.org.br is located in San Paulo. It is a democratic multicultural school with a proposal based on the most advanced technologies through which children learn in an interactive and universal way. At this new school (founded in 2003) with 40 children form ages 2-10, the educator has the role of mentor or tutor of all students, listening, stimulating and guiding learning itineraries as the children follow their interests.

Democracy presupposes the participation of everybody. For this Lumiar works with small groups, making sure everybody participates. At weekly meetings each participant, student or adult, has one vote. School decisions run the gamut from behaviour, video game rules, school projects, or the color of walls to where and when to go on outings. Monthly council meetings with students, parents, and teachers decide on school calendars, reports and reforms.

Children of various cultures and social background learn without hierarchy, acquiring the capability of respecting the differences. At Lumiar, knowledge is respected - professional experts from, various area share with the children their passion for knowledge and the study groups are formed based on common interests.

"Anyone who thinks children are the leaders of tomorrow is only procrastinating." CWC Annual Report 2003

Germany: Berlin's "Sudbury Valley"

The Sudbury-Schule Berlin-Brandenburg is a democratically run, non-graded, private school. With no set curriculum, students are challenged to figure out what they want to do and how to do it. Recognizing that many students do not do well in traditional schools because they are made to study things in which they have no interest, Sudbury redefines learning as studying what you enjoy. Students learn at their own pace, and they learn well because they are passionate about what they are discovering. Students end up with a broad perspective on life with greater personal resources and a sense of individual responsibility only an environment of freedom can offer.

As well as being responsible for their own education, students are responsible for the whole school community in conjunction with others. The school is managed during weekly School Meetings and this is basically where the day-to-day policies are created.

Another group called the Assembly—which includes students, staff, and parents—meets to deal with broader school policies. A judicial system, which is an arm of the School Meeting—meets daily and investigates written complaints about possible rule violations.

The Judicial Committee (JC) is made up of students, 2 of whom are elected and 5 of whom are selected by lot from the various age groups, and a staff member chosen on a daily basis. This group is like a little court system—investigating complaints and deciding what will happen. Trails sometimes result, and depending on the verdict, sentences given to learn more about the Berlin program write Martin Wilke martin.wilke@gmx.net

"What happens in the classroom will, in the final analysis, reveal how deep are the roots of our democratic commitment." H. G. Hullfish

Japan: School Refusers

During his workshop "Free School Network" Kageki Asakura discussed the 1980s when the Japanese public schools experienced an increase in school disaffection. Some students stopped going to school and became what are now known as "school refusers" (or "futoko" in Japanese). In 1985, school refuser Ms. Keiko Okuchi and parents of other school refusers started an democratic alternative of choice to the traditionally large and very competitive government schools, where bullying was also an issue. Since the Tokyo Shure www.shure.or.jp free school opened, the movement has grown. In 1999, various students form Tokyo Shure started the Shure University. In 2001 a free school network www.freeschoolnetwork.org was founded to support other free schools. Presently there are 126,000 school refusers in Japan. The group publishes *Fonte,* the "futaoko" newspaper www.futoko.org. They have also established the Home Shure organization for Japanese homeschoolers www.homeshure.jp.

"And while the work of preparing citizens for a democracy must include more than the schools, the schools are the public institution best positioned to affect the vast majority of young people." Westhiemer and Kahne.

South Korea: Alternative schools of choice

In South Korea, alternative schools are places that provide learning opportunities for students who have dropped out of school or who have not had a chance to attend school.

After the 1980s school attendance in South Korea increased, yet many youth had trouble adjusting and left school. As a result, various private organizations began programs for these disaffected youth. In 1990, legislation provided government approval of some of these options.

Presently, there are regular public alternatives, many of which are boarding schools in rural areas. In Seoul, 13 small Urban Alternative Schools operated by city youth centers or private groups work with around 300 middle and high school students. To support these many public and private options of choice, alternative educators created the Seoul Alternative Learning Community Network (SALCN) www.activelearning.or.kr. Although these current options are not democratic, one of the main reasons why the South Korean delegation attended IDEC, was to introduce the advantages for students/teachers of shared decision-making.

An interesting point to be made here is that these Asian options reflect an appreciation for genuine alternatives, alternatives **to** the traditional schooling approach. Currently, in the United States, there is a proliferation of alternatives **of** the traditional schools where students do not attend by choice. These programs are alternatives in name only: pseudo-alternatives that represent ineffective and punitive approaches that isolate and segregate from the mainstream students who can be difficult (Loflin, 2004).

The educators from both countries were very amazed that the majority of alternative programs/schools in USA are the at-risk/rehabilitative options where only bad kids are sent to be "fixed" and then reassimilated. They were also not aware of the history of alternative education and the changes it has gone through to the extent that alternatives now have a stigma (Loflin, 2000).

Teaching students to share responsibility for their learning and school governance while also teaching and learning with them the ways to resolve issues and conflicts is to experience life in a democracy. Institute for Democracy in Education Australia

The Booroobin School: Democracy's finishing school

The school provides for self-directed learning for students 4 to 19 years of age and is based on the Sudbury Valley School model of education. It was approved by the Queensland Education Dept as a non State School in January 1996 and commenced operation in February 1996. The school is a democratic place of learning founded on important principles not found in most other schools in Australia. These unique principles lay important foundations for life beyond school. The principles are that:

— Equal status is given to students and staff (there is no hierarchy);

— The individual interests of students and staff determine a curriculum with equal status being given to all learning pursuits;

— Individual responsibility is implicit in being enrolled at the school; and

— Learning is best fostered by self-motivation, self-regulation and self-assessment.

These principles are supported through a weekly School Meeting which all students and staff can attend to make all the day to day operational decisions in the school; a Law Book containing all the rules which apply in the school, composed and decided only through the School Meeting; a justice system mainly comprised of students which upholds the rules; School Corporations which are special interest groups of students and staff completely deal with their own affairs; and by the wisdom, life experience and support of staff who are elected annually by secret ballot by voting members of the School Meeting.

Booroobin believes that children are naturally curious, creative, generally intelligent an want to learn. The school provides an environment for students to express and explore these qualities, with responsibility, in ways that best suit them as individuals regardless of how old they are.

Currambena: Learning as a natural process

Currambena www.currambena.nsw.edu.au opened in 1969. The school believes all children are individuals with common needs for both security and challenge in their learning. The curriculum—all the learning experiences of the child— develops from the view that children are adventurous in acquiring knowledge, intellectually curious, keen to find out and actively engaged in making sense of their world. Although the children decide topics in the classroom, it is up to the teachers to draw upon the New South Wales curriculum to ensure appropriate skills in all areas are acquired.

It has no school uniforms and children are individually assessed without competitive exams. It cares about the whole child, balancing academics with social, emotional and physical needs. This is especially the case as children are encouraged to express their needs, stand up for themselves, take responsibility for their actions and make their own decisions.

The children participate in running the school through weekly school and class meetings, chaired by children. They make school rules by majority vote and discuss matters of day-to-day importance ranging from rules about bringing balls to school to what equipment to include in the school playground. Debate and discussion of current issues are encouraged. Along with student input, the school is run by the School Council, which consists of a majority of parents and some teachers.

"We children bear the brunt of the school's failure to implement and design child-centered policies and programs." CWC Annual Report 2003

United States

New York Albany Free School: School democracy on call at any time founded in the state of New York in 1969 by Mary Leue, the Albany Free School (AFS) www.albanyfreeschool.com is the oldest inner-city independent alternative school in the United States.

According to workshop presenter and former AFS teacher Michael Yoken, two important democratic developments that came out of that initial year. First, teachers and parents hammered out, in a series of intense sessions, the policy that only those actually present day-to-day in the building could determine the school policy. Others were welcome to attend meetings and to advise and suggest, but that would be the extent of their power.

This absolute internal autonomy remains an operational cornerstone. Next, in order to empower the kids to participate in school governance, and to give them a way to nonviolently work out their differences (which were many in that initial period), Mary and the other teachers instituted a "council meeting" system, whereby anyone with a serious problem could call a meeting at any time, with everyone dropping what they were doing and attending. Robert's Rules of Order would run meetings. Therefore anyone, with sufficient support, could set policy, make or change rules, and establish consequences for anti-social behaviour. The council meeting structure provided a safety net for everyone, guaranteeing that, borrowing A.S. Neill's phrase, freedom didn't become license.

At the present time, the school's enrollment stands at about fifty-five, and approximately fifteen families and various individuals make up the Free School community. With no curriculum or any mandatory classes, AFS stress personal growth and field trips over blackboards, worksheets, memorization, and tests. Thus students, ages 2-14, determine what they'll learn, when they'll learn it, how they'll learn, and where they'll learn it. This openness and freedom allows for a diversity that remains one of AFS's hallmarks. Approximately half of the kids come from the inner city, one-fourth from uptown neighborhoods, and the remainder from outlying suburbs and towns. Interestingly, this has brought about a situation where students with ADHD do not need Ritalin; they only needed freedom. At AFS, the behaviour students get in trouble for in regular schools— restlessness, boisterousness, being flighty—are considered normal.

California Global Village School: A global school for peace and diversity

The Global Village School (GVS) www.globalvillageschool.org is an accredited private democratic k-12 independent study school preparing students to be global citizens, informed leaders, and effective agents of social change. Self-directed learning based on a student's learning style creates a school climate of independence and personal responsibility. To increase peace and understanding in the world GVS educates its student about the culture and contributions of all groups of people and presents role models and examples of peaceful coexistence.

A workshop "Honoring Learning Styles as a Pathway to Peace" by teacher GVS Sally Carless illustrated the school's philosophy: *Peace and harmony is letting people be who they are.* Problems occur in the classroom when students are forced to fit into the mold of, "Sit still, be quiet, and listen." When students are given the freedom to be different, to be themselves and are thus accepted for who they are, misunderstandings disappear. Workshop attendees were given a sort of "disposition inventory" to see if they were of the performing, producing, inventing, relating, or thinking disposition.

Once a student's disposition/learning style, who they are, is respected, then activities formerly considered inappropriate or disruptive (i.e. talking a lot, needing to move around, wanting to work in groups, likes fun or is serious) less problems manifest.

Indiana A Learner's Bill of Rights: Preserving curiosity

The Learner's Bill of Rights (LBR) concept was presented at the conference. The LBR deals with learning and the processes involved with acquiring knowledge in a way so as to reduce anxiety and promote the joy and passion for learning. It tries to investigate the issues/factors involved motivation, joy, and passion. It also attempts to address the student's relationship with "self", the teacher, and learning—how the student views learning, "self", and how the learner is viewed by the teacher/school.

Since virtually all children are born with the motivation to learn—this is a characteristic of our species—the objective of the initiative is to preserve the child's integrity, self-worth, and innate curiosity. Thus the problem is defined as the inability of the child and/or the school system to retain and maintain the qualities of curiosity and motivation. The solution proposed by the LBR is to provide a form to address the needs of the child by enabling the child to develop the assertiveness necessary to desire the best and to require the best from those involved in the education process.

Beginning in mid-January 2005 a public school from central Indiana and the Mumbai's Dayanand Anglo Vedic Public School (DAV) will conduct a cross-cultural study of the affects of the Learner's Bill of Rights concept. A 4th and 7th grade class from each school will be involved. Students/staff will communicate via a LBR Yahoo group. Contact johnharrisloflin@yahoo.com

Children's Participation

The major theme of IDEC 2004 was: *Participation is a natural instinct*. From the moment they are born, children begin to participate. They participate in order to communicate and to establish links with their environment. They participate in order to gain an identity and a membership in the community. They find meaning in their lives through their participation. Gradually, through their participation, they intervene in their external environments.

Children are attempting to participate all the time. IDEC 2004 illustrates this. There are many groups of children especially working children's unions and movements that have demanded and occupied space to participate, including political space. Also the IDEC presentations by free school and democratic schools students and staff proves that children can direct their own learning and can be a part of the classroom, school, and community decision-making process.

Children's classroom, school, and civic participation is not a project, it is not event based; it is a running theme through every action or intervention and it requires a major paradigm shift. The understanding of participation and the way it is translated into action varies and seems to be defined by the socio-cultural context of the child and the ideological frame surrounding this understanding. However, it is important to arrive at a culturally neutral definition of children's participation, where the principles are common, though the manifestations may vary according to the situation of children.

When children's participation is seen within the frame of protagonism it takes on another dimension: The right and the ability to advocate on one's own behalf, to be in control and to be a part of decision making processes and interventions. This form of participation of children and youth enhances the concept of civil society participation and strengthens democratic processes. We must ask the question, *what is the role of the public schools in a democratic society?* CIDEC believes democratic education is the responsibility of our public schools. And, this is what we all must help our public schools do.

Adults in central Indiana can play a proactive role if they wish to enable children's civic participation. The business community, social organizations, the religious community, our political parties, labor and trade unions, community groups and agencies, as well as public health organizations must support the public schools in fostering democratic education. However, in order to perform this role adequately, adults need to prepare themselves. This has to be done with utmost seriousness and honesty. And perhaps the first lesson is that adults will have to "unlearn" many things before they can foster, in our own public schools, the very democracy we want for the world.

Remember, what happens in the classroom in the public schools of the United States will, in the final analysis, reveal how deep are the roots of our democratic commitment. This is the theme of Central Indiana Democratic Education Consortium.

International Democratic Education Conference 2005

The 13th International Democratic Education Conference (IDEC) took place from July 30th until August 7th 2005 in Germany in Berlin at Humboldt University. The main purpose of IDEC was to feel and understand different democratic schools in the world. Nearly 200 participants attended this from 25 countries such as Israel, India, Russia, UK, USA, Canada, Germany, Australia and others. There is extensive information on website: http://idec2005.org

What is Democratic Education?

Democratic Education or Democratic school means to allow voices of children in the entire school governance. Teach children what they wish to learn, not to force any ideas, to allow democratic values such as trust, expression and respect to prevail which don't happen in traditional or mainstream schools in the world over. In democratic education, students influence class/school for the larger interest of students. Teacher is there to clarify if anything is misunderstood. A Russian Democratic Educator says, "our schools are not known by building but by students. Democratic schools create democratic conscience". I can be free with children – a Canadian teacher.

What does IDEC talk about?

Global schooling scenario is similar in terms of teacher's attitude, school governance and institutional values. Teachers all over the world are not responsible and caring of students. Generally teachers don't use innovative educational methods to involve students in the classroom. Teachers are subject-focused and not equipped with an art of teaching. So there is a call for Democratic Education.

Our schools and teachers need re-orientations. Democratic school talks about children needs and concerns. To experience Democratic Education, one needs to swim in the concept.

Allow child to be: A child in class was looking up on ceiling while leaning on the bench. Teacher asked what are you doing, he said, "I am looking at the pattern of ceiling". "I allow children to do project of their own choice. We do meeting in the class also." – a Canadian teacher.

Some of the best democratic methods include trusting relationships, really engaging every kid, respect every other human being, and love and acceptance of children. These are the fundamental values, which are not even practiced in schools. These are the basis of Democratic Education. The crux is, increase child participation in schools and also families. According to a young German mother, "In raising my children, I don't use any fixed methods. You have to experience only for yourself as a mother".

There is need to change traditional schools to democratic ones

Today's children are very much engaged in body and mind issues and the schools all over the world are not able to go beyond framed syllabi. So schools disinterest children and adolescents, as there is a lack of harmony between what schools do and what students expect. A Spanish teacher says, "if a child, in Spain, is crying or laughing, he is told not to do so. Expression of emotions is not allowed". According to an Israeli parent, "my daughter is not in touch with what is happening within her. She is all the times doing math, English or science etc". Hence there is an urgent need for traditional schools to be open and change as per needs and concerns of children. According to an American democratic educator, "there is a strong need for a safe learning environment in school and for a child to be accepted as he / she is".

Democratic Education talk about individual values and interpersonal sensitivities. Schools need to organize sensitivity programs for teachers on democratic approach of schooling, as Tim, an Australian teacher says, "I trust my students and respect them". Using democratic principles of Democratic Education by teachers would be one way to start democratizing traditional schools. So train teachers for Democratic Education.

For introducing Democratic Education in Indian schools, we also need to assess responsive readiness on part of children, parents, teachers and school managements. There is a need to create awareness of the concept in the community. There is a need for creating democratic educational environment through cooperative learning and providing universal skills to children which they can use in life; not simply to prepare children to prove in subjects.

What is the big role of democratic schools?

Children are searching for a baseline meaning for their life. They need an open environment in which they can express and experiment with their original and novel ideas. At present most schools and teachers are unable to tap and develop the creativity in children, which is in abundance in them. Informal and formal structures of the school do impact on the child's learning, creativity and the way they absorb values, which they will unconsciously use when they grow into adults.

Some of the Indian group of schools such as DAV schools link classroom learning with democratic values. Bright learner support / empower average learner. No exams and no failure at the lower grades provide support mechanisms to students, and at the same time, minimum learning is ensured. But largely Indian schools need to be democratized where children have the right to decide over matters that concern them in learning and education. The world needs democratic schools where children no longer suppress themselves but instead feel free to experience life the way they wish, and develop the natural potential they are endowed with and that suit their individual personality. Democratic schools offer a lot of opportunity for innovation in the school that the children enjoy.

We need to look at the role of democratic schools in developing future societies. What competencies these schools shall be offering? What ideology shall they be developing? We also need to understand the schools broadly to deal with community issues and essentially play the role of a dynamic integrator of societies of the world. Democratic schools are an earnest effort towards democratizing communities and societies around us. Schools are essentially instrumental in building societies and integrating cultural expectations.

IDEC members of Australia invite the next IDEC in 2006.

Internalization of Democratic Values in Educational Institutions

For realizing the vision of true democratic society, we need to strengthen the democratic sensitivities and aspirations. For this we need to urgently substitute our teaching and learning strategies. There should be an urgent shift from structured external trappings of democracy to earnest internalization of values of democratic principles and perceptions. We need to analyze the academic rhetoric and political orchestrization and initiate our learner to appreciate the values like equality and expression, esteem and respect, opportunities for all, and free development.

To achieve this, the school should not only integrate democratic practices cosmetically but should provide real opportunity of active and chaotic participation. Of course, this means more challenges, more problems, more discomforts but they are all worth for realizing the democratic mission.

Internalization of democracy means liberate the learner, restore his rights, affirm the faith in the fundamental educational principles of 'learner first'. The internalization shall be achieved through more interactive and innovative flow of responses, arrangement and re-arrangement of curriculum elements and sensitive evolution of interest centered activities and projects. The internalization should also mean a revolutionary paradigm shift where the emphasis should shift from institution to individual, from perception to subscription, and acceptance to inquiry.

How to change Indian schools into democratic ones? We need to understand the psychology of democratic education. We need to find out first how do children feel, and how do teachers behave in democratic schools. Happy schools are those where children are allowed to make a noise on matters that relate to them; parents can have a voice on issues that concern their children; and teachers are encouraged to experience emotionally poise. We need to restore basic child rights in school system and learning process.

Some Indian data reveal the following Negativities in Indian schools. We need to understand the nature of negatives that continue in our school education and hamper the creative experiences in children. These problems, more applicable to some countries than others, are mentioned below:

- Academics are viewed as more important than anything else.
- Children are caught in-between, like a ball thrown back and forth.
- Faulty examination systems.
- Indifference of parents and lack of teachers' involvement.
- Lack of a school counsellor whom the parents and children can talk to.
- Lack of knowledge on developmental issues and theories on the part of teachers.
- Lack of laboratory/audio-visual equipment.
- Lack of qualified people in the school system.
- Lack of resources for special or gifted children.
- Large number of students in classrooms.
- More memory oriented, stress on rote learning.
- Multiple sharing of blame between parents and teachers.
- No leisure time for students or teachers.
- No respect for a child's individuality.
- Parental pressures on children to perform.
- Physical and sexual abuse of children.
- Rigid and restricted school life.
- Teachers burdened with an excessively large syllabus.
- Teacher-student relationship is non-existent.

One needs to ask: where are we heading children amidst these negative aspects in schools? Schools definitely need a positive change, an optimistic mind-set.

Approach to Internalizing Democratic Values in Indian Educational Institutions

I. Voice of children, teachers and parents will evolve real values in school.

Voice of children, teachers and parents is lacking in Indian schools and also in the rest of the world schools. It's very strange to notice that whom the education matters don't have say in it. Something seriously wrong which need immediate attention.

II. Process of internalizing democratic values would involve:

How to internalize democratic values in Indian schools depends upon the following actions:

Regular interactions for problem solving:

Children, teachers and parents need to regularly dwell upon understanding day-to-day issues that crop up as regards studies as well non-study aspects of schooling.

Proactive philosophy and approach:

The school managements and authorities must believe in proactive philosophy and approach, which are child focused and child friendly. In the processes of managing administrative, commercial and infrastructural matters and affairs in schools, the child as a person has been largely neglected. The child's personality is out of focus in school.

Orientation of stakeholders on democratic values:

The principals, children, teachers, education officers, managements and parents need to be re-oriented on democratic values, rights and responsibities. These stakeholders need to participate actively in the school affairs and proceedings.

III. Changing Scenario of Indian Educational Institutions towards Democratic Values

a. **Collective approach poses lots of challenges to deal with:** working democratically in school would pose lots of ego problems at all levels of the stakeholders, which need to be understood and managed appropriately.

b. **Educational get-togethers:** seminars and conferences on democratic schooling systems need to be organized for creating awareness and consciousness in the schools.
c. **Involvement of policy planners:** the government representatives on State education departments need to be involved at all democratic interventions in schools.
d. **Transparency is foremost:** openness is the key to stabilizing democratic philosophy and values in schools failing which this experiment is most likely to fail.
e. **Long-term approach:** democratic schooling experiments are not producing results in a short time, the schools can expect positive results in 2-3 years. It requires continuous efforts to change from the traditional system of schooling to the democratic one.

Finally, we need to look at the role of democratic schools in developing future societies. What competencies these schools shall be offering? What ideology shall they be developing? We also need to understand the schools broadly to deal with community issues and essentially play the role of a dynamic integrator of societies of the world. Democratic schools are an earnest effort towards democratizing communities and societies around us. Schools are essentially instrumental in building societies integrating cultural expectations.

It is also very necessary to understand as to why victimization in school children is not a concern of social policies of the State and Central Governments when such a large number of children (98% as revealed in qualitative analysis) are exposed to victimization of one or another kind in schools. Victimization of any kind of school children is a crime; it needs to be curbed by strict laws. The national and the state bodies of the human rights commission need to intervene.

Question for Readers

What is the concept of democracy in school? Is classroom democratic for children?

14

Democratic Education, Disaffection, Dropout, and Underachievement Rates of Children and Youth in School

'Listen, create an environment where students feel that their voice is taken seriously and acted upon, and then involve them in school decision-making. The positive action and school improvement follows as sure as night follows day.'

—Derry Hannam, School Inspector, United Kingdom

Popularized by the rise of democratic governments in the former Soviet Union, South Africa and South Korea, and the events surrounding the failed democracy movement in China, citizens around the world are more than ever looking to democratic ideals and democratic governments to replace non-elected ones. This is also illustrated by the growth of third parties in America, the pro-democracy movement in Myanmar (Burma), the drafting of constitutions in Afghanistan and Iraq, and the opening-up of the election process in Egypt and Saudi Arabia.

Why are democratic ideals being studied and acted upon? Why, in some cases, are people fighting and dying for democracy? Is it that democracy allows people control over their lives? Does democratic decision-making about issues that affect the lives of citizens decrease apathy, stress, alienation, disenfranchised, and violence; and, does it increase hope, involvement, belongingness, ownership, responsibility and peace? Is the American ideal, "Of the people, by the people, and for the people," resonating throughout the world?

The answer to these questions is obviously, yes. And this "yes" begs other questions. With respect to education and schooling around the world: Can democracy affect the high disaffection, dropout, and the underachievement rates of children and youth in school? Those who support and attend the 13th International Democratic Education Conference (IDEC) think so, and they have proof to support their contentions. The conference was held recently in Berlin, Germany. Over 200 people, ages 15 to 70, representing schools, organizations, and individuals from 28 different countries attended.

What is IDEC?

Started in 1992 by a small group of international educators who were concerned with school disaffection, IDEC gave voice to proven democratic education approaches to prevent school disaffection. IDEC are annual international conferences that provide the opportunity for students of all ages, parents, educators at all levels, elected and government officials, private and public schools and programs, business, youth, labor, religious, education, and community organizations to meet, hear speakers, attend workshops, and pass resolutions on the potential of democratic education.

The theme this year was "Curiosity or curriculum" emphasizing the power of individual curiosity over a common and mandated state curriculum. Coordinated by the Berlin children rights group KRATZA (www.kraetzae.de) the conference spent many hours discussing human rights and democracy as they applied to children and thus the extent to which parents, teachers and/or the state should have control over the lives and school/learning decision of children and youth. See more at www.idec2005.org.

The participants agreed upon the following statement: We believe that, in any educational setting, young people have the right to decide individually how, when, what, where and with whom they learn, and to have an equal share in the decision-making as to how their organizations—in particular their schools—are run, and which rules and sanctions, if any, are necessary. The 2006 conference will be held in Sydney, Australia. See www.idec2006.org

Globally: A third wave—democratic education

This same sense of a new wave of global change with respect to democracy comes from the world-class Institute for Democratic Education (IDE) in Israel, and further illustrates the international presence and possibilities of democratic schools. Touting the theme, "Democratic Schools—the educational answer to the 21st Century," this group of alternative education advocates promotes: "Educational innovativeness from a democratic point of view." See **www.democratic-edu.org**

This institute finds it is very important to compare the present situation in the educational system with past phenomena in order to prepare for the future. There have been three distinct waves in alternative education in the 20th Century: The first wave occurred during the twenties and the thirties and was called "new education" or "progressive education." The second wave took place during the seventies and was called "open and free education". The present wave, which started in the nineties, and was given the name "democratic education," is spreading throughout the world (Hecht, 2002).

The vision: A democratic culture

The first two waves took place when "The Wave of Traditional Schooling," which started in the middle of the industrial revolution, was at its peak. Today, the educational system is facing a severe crisis all over the world. *The world we live in becomes more and more democratic yet the schools, which prepare our children to life, operate in a non-democratic way and thus create a growing estrangement between school life and real life situations.* This brings about the emergence of the third wave of democratic education that may transform a society based on democratic procedure into one that cultivates a democratic culture (Hecht, 2002). According to the IDE:

Democratic education views the purpose of learning as creating a developmental process, which accompanies people throughout their lifetime. Such a process promotes the multi-facet development of one's personality, encourages independence and authenticity, fosters respect to human rights and increases social and environmental responsibility.

Democratic education views the right of every human being to be recognized as a unique individual, and to express his uniqueness, as the basis for educational interaction centered on respect, tolerance, and love.

Democratic education views the right of every human being to direct his life in general, and his life within the school system in particular, as a preliminary condition for the promotion of independent, responsible, creative, and authentic individuals.

Democratic education views the educational field as comprised of all aspects of life, such as family, play, work, school, culture, and the environment.

Democratic education views every democratic educational system as a "laboratory", and every person involved in implementing democratic education as an "education researcher" who aims at creating new methods and breakthroughs in the fields of learning and education.

More evidence of the 3rd wave: England's national democratic education

In England, as in America, people are concerned about school disaffection in the form of academic attainment, attendance and exclusions. Over the last 10 years a handful of British educational researchers have been listening to students' opinions about schools and the curriculum. This brought the realization that students had insights into what would make schooling work. Following the implications of the researchers, the national Education Ministry created a Children's and Young Peoples Unit and funded a more elaborate study. As a result of this extensive study, as of the fall of 2002, due to the Citizenship Order, all English secondary schools were encouraged to have students "participate" in important school and community decisions. For the full report see www.csv.org.uk/csv/hannamreport.pdr. The "Student Participation Report" showed how shared school and community decision-making with all students improved academics, behaviour, attendance, school climate, and lowered suspension and expulsion rates. The report concluded these positive factors were, "...a consequence of higher self-esteem and a greater sense of ownership and empowerment of students leading to a greater motivation to engage with learning across the curriculum" (Hannam, 2001).

"Student Participation" as defined in Section 176 of the Education Act 2002

The Education Ministry's working definition of student participation can be a help to us. It refers to student participation as 'learning to collaborate with others (peers/adults), in the identification of needs, tasks, problems within the school or the wider community, to ask appropriate questions and gather appropriate information, to discuss and negotiate possible courses of action, to share in the planning and decision making, to share the responsibility for implementing the plan, to evaluate/review/reflect upon the outcomes and to communicate these to others' (Hannam, 2001). These are the activities of a democratic school climate that will challenge the factors of contributing to school disaffection. For information on school councils or to purchase School Council Tool Kits see School Councils UK at **www.schoolcouncils.org**

Outcomes of Research on Democratic Education in the UK

In secondary schools that practiced democratic education, compared to similar schools that did not, for a significant number of students involvement in school and classroom decisions:

- Enhanced learning across the curriculum and the full range of academic abilities—sometimes in unexpected and unpredictable ways
- Helped them gain important organizational and time management skills
- Required them to take initiatives and make decisions
- Supported the learning of communication and collaboration skills
- Facilitated quality outcomes, which both intrinsically and through recognition from others, led to enhanced self-esteem
- Fostered an all over sense of personal and social efficacy
- Brought a greater sense of ownership and personal empowerment leading to greater motivation to engage in school activities
- Made both females and males feel more independent, trusted, and responsible—feeling more a part of the school and the surrounding community

In schools that practiced democratic education, compared to those that did not:

- Disruptive behaviours in classrooms and hallways were significantly lower
- Attendance improved in all students, but significantly in the less academic and potentially alienated students
- Suspensions and expulsions were significantly lower
- School violence was down significantly
- School climate became more positive and the attitudes of teachers and staff improved
- Real-life benefits were brought to the relationships between students and teachers
- The experience did not cause anxiety to parents and teachers

*(From Executive Summary "Student Participation" Report for DFES, Hannam 2002; *School Councils School Democracy and School Improvement*, Trafford, 2003)

Shared decision-making in the classrooms and schools: Why teachers and students need it

Most educators are aware of the phenomenon known as burnout—there are days when it seems that nothing is working and enthusiasm disappears. Many times, dealing with student behaviour is an issue. Most behavioural interventions involve some sort of punishment or negative consequences or some manipulation designed to correct disruptive actions. Yet, experience tells us that punishment does not work at all with many students, particularly those with low self-esteem (Kohn, 1993). The repeat "offenders" in school detention/suspension rooms are a daily confirmation of the failure of punishment. So, who is really being penalized? Who's really in distress here? *It is the teachers—they are burning out from trying to coerce students into obedience.*

What about students? Does burnout lead to disengagement, apathy, or conversely, thoughtlessness or aggression? The fact is students often act this way (Kohn, 1993). But, now let us ask what we have learned from the workplace about *what causes burnout:* the best predictor, it turns out, is not too much work or overtime, bad supervisors, too little pay or problems with co-workers—rather *it is powerlessness*—a lack of control over what one is doing (Kohn, 1993). Even an amateur psychologist knows feelings of impotence lead to stress.

Instead of writing names on the board, using group punishments and rewards, corporeal exercises, escalating detention time, or threatening suspension why not use something that will strengthen student empowerment and responsibility while affecting the factors that contribute to stress and burnout? Many educators suggest a proven strategy: shared decision-making with students in creating classroom climate (Beadi, 1996; Freiberg, 1996; Gathercoal, 1991; Gerzon, 1997; Schneider, 1996; Slater, 1994; Zachlod, 1996).

Enlightened societies do not want to create adults who never vote or who are not responsible citizens due to the fact that in the classroom and school they were treated in such a way as to feel powerless, burned out, compliant, controlled, and silenced (Kohn, 1993).

The relationship between estrangement and disruptive behaviour: Can democratic classrooms and schools have an effect?

According to Abraham Maslow, we all have a need for recognition—a sense of significance, and if it cannot be obtained legitimately, it will be obtained...somehow. When our need for recognition, our affirmation is blocked, we become assertive. If our assertiveness is blocked and we still do not get the recognition we are searching for, we may become aggressive. If others continue to ignore us no matter what we do, the soil is made ready for the seeds of disaffection, hopelessness and apathy, and we may be inclined to violence.

Students have a voice. And they want to be heard. They want to be involved. They want to feel important, to have a sense of power that is more a personal, psychological or social power—the power to be able to assert oneself, to exercise influence on the world, to make a difference, a power that affirms their existence.

The problem is: in order to decrease the potential of disaffection, *we must recognize the underlying causes of the social disease of impotence*. Apathy is the stage before violence. Power corrupts, but so does powerlessness. By trusting and then welcoming students to share in significant classroom and school decisions, schools meet the psychosocial needs of students for recognition, and assertiveness, while eliminating the situations that lead to disengagement, aggressiveness, or even violence.

Democracy as deliberation as self-affirmation as belongingness

Democracy teaches deliberation. Democracy is a way, a system of talking things over. The system is made up of reasoning, consideration, reflection, compromise, fair discussions, and working things out. Tolerance, respect, a willingness to learn from each other—these are the values self-affirmation on which democratic nations thrive. They are the values that schools must teach and practice if they want to counter disaffection. Democracy provides a system to allow individual voices and ideas to be heard, considered, respected, recognized, and used. *Democracy is self-affirmation*. When these basic needs for recognition and connection are met, disaffection disappears and aggression is unnecessary.

Democracy as deliberation as self-affirmation not only produces better, more fully supported decisions; the process also builds community and provides a model of civic society for students. Violence and communication are mutually exclusive. Simply put, it is hard to talk to your enemy—and if we can talk with that person, that person ceases to be your enemy. Divisive issues do not have to paralyze schools and disaffect students.

As well, a significant part of moral development comes through democratic dialogue, reflecting on experience, and looking at how our behaviour affects others. Each student may not get what they want; but democracy is also about compromise, building consensus, thinking about the other student's needs and views, and the commitment to the larger community. This cannot happen if students feel they are not respected because they are not a part of the school and classroom decisions that directly affect them.

If violence is the expression of impotence, then not being indifferent and empowering students by giving them a voice in classroom and school deliberations and the decisions and responsibilities that follow, school staff will meet the need for recognition and provide a sense of personal power—that one can make a difference—at such a basic psychological and community level, seeking significance negatively or anti-socially, or just being disaffected and dropping out will be less likely.

So, what are democratic schools?

Democratic schooling allows the voices of children and youth to be heard in school governance. Democratic schools are both public and private. Democratic schools run the gamut of democratic possibilities. Student councils or student governments are popular. When school or student problems arise, these groups help solve them. In many situations, students are involved in day-to-day activities of the school, solving misunderstandings, helping create school rules and determining what happens if they are broken, or attending committee and teacher meetings. Some schools have students help in the hiring of teachers, budget and scheduling decisions, or solving problems in the school's neighbourhood or community. In some instances, students have input into classroom decisions such as the best way to learn and assess learning. The more democratic schools tend towards teaching children what they wish to learn, to not force any ideas, to allow democratic values such as trust, expression, and respect to prevail, which does not happen in traditional or mainstream schools in the world over. Teachers are there to clarify if anything is misunderstood. In democratic education, students influence classrooms and schools for the larger interest of students.

In the United States, advocates of democratic education believe that students, if they are to acquire the skills, knowledge, and values they need to perform their roles as citizens in a democracy, should receive a type of education that actively engages them as citizens in their own schools and communities. For example, they believe that students should participate in the governance of the school and engage in service-learning activities in their local communities (ASCD, 2002).

The UN's Rights of the Child Article12—Free Expression of Opinion states children have a right to express an opinion in matters affecting them and to have that opinion be heard.

Proponents of democratic education agree. They know that getting students involved in classroom and school decisions make them full participants in their education. *It is this climate of disengagement that those who support democratic education strongly believe is at the core of school disaffection.*

Examples of democratic schools and organizations

The Concerned for Working Children (CWC) is a secular,

democratic, private development agency in the state of Karnataka, India. See **www.workingchildren.org.** Since 1979, it is one of the first groups in India to work exclusively on the issues of child labour and children's rights. The Bhima Sangha, a union of, by, and for working children with thousands of members, is one of the results of this process. CWC also facilitates Children's Village Councils which enable all children of an area to participate in governance.

CWC recognises working children as the primary stakeholders in its work because they believe children's participation in developing strategies is critical to the effectiveness of the program. CWC enable children to access appropriate information, skills and tools in order to realise their rights. Over the years children have played a leading role in the making of government policy with regard to such problems as concern children: the disabled, the environment, pollution, degradation of resources, biodiversity, education and training, HIV/AIDS and health issues such as drinking water, substance abuse, child marriage, child labour, and child neglect and abuse. Children discussed the problems and issues, prioritized them, did the research, wrote the materials, presented the policy recommendations, lobbied for their passage, and monitored their implementation and usefulness.

Through experiencing democracy, these children have gained political recognition and space for political participation. This is ownership. This is including children at all levels of solving problems that concern children (National Movement of Working Children, 2003), not adults. There is no disaffection here.

This same approach to eliminating disaffection is also taking place in the two groups in New Delhi. Don Bosco Ashalayam is an organization committed to empowering youth at-risk to be agents of personal and social transformation in the participatory approach. Through the democratic involvement of youth leadership, the organisation has created programs that concern children and thus discourage disaffection: drop in centers, night shelters and outreach programs for children living a life of neglect around railway stations, religious places, and markets; homes for working boys; Asha Placement that trains and places youth in jobs; the street children initiated and co-administered Youth Bank; and, CHILDLINE, a national help-line for children in distress.

The Butterflies program for street and working children in the state of Delhi began in 1988. Butterflies believes children have the right to protection, respect, opportunity and democratic participation in their own growth, development and in decisions that affect them. Including children in the processes, the Bal Sabha for Children's Council meets to discuss problems such as police harassment, employment, saving schemes, gambling and drugs. Out of such discussions have come the meals-on-wheels Butterflies restaurant, and a Child Worker's Union.

What is particularly pertinent here is the Butterflies alternative education democratic free school. Having lived on the street for a longtime and by being wage earners, the school's curriculum is based on the strengths of the children—their knowledge, work situation, environment and life—not that of the state. Children choose when, how, and what they learn. Through school meetings, they are a part of school decisions that affect them. This kind of respect and approach discourages school disaffection.

School disaffection is a problem in Japan. Presently there are approximately 126,000 school refusers in Japan (Asakura, 2004)., School refusers are students who refuse to attend Japan's public schools. Due to increased pressure for economic development in the 1970s, Japanese society became oriented towards higher education. School children became "human capital" and were forced to absorbed high amounts of knowledge. Efficiency, competition, and control took over. Teachers in large classes taught in a uniform way and gave commercial chapter tests. Many fell behind and were force to go to "cram" schools. Children's behavior, clothes, and how to raise their hands or walk in hallways were regulated. Bullying and corporeal punish became daily events. This, along with pressure to perform on tests and get into the best universities, produced delinquency, stress and self-repression, which led to the most serious problem: teen suicide.

In 1985, former school refusers created Tokyo Shure, a democratic free school. Shure values center around respect for freedom, the individual, and children's autonomy. See **www.shure.or.jp.** Today, the K-12 school and many other free schools around Japan give families and students a choice. See **www.freeschoolnetwork.org.** These democratic schools give students a say in what, when, where, how and with whom they learn. Students can learn at their own pace following their own interests without fear. In 1999, students formed Shure University, which has a democratic free learning climate as well. See **www.shureuniv.org**

Moscow's School of Self-Determination opened in 1987. **See www.734com1.ru.** This public school has over 1000 students K-11. The school founders realized that a democratic school climate could not exist without the honor and respect for the dignity of the individual person. Thus, the school helps students realize their own individuality, to become personalities, and teaches them to self-educate, thus self-determine: I determine myself. I determine my limits and the reach them. It is in these conditions of real freedom that it is impossible to do without self-respect. And this leads to the school's main idea—to learn to respect the other person and listen to their point of view. These values enable the school to be run democratically by the staff and students.

Noted democratic educator and the school's director, Dr. Alexander Tubelsky, says, "Our schools are not known by the building, but by the students. Democratic schools create democratic conscience." Here, school democracy is the opposite of school disaffection.

Luminar is a private school where "children can be responsible in a democratic space" located in Sao Paulo, Brasil. See www.luminar.org.br. Learning is student centered and teachers are mentors and guides. Children, ages 2-12, of various cultures and social backgrounds learn without hierarchy.

Democracy presupposes the participation of everybody. Students and staff attend weekly school meetings, where each has one vote, and all discuss and decide on school issues from the color of walls to where to go on outings to behaviour problems. A monthly staff and parent council decides on school budget, hiring, calendar, and other school topics. School disaffection is not a problem at Luminar because by definition everyone is involved in decisions that directly affect them.

All of these school countered school disaffection with, freedom, respect for the individual strengths, interests, and learning styles as a democratic say in the daily and comprehensive activities of the school.

Democratic schools are now a worldwide phenomenon. See democraticschools@educationrevolution.com. As well, in Europe, secondary students have formed organizations that look out for the interests of youth in school. The English Secondary Student Association (ESSA) See **www.studentvoice.co.uk**, Ireland's Union of Secondary Students (USS) **www.ussonline.net**, and Europe's Organizing Bureau of European School Students (OBESSU) **www.obessu.org** are examples. These organizations make sure educators, schools, and government provide students with the best schools and education possible.

And, according to the UN Rights of the Child Article15: Freedom of Association, children have the right to freedom on association and freedom of peaceful assembly. These students have this freedom to form associations, unions, and groups to meet, discuss, and act upon mutual interests.

There is need to change traditional schools to democratic ones

In many aspects, the global schooling scenario is similar in terms of teacher's attitude, school governance and institutional values. Teachers all over the world are not responsible and caring of students. Generally teachers do not use innovative educational methods to involve students in the classroom. Teachers are subject-focused and not equipped with an art of teaching. So there is a call for democratic education.

Our schools and teachers need re-orientated (Kaila, 2005). Democratic education talks about children's needs and concerns. To experience democratic education, one needs to swim in the concept. Some of the best democratic methods include trusting relationships, really engaging every child, respect every other human being, and love and acceptance of children. These are the fundamental values, which are not even practiced in schools. These are the basis of democratic education. The crux is, increase child participation in schools and also families.

Today's children are very much engaged in body and mind issues and schools all over the world are not able to go beyond framed syllabi. So schools disinterest children and adolescents, as there is a lack of harmony between what schools do and what students expect. Hence there is an urgent need for traditional schools to be open and change as per needs and concerns of children.

Democratic education concerns individual values and interpersonal sensitivities. Schools need to organize sensitivity programs for teachers on a democratic approach to schooling. Training teachers in the use of democratic principles of education would be one way to start democratizing traditional schools (Meier, 2005).

For introducing Democratic Education in Indian schools, we also need to assess responsive readiness on part of children, parents, teachers and school managements. There is a need to create awareness of the concept in the community. There is a need for creating democratic educational environment through cooperative learning and providing universal skills to children which they can use in life; not simply to prepare children to prove in subjects.

What is the big role of democratic schools?

Children are searching for a baseline meaning for their life. They need an open environment in which they can express and experiment with their original and novel ideas. At present most schools and teachers are unable to tap and develop the creativity in children, which is in abundance in them. Informal and formal strûctures of the school do impact on the child's learning, creativity and the way they absorb values, which they will unconsciously use when they grow into adults.

Some of the Indian group of schools such as DAV schools link classroom learning with democratic values. Bright learner support / empower average learner. No exams and no failure at the lower grades provide support mechanisms to students, and at the same time, minimum learning is ensured. But largely Indian schools need to be democratized where children have the right to decide over matters that concern them in learning and education. The world needs democratic schools where children no longer suppress themselves but instead feel free to experience life the way they wish, and develop the natural potential they are endowed with and that suit their individual personality. Democratic schools offer a lot of opportunity for innovation in the school that the children enjoy.

We need to look at the role of democratic schools in developing future societies. What competencies these schools shall be offering? What ideology shall they be developing? We also need to understand the schools broadly to deal with community issues and essentially play the role of a dynamic integrator of societies of the world. Democratic schools are an earnest effort towards democratizing communities and societies around us. Schools are essentially instrumental in building societies and integrating cultural expectations.

Conclusions

Democratic education can counter school related factors that lead to dropping out. Bella and Mputu (2004) concluded that school related, not personal or external problems are central in early dropout decisions. They suggested a wide approach and a change in the education system—addressing roots causes, not symptoms—as policy.

School factors such as grade retention, failure in language

and math, quality of teaching and teacher relationships, school climate, guidance to jobs or university, relevance of the course are all factors can be challenged and reduced by democratic education. Why? Research on democratic and free schools show students can take charge when respected and give the opportunity and guidance. When given accountability, in a democratic climate where they share in decisions and responsibility, children and youth will make sure they attend good schools and receive the best education available. Those closest to the problem have insights into solutions. Student input, research, policy recommendations, and actions on how to best counteract the above school factors are a valuable resource in address the root causes of school disaffection.

Most education is designed to formalize learning. The routines of systematic approaches tend to make educators forget that children and youth are first and foremost individuals. Yet, as has been shown, regard for the individual is the essence of democratic education.

Presently, many students believe school is not the place for them, and they are right. They may have a desk, but are not provide a place at the table where decisions are made. Democratic education provides that place, a place that allows them to share in classroom and school decisions. Educators must realize it is not naive or Utopian to think that students can make responsible decisions about their school, classroom, and their own learning.

Totalitarian regimes and social elites use schooling to perpetuate the status quo and will discount democratic education. However, for those who have the insight and truly care about children, finding as many ways as possible for students to take responsibility for the daily life of the school will be one of the best policies to address the problem of international school disaffection.

Question for Readers

How are creativity in school children and economic development of a country connected?

Bibliography

Achenbach, T.M and Edebrock, C. (1983). Manual for the behavior and checklist and Revised Child behavior profile, U.S.A Queen City Printers Inc.

Adaval, S.B. (1952). An Introduction into the qualities of the teachers under training. PhD. Edu. Allah. Univ.

Adelson, J. (1980). Handbook of Adolescent Psychology, New York, John Wiley & Sons.

Ahlsio. B, Britton, M.Murray and T.Theorell (1984). Disablement and quality of life after stroke, Stroke, 15, No. 5, 886-890.

Allport, G.W., Vernon; P.E. and Lindzey, G. (1960). A study of values. Boston: Houghton Mifflin.

Anderson, G. M., Hoshino, Y. (1997). Handbook of autism and pervasive developmental disorders. Neurochemical studies of autism. In D. J. Cohen & F.R. Volmar (eds.), Toronto: Wiley.

Andorson, H. J. (1931). Correlation between Academic Achievement and Teaching success, Elementary school, Jr. 32: pp 22-29.

Andorson, H.M. (1954). Study of certain criteria of Teaching Effectiveness, Jr of Edu Res 23: pp 41-71.

Anita Sharan (1998). The overburdened child. The Independent Journal of Politics and Business. (Society). Pg. 17.

Anne-Marie Ambert (1994). A Qualitative Study of Peer Abuse and Its Effects: Asian Journal of Psychology and Education Vol-27, No 9-10, 1994, page-20-28.

Anton Dosen, Anton, M.D. Dosen, Kenneth Day (2001), Treating Mental Illness and Behavior Disorders in Children and Adults with Mental Retardation. American

Psychiatric Association 1st edition (Netherland).

Arendell T. (1997). Contemporary parenting: challenges and issues. Thousand Oaks, Calif: Sage Publications.

Arora, K (1978). Difference between Effective and Ineffective Teachers, S. Chand and Co, Ltd. New Delhi.

Arthur T. Jersald and David W. Brook. Psychology of Adolescent. 3 ed. McGraw Hill Comp.

Arulmani G. (1989). Patterns of coping with psychological stressors among Indian adolescents. Unpublished M.Phil. Bangalore: Bangalore University.

Asakura, K. (December, 2004). Statement made as Tokyo Shure session, "You can learn anything." IDEC 2004, Bhubaneshwar, State of Orissa, India.

Asamen, J.K. (1983). The effects of perceived prejudice, alienation and acculturation on the self-concept of Japanese and Chinese Americans. DAI, (1984). Feb.44 (8). 2398-A.

ASCD. (2002). *A Lexicon of Learning: What Educators Mean When They Say...* Association of Supervision and Curriculum Development.

Autism Society of America (ASA) website - The Voice of Autism. http://www.autism-society.org/site/PageServer?pagename=WhatisAutism

Azar Sandra T, Nix Robert L, Makin-Byrd, Kerry N ; Parenting Schemas and the process of change; Journal of Marital and Family Therapy; Jan 2005; Pg 1-7.

Bailey, A., Le Couteur, A., Gottesman, I., Bolton, P., Simonoff, E., Yuzda, E. and Rutter, M. (1995). Psychological Medicine. Autism as a strongly genetic disorder: Evidence from a British twin study, 25.

Balchandran, E.S. (1981). Teaching Effectiveness and students Evaluation of Teaching, Ph.D Edu, Madras University.

Barbara R.Sarson, Irwin G. Sarson (1993), Abnormal Psychology: the problem of maladaptive behavior. Pearson education Tenth edition (New Jersey), page no. 504.

Barlow D.H, Durand V.M (1999), Abnormal Psychology, An integrative approach; 2nd edition; New York : Brooks/ Cole Publications, Thomson Learning Inc.

Barr A.S. (1929). Characteristics Differences in Teaching Performance of Good and Poor Teachers of social studies, Bloomington, III Public School Publishing Co.

Beadi, N. (Fall, 1996). From teacher as decision maker to teacher as participant in shared decision making. *Teacher College Record*.

Becvar Stroh Dorothy,Becvar J. Raphael;1988; Family Therapy: A Systemic Integration; Allyn and Bacon, Inc., Massachussets.

Beels Christian; A cultural history of family therapy; Family Process; Spring 2002; http://www.findarticles.com/p/articles/mi m0AZV/is 1 41/ai 84540247.

Bell, H.M. (1937). Consulting Psychologists. Press Inc. Palo, Alto, California.

Bella, N. and Mputu, H. (2004). Dropout in primary and secondary school: a global issue and an obstacle to the achievement of the Education for All goals. *The International Journal of School Disaffection.* Staffordshire, UK: Trentham Books. Vol 2 #2 p 14-30.

Benton S.A., Robertson J.M., Newton F.B. and Benton S.L. (2001). Dramatic increases seen in college students' mental health over last 13-years. Professional Psychology: Research and Practice, vol no. 34, issue 5, pp123-130.

Berna, J. (1993). The worst experiences of adolescents from divorced and separated parents and the stress responses to those experiences. Unpublished doctoral dissertation, Temple University, Philadelphia, PA.

Bhagoliwal, S. A. (1962). Study Personality characteristics associated in Teaching effectiveness as seen through Research techniques, PhD Edu, Allahabad University.

Bhattacharya, S. Psychology of Child Development. Sterling Publishers Private Ltd, New Delhi.

Bombay Times (1999). All work and no play sends kids to the counselor; 21 Jan. 1999, Mumbai.

Bonanno G.A. (2004). Loss, trauma, and human resilience: Have we underestimated the Human capacity to thrive after extremely aversive events? American Psychologist, vol no. 59, pp 20-28.

Bosma H. and Jackson S. (1990). In: Gibson-Cline J (Eds). Adolescence: From crisis to coping: A thirteen-nation study. Butterworth-Heinmann Ltd. Jordan Hill. 3.

Boyce, A. C. (1912). Qualities of Merit in Secondary School Teachers, Journal Edu Psychology, 3 : pp 144-57.

Brazelton T.B., Coles R., Comer J.P., Insel T., Kline K.K., Poussaint A., Schore A.N., Spear L., Suomi S.J., Wallerstein J. (2003). Hardwired to connect: The new scientific case for authoritative communities. Institute for American Values.

Brookover W.B. (1945). The relation of social factors to teaching ability, Jr. of Experimental Education, 13 pp. 205.

Burgess, A. W., Hartman, C. R. and McCormack, A. (1987). Abused to Abuser: Antecedents of Socially Deviant Behaviors. American Journal of Psychiatry, 144 (11). 1431-1436.

Butcher, Carson, Mineka, Abnormal psychology and Modern life (2002) 11th ed (New York) page no. 523.

Carins R.B., Leung M., Gest S.D. and Cairns B.D. (1995). A brief method for assessing social development, structure, reliability, stability and developmental validity of interpersonal competence scale. Behav Res Ther; 33(6). 725-36.

Carlile, A.F. (1954). Predicting Performance in the teaching profession. Jr. of Edu Res. 57: pp 641-688.

Carson R.C., Butcher J.N. and Mineka S. (1998). Abnormal Psychology and Modern Life. (10th ed.). New York: Wesley Longman Inc.

Center for the Study of Autism (CSA), Salem/ Portland. Information about Autism to parents and professionals and research on efficacy of therapeutic interventions. Research on collaboration with Autism Research Institute, San Diego. http://www.autism.org/contents.html

Chakrabarty, N. (1993). Students under stress: a comprehensive study. Unpublished project report, Bangalore: Rajiv Gandhi Research programme.

Chandrashekhar, C.R. (1979). Mental illness in Research students: Relationship with attitudes and life stresses unpublished M.D.-Thesis, Bangalore: NIMHANS.

Chauhan, N.S. Jain; R (1976). Teaching Efficiency Scale, Agra: APRC.

Chu, J.A. and Dill, D.L. (1990). Disassociative symptoms in relations to childhood physical and sexual abuse. American Journal of Psychiatry 147 (7). 887-892.

Claes M.E. (1992). Friendship and personal adjustment during adolescence. J. Adol; 15(1); 39-43.

Cohen S. and Williamson G.M. (1991). Stress and Infectious Diseases in Humans. Psychological Bulletin. americanpsychologicalassociation.org.

Cohen S., Doyle W.J., Skoner D.P., Rabin B.S. and Gwalfney J.M. (1997). Social ties and susceptibility to the common cold. Journal of the American Medical Association, vol no. 4, issue 1, pp100-112.

Cohen. David. (2001) B, B.A., Ph. D. Depression (Psychology). Encarta Encyclopedia, Deluxe.

Compass, B.E., Daviss, C.E. and Forsythe, C.S. (1985). Characteristics of life events during Adolescence. American Journal of Community Psychology 13. 677.

Conger, J.J. (1979). Adolescence: Generation under pressure. Curacao The Life Cycle Series, Willemstad, Multimedia Publications, Inc.

Cowen P, Gath D , Gelder M , Mayon R (1996), Oxford Textbook of Psychiatry; 3rd edition, New York, USA : Oxford University Press Inc.

Cox, T. (1988). Psychological factors in stress and Health. In S - Fisher and J Reason (eds). Handbook of life stress, Cognition, and Health, N.Y. John Wiley and sons Ltd.

Coy D.R. (1995). The need for a school suicide prevention policy. NASSP Bulletin, vol no. 79, issue 9, pp 32.

Crooks. R. and Jean. S. (1998). New York, New York: Holt, Rinehart & Winston.

Curcio, K. (1994). Stress symptoms of special education students diagnosed with conduct disorder. Unpublished doctoral dissertation, Temple University, Philadelphia, PA.

CWC (2005). A Unique Revolution: Children lead the way to decentralization and civil society participation.

Concerned for Working Children: Bangalore, India.

D'Amico A. and Cardaci M. (2003). Problem behaviors and academic achievement. Psychological Reports, vol no. 92, issue 10, pp 745.

D'Arcy, C. and Siddique, C.M. (1984). Psychological Distress Among Canadian Adolescents, Psychological Medicine, 14, 3, 615.

Dalal M. (1989). Prevalence and pattern of psychological disturbances in school-going adolescent girls. Unpublished M.Phil. dissertation submitted to Bangalore University.

Dalal S., Kapur M. and Subbalakshmi D. (1990). Prevalence and pattern of psychological disturbances in school going adolescent girls. Indian journal of clinical psychology 17: 83-84.

Dalal, M. (1989). Prevalence and pattern of psychological disturbance in school early adolescent girls. Unpublished M. Phil. Bangalore University, Bangalore, India.

Daniel, E. (1989). Students of disorders of emotion and conduct. The International Journal of School Disaffection. International Consortium of School.

Datta, V. (1991). Teachers Effectiveness and Academic Achievement, Asian Jr. of Psy and Edu, Vol 24, No 7-8, pp 8-12.

David A. Wolf, Eric J. Mash (2004), Abnormal child Psychology Wadsworth publication. Second edition (New York), Page no.230.

David Eitle; Tamela McNulty Eitle (2003). Segregation and School Violence. Social Forces, Vol. 82, No. 2. (Dec., 2003), pp. 589-616.

David H. Barlow, V. Mark Durand (2002), Abnormal psychology Thomson, brooks/cole publications, second edition (calfornia), page no.438.

Dean, D.G. (1961). Alienation: Its meaning and measurement. American Sociological Review (Oct). 26, 753-758.

Debnath, H.N. (1971). Teaching efficiency: Its measurements and its determinants Ph.D Edu, Vishwa Bharati, Univ.

DeMan, Anton and Devisse, T. (1987). Locus of control

mental ability, self-esteem and alienation. Social Behaviour and Personality 15(2), 233-236.

Department of Health Sciences. americanpsychologicalassociation.org.

Depression in Children. www.divorceinfo.com/depressioninchildren.html.

Dera, R.C. (1966). Prediction of Student- Teaching Success, Ph.D Edu, AMU, Aligarh.

Deron. Deborah. Children & Depression. www.wingofmadness/articles/children.html.

Development Program Schools. The Journal of Negro Education, Vol. 65, No. 3, Educating Children in a Violent Society, Part I. (Summer, 1996). pp. 308-314.

Dharitri R. (1996). Identification and Presentation of Emotional Disturbance as a Stress Reactor among Students. Indian Journal of Clinical Psychology Vol 23: No.1, P-12-15.

Diener E., Lucas R.E., Oishi S. (2002). The handbook of positive psychology. New York: Oxford University Press.

Durand, Barlow. Abnormal Psychology. 2nd Ed, Thomson Inc., New Delhi.

Ebata, A.T., Moos R.H. (1991). Coping and adjustment in distressed and health adolescents. J Appl Dev Psychol; 12:33-54.

Edelson, S. M. Overview of Autism. Center for the Study of Autism, Salem/ Portland. http://www.autism.org/overview.html

Education Commission (1970). Education and National Development, Report of the Education Commission 1964-66, NCERT, p xvi.

Egeland B., Carlson E., Sroufe L.A. (1993). Resilience as process. Development and Psychopathology, vol no. 5, pp 517-528.

Eliassen, R.H, Morti, R.L (1940). Pre-training Selection of Teachers during 1937-39. Edu. Adm 8, Supe, 26: pp 481-492.

Eme, R.F. (1979). Sex Differences in Childhood Psychology: A Review, Psychological Bulletin. 86 575.

Erikson E.M. (1968). Identity, Youth and Crisis, New York: Norton.

Eysenck, H.J., and Eysenck, S.B.G. (1975). Manual of the Eysenck Personality Questionnaire. Kent, Hodder and Stoughton.

Feldman. Robert. 4th Ed (1995). Understanding Psychology. New York, McGraw – Hill.

Fergusson D.M., Horwood LJ, Lynskey MJ. (1993). Prevalence and co-morbidity of DSM III R diagnosis in a birth cohort of 15 year old. J Am Acad Child Adol. Psychiatr. 32; 1127-34.

Forehand R. and Neighbours B. Wierson (1991).The transition to adolescence. The role of gender and stress in problem behavior and competence. J Child Psychol Psychiatr. 32 (6), 929-1002.

Freiberg, H. J. (Sept., 1996). From Tourists to Citizens in the Classroom. *Educational Leadership*.

Garmezy N. (1985). Stress resistant children: The search for protective factors. In J. Stevenson (Ed.). Research in developmental psychopathology. Oxford; Pergamon, pp 213-33.

Gathercoal, F. (1991). *Practicing Judicious Discipline: An Educator's Guide to a Democratic Classroom*. Edited by Barbara McEwan. San Francisco: Caddo Gap Press.

Geertz C. (1975). On the nature of anthropological understanding. American Scientist, vol no. 63, pp 47-53.

Gehlot P.S. and Nathawat S.S. (1993). Suicide and family constellation in India American journal of psychotherapy, 27, 273-278.

George S Baroff, J Gregory Olley (1999). Mental retardation: Nature, cause, and management, Brunner-Mazel Inc. (U.S.)

Gerzon, M. (Feb., 1997). Teaching Democracy by Doing It! *Educational Leadership*.

Gibson-Cline J. (1995). Adolescence: From crisis to coping: A thirteen-nation study. Butterworth-Heinmann Ltd. Jordan Hill. 3.

Gohm C.L., Oishi S., Darlington J., Diener E. (1998). Culture, parental conflict, parental marital status, and the subjective well being of adults. Journal of Marriage and the Family, vol no. 60, pp 319-334.

Goldberg D. (1972). The determination of Psychiatric illness by Questionnaire, London, Oxford University.

Goldberger L. and Brenitz S. (Ed). (1982). Handbook of Stress: Theoretical and Clinical aspects. New York: Macmillan Publishers Inc.

Goldwater, A. (1993). Attributional styles and stress symptoms in children exposed to Hurricane Andrew. Unpublished doctoral dissertation, Temple University, Philadelphia, PA.

Goodyear, I.M., Kolrin, I. and Gatzanis, S. (1986). Do Age and Sex influence the association between the Recent Life events and Psychiatric disorders in children and Adolescents: A controlled enquiry, Journal of Child Psychology and Psychiatry 27, 681.

Gormly, Anne V., Brodzinsky, David M. Lifespan Human Development. 4th Ed, Holt, Rinehart and Winston inc., Chicago.

Gould, L.J. (1969). Conformity and marginality. Two faces of alienation. Jl. of Social Issues, Spring, 25(2). 39-63.

Grant K.E. and Compas B.E. (1995). Stress and anxious-depressed symptoms among adolescents. Searching for mechanism of Risk. J.Consult Clin Psycol; 63(5), 1015-23.

Grey. Stanley. Psychology in Use. New York, American Book Company.

Groer M.W., Shoffner D. and Thomas S.P. (1992). Adolescent stress and coping - a longitudinal study. Resident Nursing Health, 15(3), 209-23.

Gupta A. (1994). Success in life and its correlation with early educational background Indian express, July 14, New Delhi.

Gupta, R.C. (1976). Prediction of Teachers Effectiveness through Personality test, PhD Edu.

Guthrie, E.R. (1927). Measuring student opinion of Teachers, school and society.

Haines. Cynthia. (2005). Types of Depression. www.psychodirect.com/printfriendly.com/dtypesprint.html.

Halkias, D., Fakinos, M., Hyman, I., Cohen, I., Mahon, M., Akrivos, D., Snook, P., and Ducette, J. (2002). Victimization of children in schools: Traumatic symptoms and stressors in Greek and American schools. Paper presented at the XVI Congress of The international Association for Cross Cultural psychology, Yogyakarta, Indonesia.

Hall, V.C. (1965). Former student evaluation as a criterion for Teaching Success, Jr. of Experimental Edu; Vol. 34 No.1 pp. 1-19.

Hancock D.R. (2001). Effects of test anxiety and evaluative threat on students' achievement and motivation. Journal of Educational Research, vol no. 94, issue 8, pp 284.

Hannam, D (2001). Executive Summary of Derry Hannam's "Student Participation" Report for DFES. derry@demo51.freeserve.co.uk

Hannam. D. (2005). Education for democracy and education through democracy. *Teaching Citizenship*.

Hart, J.W. (1971). Teachers and Teaching as a function of creativity, Intelligence and intercept, PhD Psy, Agra Univ.

Hecht, Y. (2002). *Educational Innovativeness from a democratic point of view.* Tel Aviv, Israel: The Institute for Democratic Education.

Heim. Christine (2000). Pituitary-Adrenal and Autonomic Responses to Stress in Women After Sexual and Physical Abuse in Childhood. The Journal of the American Medical Association. Vol. No. 284, Issue 5, Aug , pp – 592-597.

Henderson N., Bernard B., Sharplight N. (1999). Resiliency in Action: Practical Ideas For Overcoming Risks and Building Strengths in Youth, Families, and Communities. San Diego, CA: Resiliency in Action, Inc.

Henderson N., Milstein M.M. (1999). Resiliency in schools: Making it happen for students and educators. Thousand Oaks, CA: Corwin Press.

Herman. J. L., Perry. J. C., Van der Kolk. A (1989). Childhood trauma in borderline personality disorder. American Journal of Psychiatry 146 (4). 490-495

Hindustan Times (1998). Parents, society may drive students to the hilt, 25 march, New Delhi.

Hoeksema, Nolen Susan. Abnormal Psychology. 3rd Ed, McGraw-Hill Companies, New Delhi.

http://www.findarticles.com/p/articles/mi_qa3658/is_200501/ai_n9520948.

http://www.ninds.nih.gov/disorders/autism/detail_autism.htm (Could not access this website again due to some internet problems)

Hurlock, E.B. (1962). Adolescent Development. N.Y., McGraw Mill Book Co. Inc.

Hyman, I. (1990). Reading, writing, and the hickory stick: The appalling story of physical and psychological abuse in American schools. Lexington: Lexington Books.

Hyman, I. (1997). The case against spanking: How to discipline your child without hitting. San Francisco: Jossey-Bass.

Hyman, I. and Snook, P. (1999a). Dangerous schools: What we can do about the physical and emotional abuse of our children. San Francisco: Jossey-Bass.

Hyman, I. and Snook, P. (1999b). Use of the My Worst Experience Scales for diagnosis and treatment of posttraumatic stress disorder in children. Paper presented as part of a mini-skills workshop at the 1999 National Association of School Psychologists Annual Convention and Exposition, April 9, 1999, Las Vegas, NV.

Hyman, I. and Snook, P. (2000). Student alienation syndrome: Theory, assessment and application. Paper presented at the 108th National Convention of the American Psychological Association, August 6, 2000, Washington, DC.

Hyman, I. Zelikoff, W., and Clarke, J. (1988). Psychological and physical abuse in the schools: A paradigm for understanding post-traumatic stress disorder in children and youth. Journal of Traumatic Stress, 1, 243-267.

Hyman, I., Berna, J., Snook, P., DuCette, J., and Kohr, M. (in press). Manual for the My Worst Experience Scales. Los Angeles, CA: Western Psychological Services.

Hyman, I., Cavallo, F., Erbacher, T., Spangler, J., and Stafford, J. (1997). Corporal punishment in American: Cultural wars in politics, religion and science. Children's Legal Rights Journal, 17(4)., 36-46.

Hyman, I., Dahbany, A, Blum, M., Brooks Klein, V., Weiler, E., and Pokalo, M. (1997). School discipline and school violence: The teacher variance approach. Needham Heights, MA: Allyn and Bacon.

Indian Council of Medical Research (1983). Unpublished final report of the task force project 'Multicenter study of the patterns of child and adolescent disorders. New Delhi: ICMR.

Informal communication with Dr. Usha S. Nayar, Dy. Director, TISS, Mumbai.

Informal communication with Mrs. Ravi Vijayam, Principal, S.S. Singhania School, Thane.

International Democratic Education Conference. (2004). December 3-12, 2004, Bhubaneshwar, Orissa, India.

Iyenger S.S. and DeVoe S.E. (2001). Rethinking the Value of Choice: Considering Cultural Mediators of Intrinsic Motivation. Invited Article to appear in the Nebraska Symposium on Motivation.

Jackson PW, Getzells TJ (1963). In: Garrison and Garrison.(Eds). Psychology of adolescence. N.Y. Prentice Hall. 259.

Jane D. McLeod; James M. Nonnemaker (2000). Poverty and Child Emotional and Behavioral Problems: Racial/Ethnic Differences in Processes and Effects. Journal of Health and Social Behavior, Vol. 41, No. 2 (Jun., 2000)., pp. 137-161.

Jayamma, M.S. (1962). Constitution and standardization of an Inventory for predicting Teachers Efficiency, Ph.D. Edu. Kerala: Kerala university.

Jefferson. J. W. and Greist. J. H. rev. ed. (1997). Depression and Antidepressants: A Guide.

Jensen (1951). Determining critical requirements for Teachers, Jr. of Expl. Edu 20: pp 79-85.

Jitendra Mohan, Nisha Mahajan, Neeraj Kakkar (1999). A study of alienation among adolescents, Asian Journal of

Psychology and Education Vol. 32, No. 1-2, Page 11-16.

Jones RW (1993). Gender-specific differences in the perceived antecedents of academic stress. Psychol Rep; 72(3): 739.

Jones, M.L. (1956). Analysis of certain prospects of Teaching Ability. Jr: of Expl. Edu; 25; pp 103-108.

K Eileen Allen, Ilene S Schwartz, Eileen K Allen (2000). The Exceptional Child: Inclusion in Early Childhood Education, Thomson learning ltd (New York). page 83.

Kaila H. L. (2003). Parenting Function; Icon publications pvt. ltd. New Delhi.

Kaila H.L. (2001). Social Development of Teenagers, Social Welfare Vol. 48, No. 3, June Issue.

Kaila H.L. (2002). "School Based Approaches of Child Guidance and Counselling Services in Mumbai City" a paper presented in the Symposium on 'Alternative Models of Child Guidance Services' organized by The National Institute of Public Cooperation and Child Development as part of International Congress of Child and Adolescent Psychiatry and Allied Professions at Hotel Ashok in New Delhi on 1 November 2002.

Kaila H.L. et al (2002). Counseling for Growth. New Delhi: Himalaya publishing house.

Kaila, H. (March, 2005). Democratizing schools across the world to stop killing creativity in children: An Indian perspective. *Counseling Psychology Quarterly*. 18(1): 1-6.

Kaila, H.L. (2003a). Counselling young people: Issues and Experiences. Paper presented at a workshop on "Youth in a Globalizing World: Dynamics, Challenge and Strategy" organized by the Unit for Child and Youth Research, TISS, held on 3 and 4 February 2003.

Kaila, H.L. (2003b). Parenting Function. New Delhi: Icon Publications Pvt. Ltd.

Kaila, H.L. (2005). Democratizing schools across the world to stop killing creativity in children: An Indian perspective. Guest Editorial, Counselling Psychology Quarterly, March 2005; 18(1): 1–6.

Kaila, H.L. (2006). Counselling in Schools. New Delhi: Icon

Publications Pvt. Ltd.

Kanner, L. (1943). Nervous Child. Autistic disturbances of affective contact, 21.

Kanungo, R.N. (1979). The concepts of alienation and involvement revisited. Psychological Buletin, 86, 119-138.

Kaplan H.I , Sadock B.J. (1995), Comprehensive Textbook of Psychiatry, 6th edition, volume 2, USA : Williams and Wilkins Publications.

Kaplan, M. Robert and Harari Herbert (1977). Psychology: personal and social adjustment N.Y. Harper and Row Publishers.

Kapur M (1990). Early childhood stimulation and optimum mental development. Unpublished data. WHO-NIMHANS project.

Kapur R L (1969). Student Wastage: An Epidemiological Inquiry into psychiatric and Allied factors contributing to it. Ph. D thesis submitted to University of Edinbrugh.

Kashani JH, Beck NC, Hoeper EW, Fallahi C, Corcoran MA, McAllister JA, Rosenberg TK, Reid JC (1987). Psychiatric disorders in a community sample of adolescents. Am J Psychiatr, 144; 584-9.

Kate Friendlander (1951). Psycho Analytic Approach to Juvenile Delinquency. McGraw Hill Comp.

Kaul, L (1972). Factorial Study of certain Personality variables of popular Teachers in secondary schools, PhD Edu. Kurukshetra Univ.

Kaur S (1987). A clinical study of somatoform disorders in children. Unpublished M. D. thesis. Postgraduate Institute of Medical Education and Research. Chandigarh.

Killian K.D (July,1994), Fearing Fat : A Literature Review of Family Systems Understandings and Treatments Of Anorexia and Bulimia, Journal of Family Relations Published by National Council on Family Relations, Volume No. 43, Issue 3, pp 311-318.

Kilpatrick D.G., Ruggiero K.J., Acierno R., Saunders B.E., Resnick H.S. and Best C.L. (2003). High percentage of youth in the U.S. report symptoms of Posttraumatic Stress and other disorders. Journal of Consulting and Clinical Psychology, vol no. 71, issue 4, pp 231-241.

Kitayama S., Suzuk T., Connor A., Markus H. R. (2001). Culture, self, and dissonance: Post-decisional attitude change in Japan and the United States. Unpublished manuscript.

Klerman. L. G. and Weissman (1989). Increasing rates of Depression. The Journal of the American Medical Association. Vol. No. 261, Issue 15.

Knight, F. B. (1922). Qualities Related to Success in teaching, Teachers college in Columbia Univ. Contribution of Edu. No 120.

Koegel, R. L., Koegel, L. K., and McNerney, E. K. (2001). Journal of Clinical Child Psychology. Pivotal areas in intervention for autism, 30.

Kohn, A. (Sept., 1993). Choices for Children: Why and How to Let Students Decide. *Phi Delta Kappan*.

Kohr, M. A. (1996). Validation of the My Worst Experience Survey. Unpublished doctoral dissertation, Temple University, Philadelphia, PA.

Kukerti B.R (1990). A study of some psychological correlates of successful correlates of successful Teachers, PhD Edu Rohilkhand Univ.

Kukreti B.R (1993). Qualities Needed for Successful Teachers; An Investigation.

Kukreti, B.R (1993). How to measure Teacher Effectiveness? A review, Indian Psychological review Vol-40 No: 9-10, pp. 1-10.

Kukreti, B.R (1993). Teaching Aptitude and successful teachers: A co relational study, Indian Psychological review, Vol 40 No.5-6, pp: 7-14.

Kulandairel .K Rao (1968). Qualities of Good Teachers and Good Student (A Study in student ratings). Sri. R.K Mission Vidyalaya Teachers College, Coimbatore,

Kuwana, E. Y. Neuroscience for Kids: A Case Study http://faculty.washington.edu/chudler/aut.html

Lal, N and Sethi, BB (1977). Estimate of mental ill health in children in an urban community, Indian J. Paediat. 4 55- 64.

Lambert, C. (1990). Factorial structure and reliability of a scale measuring stress responses as a result of maltreatment in the schools. Unpublished doctoral dissertation, Temple University, Philadelphia, PA.

Lamke, T.A (1951). Personality and Teaching Success, Jr. of Experimental Edu. 20 pp. 217-259.

Latna H. (1983). Psychological problems of students and role of conselling. Unpublished Doctoral thesis. University of Bangalore.

Lehrer P.M. and Woolfolk R.L. (1993). Principles and Practice of Stress Management. (2nd ed). New York: The Guilford Press.

Leslie, S.A (1974). : Psychiatric Disorder in the Young Adolescents of an Industrial Town. British Journal of Psychiatry, 125,113.

Lester D. Crow and Alic Crow (1962). Adolescent Development and Adjustment. 2 ed McGraw Hill Comp.

Levinson R , Powell B, Steelman L.C, (Dec,1986), Social Location, Significant Others and Body Image Among Adolescents, Social Psychology Quarterly Published by American Sociological Association, Volume No. 49, Issue 4, pp 330-337.

Lewin, K., r. Lippit and R. White (1939). Patterns of aggressive behaviour in experimentally created climates. J. Soc. Psyschol., 10, 271-299.

Linda Lantieri; Janet Patti (1996). Waging Peace In Our Schools. The Journal of Negro Education, Vol. 65, No. 3, Educating Children in a Violent Society, Part I. (Summer, 1996)., pp. 78-91.

Loflin, J. (2000). Alternative Education's Spoiled Image: When it happened, how it happened, why it happened, and what to do about it. Published by the Iowa Association.

Loflin, J. (2003). Common Sense: Explaining low voter turnout: More key reforms to reverse the increase in voter apathy. Indianapolis, IN: Democratic Education Consortium.

Loflin, J. (2004). (DOC). jsmink 12 National Dropout Prevention Center. Trentham Books Limited: London.

Major, C.L. (1938). The Percentile Ranking on the Ohio State University psychological test as a factor in forecasting the success of Teacher's in Training, school society, 47: pp 582-584.

Malavika Kapur. (1990). Psychological Perspective on Stress and Health, Sage: New Delhi. pp. 268 – 272,

Malhotra, S, Kaur, R and Nehra R (1992). Life events in psychiatrically sick children. Indian Journal of Psychiatry, 34, 222-230

Malhotra, S, Malhotra, A and Verma, V.K. (1992). Child Mental Health in India Macmillian Ind. Ltd. Delhi.

Mani Pande (1994). Pushing the kids into neurosis.The Tribune, Chandigarh, February 13, pp. 73-74.

Mann S.S. (1980). Some correlates of success in Teaching of secondary school teachers. PhD Edu. Chandigarh: Punjab Univ.

Mansoor E. and Grus C.L. (2005). Social acceptance and academic achievement. Journal of Developmental and Behavioral Pediatrics, vol no. 26, issue 1, pp 338-342.

Marano. E. Hara. (2005). More Women Suffer Depression. www.cms.psychologytoday.com/articles/pto-20030718-000003.html.

Mariam, L. L. (1906). Normal School Education and Efficiency in Teaching, Contribution o education. No. 1 Columbia Univ.

Martin B. Saligman, David L.Rosenhan, Abnormality, page no. 307.

Martin H. Neumeyer (1961). Juvenile Delinquency in Modern Society. 3 ed. New York.

Mary Beirne-Smith, James R. Patton, and Shannon H. Kim (2001).

Mash, Eric J., Wolfe, David A. Abnormal Child Psychology. 2nd Ed, Wadsworth, California.

Masten A.S. (2000). Children who overcome adversity to succeed in life. University of Minnesota.

Masten A.S., Hubbard J.J., Gest S.D., Tellegen A., Garmezy N., Ramirez M. (1999). Competence in the context of adversity: Pathways to resilience and maladaptation from childhood to late adolescence. Development and Psychopathology, vol no. 11, pp 143-169.

Mata Prasad (1996). Need of providing mental Health Services in the Schools. Presidential Address of the 22nd Annual

Conference, Indian Journal of Clinical Psychology. Vol. 23, 45-59.

Mathew R. (1980). Factorial structure of Teaching competencies among secondary school teachers. PhD Edu. Baroda: M.S University.

May, R. (1972). *Power and Innocence* New York: W. W. Norton.

McGee M.G. and Wilson D.W. (1999). Psychology, Science and Application. New York: West Publishing Co.

McMahon, Frank B. Abnormal Behavior, Psychology's View. Prentice Hall Inc., New Jersey.

Mehr J. (1983). Abnormal Psychology. New York: Holt, Rinehart & Winston.

Mehta Seema (2002). Parental pressure self esteem and academic interest of adolescents. M. PHIL. Dissertation, Mumbai: SNDT women's university.

Meier, D. (Summer, 2005). Creating democratic schools: A democratic school culture is the best professional development of teachers. *Rethinking Schools*. Milwaukee, WI p. 28-30.

Mensh, I.N and E.P. Mason (1951). Relationship of school atmosphere to reactions to frustrating situations. J. Educ. Res., 45, 275-286.

Mental Retardation: An Introduction to Intellectual Disability, Prentice Hall 7th Edition (New Jersey).

Miller J. G. (1994). Cultural diversity in the morality of caring: Individually oriented versus duty-based interpersonal moral codes. Cross-cultural research, vol no. 28, pp 3-39.

Miller J. G., Bersoff D. M. (1998). The role of liking in perceptions of moral responsibility to help: A cultural perspective. Journal of Experimental Social Psychology, vol no. 34, pp 443-469.

Mishra, P.N., Pandit S. and Hindolia, S.L. (1993). Teaching Effectiveness – A model Academic Work Load Distribution, University News, Vol XXXI No.42, pp 1-3 Oct 18.

Misra R. (Ed). (2000). Psychological perspectives on Stress and Health. New Delhi: Concept Publishing Company.

Misra R. and McKean M. (2000). College student's academic stress and its relations to their anxiety, time management, and leisure satisfaction. University of Alabama,

Mohan J. and Eysenck, H.J. and Eysenck, S.B.G. (1987). The Eysenck Personality Questionnaire. An Indian Experience. Personality study and Group Behaviour, 7(2)., 67-70.

Mohan, J. (1998). A cross-cultural experience of collaboration I research and personality. Invited address 24th International congress of Applied Psychology. San Francisco 9-14.

Mohan, J. and Joginder, (1984). Alienation of Urban youth: A study in relation to personality, achievement motivation and academic achievement. Ph.D. Theses, Punjab, University Chandigarh.

Morgan C.T., King R.A., Weisz J.R. and Schopler J. (1997). Introduction to Psychology. New Delhi: Tata McGraw Hill Publishing Company Ltd.

Mukerji A. (2005). Playschools spell hard work for toddlers. The Times of India.

Murphy L.B. and Moriarity A.E. (1976). Vulnerability, coping, and growth. New Haven and London University Press.

Murray B. (2003). Rebounding from losses. Monitor, vol no. 34. Print version, pp 42.

Mussen. H. Paul, Conger. J. John, Kagan. Jerome and Huston. C. Aletha. 6th Ed. Child Development and Personality.

Mutha, D.N. (1989). An Attitudinal and Personality study of Effective Teachers; PhD, Psy. Jod Univ.

Nandi, D N, Ajmany, S, Ganguli H, Banerjee, G,Boral G.C, Ghosh A, and Sarkar S.(1975). Psychiatric disorders in a rural community in West Bengal an epidemiolcgical study, Ind J Psychiat. I.C.M.R., 1787.

Nandini T.K., Malavika Kapur, H. Uma and D.K. Subbakrishna (1998). Perceived Stress and Adjustment in Competent and Disturbed Early Adolescents. NIMHANS Journal, 16(3)., July, pp. 181-186.

Narayan R.K (1992). Take The Burden off the Children, Indian express, April 28, New Delhi.

Nathawat S. S and Gupta Kavita (1990). Sources and management of stress in school going children and adolescents D.E.I research journal of education and psychology, 8, 35-39.

Nathawat S. S. (1997). Reducing academic burden on school students. Indian journal of clinical psychology, vol no; 1 pp. 1-2.

National Movement of Working Children. (2003). *Education-related Problems faced by Working Children and Their Recommendations.* Report submitted in Geneva to The United Nations Committee on the Rights of the Child.

National Policy on Education (1986). Programme of Action; Ministry of HRD Deptt. of Edu, Govt of India, New Delhi, p 186.

Neumann Y.E. and Reichel A. (1990). Determinants and consequences of student's burnout in universities. Journal of Higher Education, vol no. 61, issue 1, pp 70-71.

Nichols P. Michael, Schwartz C. Richard; (1991, 1984; 2nd Edition); Family Therapy: Concepts and Methods; Allyn and Bacon Inc., Massachussets, Boston, London, Toronto, Sydney, Tokyo, Singapore.

Ninan. T and Kapur, M (1981). Life Events of hysteria in early adolescents. NIMHANS Journal 7, 43-48.

Norris M. Haynes (1996). Creating Safe and Caring School Communities: Comer School of Alternative Education (IAAE).

Ojeman, R.H and F.R, Wilkinson, (1939). The effects on pupil growth of a increase in teachers understanding of pupil behavior. J. Exper Edue, 8, 143-147.

Online encyclopedia http://en.wikipedia.org/wiki/Resilience

Osborne, N D. (1978). A study of relationship of suspended and non-suspended high schools students in terms of student perception of school climate, alienation, student deviant behavior, teacher-student relationship and the extent of voluntary participation in extra class activities. Diss. Abs.Int A, 38, 5833.

Pachausi. G.K (1983). Proficiency in teaching as a function of Personality Factors; Frustration (regression and aggression). and sex, PhD Edu. Agra: Agra Univ.

Papalia. D. E, Old. W. Sally and Feldman. R. D. 9th Ed. Human Development.

Pareek, U. Rao, T.V, Ramlingaswamy, P and Sharma, B.R. (1976). Manual for Battery of Preadolescent Personality Tests Varanasi, Rupa Psychological Center.

Pares Chandra Biswas (1990). Relationship Between School Organizational Climate and Reactions to Frustration of Secondary School Children. Journal of Education and Psychology. Volume XXXXVIII No. 1-2.

Patled, G. M. (1972). Multiple prediction of student Teacher Performance in Teaching Teacher Education, 7 pp 24-32.

Patricia A. Adler; Peter Adler (1995). Dynamics of Inclusion and Exclusion in Preadolescent Cliques. Social Psychology Quarterly, Vol. 58, No. 3., pp. 145-162.

Paul H. Landis. Adolescents (1952). 2 ed. McGraw Hill Comp.

Pawlik. Kurt and Rosenzwig. R. Marle. The International Handbook of Psychology. Sage Publications India Pvt. Ltd. New Delhi.

Peterson AC, Hamburg BA. (1986). Adolescence A developmental approach to problems and psychopathology. Behav Ther; 17:480-94.

Puskar KR, Lamb JM. Bartolovic M. (1993). Examining the common stressors and coping methods of rural adolescents, Nur Pract; 18(11): 50-8.

Rangaswami, K (1995). Academic stress and Mental Health Editorial. Indian Journal of Clinical Psychology. 22 (1).

Rangaswami, K and Kamakshi G (1983). Life Events in hysterical adolescents. Child Psychiatry Quaterly, 15, 26-33.

Rao PV, Ramlingaswamy TV, Sharma BR. (1976). Manual for battery of pre-adolescent personality tests. Varanasi Rupa Psychological Center.

Rao, P.N (1978). Psychiatric Morbidity in Adolescence: An Epidemiological Survey of Prevalence and pattern of Psychological disturbances of school going early Adolescents. Unpublished dissertation, Bangalore University.

Rea, C. D. (1994). Comparisons of patterns of traumatic stress symptoms in adolescents with and without overt behavior difficulties. Unpublished doctoral dissertation, Temple University, Philadelphia, PA.

Renee R. Jenkins; Janice G. Hutchinson (1996). The Public Health Model for Violence Prevention: A Partnership in Medicine and Education. The Journal of Negro Education, Vol. 65, No. 3, Educating Children in a Violent Society, Part I. (Summer, 1996). pp. 38-49.

Reudiger, W. C. and Strayer, G.D. (1910). The qualities of Meritorious Teachers Jr. of Edu psy, 1: pp. 272-78.

Ritvo, E. A., Jorde, L. B., Mason-Brothers, A., and Freeman, B. J. (1989). American Journal of Psychiatry. The UCLA University of Utah epidemiologic survey of autism: Recurrence risk estimates and genetic counseling, 146.

Roberta G. Simmons; Dale A. Blyth; Edward F. Van Cleave; Diane Mitsch Bush (Dec., 1979). Entry into Early Adolescence: The Impact of School Structure, Puberty, and Early Dating on Self-Esteem. American Sociological Review, Vol. 44, No. 6. (Dec. 1979). pp. 948-967.

Ron Avi Astor; Ronald O. Pitner; Brent B. (1996). Duncan Ecological Approaches to Mental Health Consultation with Teachers on Issues Related to Youth and School Violence. The Journal of Negro Education, Vol. 65, No.3, Educating Children in a Violent Society, Part I. (Summer, 1996)., pp. 336-355.

Rosenberg, M. (1965). Society and adolescents self-image N.J. Princeton Univ. Press.

Rosenzweig, S. (1944). An outline of frustration theory, In: Hunt, J. McV.(Ed)., Personality and Behaviour Disorders, New York, Ronald Press, Vol.1, 379-388.

Rosenzweig, S. (1978). The Rosenzweig Picture Frustration Study: Basic Manual. St.Louis: Rana House.

Rostker, L.E. (1965). The measurement of Teaching ability, Jr. of Experimental Education, 14: pp 6-51.

Rotter, J.B. (1977). Generalized expectancies for internal vs. external control of reinforcement. Psychological Monographs, 80 (609).

Rozario J. (1988). An epidemiological survey prevalence and pattern of psychological disturbance of school going early adolescents. Unpublished M.Phil dissertation, Bangalore University.

Russell, W. (1991). Symptoms of 4-6 year old children who were sexually abused, or witness to extreme violence. Unpublished doctoral dissertation, Temple University, Philadelphia, PA.

Ruther, M. Graham, P. Chadwick, O. and Yule, W. (1976). Adolescent turmoil: Fact or Fiction? Journal of Child Psychology and Psychiatry. 17, 35.

Rutter M. (1987). Psychological resilience and protective mechanisms. Am J. Orthopsychiatry, 57; 316-31.

Rutter M. (1999). Resilience concepts and findings: Implications for family therapy. Journal of family therapy, vol no. 21, pp 119-144.

Samantaroy, G.K. (1971). A study of Teacher Attitude and in relationship with teaching Efficiency, PhD Edu; San Univ.

Sarason I.G. and Sarason B.R. (2002). Abnormal Psychology. New Jersey: Pearson Publishing Inc.

Sarkar. A. (1990). Prevalence and pattern of psychological disturbances in 8-11 year old school going children. Unpublished M. Phil dissertation. Bangalore University, Bangalore India.

Sathyavati, K. and Thomas, A. (1984). An attributional approach to locus of control, self-esteem and alienation: a clinical study. Psychological studies 29(1)., 76-82.

Satyagiriranjan, S. (1985). Competency Personality and Motivation and Professional Perception of College teachers. PhD, Edu Maduria Kamraj Univ.

Sawant P. (2005). Stress kills 11-year old. Mulund Plus, October 9th.

Scarborough, H. (1981). Adolescent development in contemporary society. London and Boston. Routledge and Kegan Paul.

Schneider, E. (Sept., 1996). Giving Students a Voice in the Classroom. *Educational Leadership.*

Sebastian, Thara (1997). Parental Pressure for achievement and academic interest, actual academic achievement, self-esteem and creativity. PH.D Department of home science, St. Teresa's college Ernakulam, Kerala, August 1997.

Seguin. L. *et. al.* (1995). Chronic stressors, social support and depression during Pregnancy. Obstretrics & Gynecology, 85: 583-589. www.greenjournal.org/cgi/content/abstract/85/4/583.

Sell. H., and R. Nagpal (1992). Assessment of Subjective Welt Being. The Subjective Well Being Inventory (SUBI). SEARO, Regional Health paper No 24, WHO, New Delhi.

Sethi, B.B. Gupta, S.C. and Rajkumar, P.K. (1972). A Psychiatric survey of 500 rural families, Indian Journal of Psychiatry. 14, 183.

Sethi, B.B., Gupta, S.C. and Kumar, K. (1967). 300 urban families - a psychiatric survey, Ind J. Psychiat 9, 280.

Shannon, A. (1993). Comparison of high successful teachers, failing teachers and average teachers at the time of their graduation from Indiana state Teachers college, Edu. Vol. LXVIII, No. 2.

Sharma M.L. (1973). An investigation into organizational climate of secondary schools I Rajasthan. Unpublished Ph.D. Thesis, M.S. Uni. Baroda.

Sharma M.L. (1975). School Climate and the role of school administrator, A system analysis. Indian Educl. Rev 10(1)., 118-131.

Sharma, R.K. and Rai, B.C. (1981). General Psychology, Lucknow; Prakashan, Kendra.

Shenoy, J. (1992). Psychological disturbances in 5-8 year old school going children. Unpublished doctoral dissertation. Bangalore University, Bangalore India.

Sigelman. K. Carol, Shaffer. R. David. 2nd Ed. Life-Span Human Development. California, Brooks/Cole Publishing Company.

Slater J. (2004). Exam fear haunts pupils. Times Educational Supplement.

Slater, R. (Jan., 1994). Making Democracy Work in Our Schools: From Theory to Reality. *NASSP* Bulletin.

Snyder C.R., Shorey H.S., Cheavens J., Pulvers K.M. and Wiklund C. (2002). Hope and Academic success in college. Journal of Educational Psychology, vol no. 94, issue 7, pp 820-821.

Sonawat R. (2001). Understanding families in India: A reflection of societal changes. Psicologia, Teoria e Pesquisa, vol no. 17, pp 177-186.

Sonpar S. (1982). The psychopathology of adolescence. A multiple approach to its understanding. Unpublished Doctoral thesis, Bangalore University.

Sonpar, S. (1988). Study of childhood hysteria, unpublished doctoral dissertation, Bangalore University. India.

Sorensen, T. (1981). Freedom and Social support Dimensions of quality of life in rehabilitation of long term psychiatric patients. Psychiatry and Social Science 1, 197 – 205.

Srivastava, B.N. (1981). the effects of self-esteem and academic performance on alienation among students in an Indian educational environment. Jl of social Psychology, 115(1). 9-14.

Steffens. C. David *et. al.* (2000). Prevalence of Depression and its Treatment in an Elderly Population. Archives of General Psychiatry. Vol. No. 57. Issue 6. pp. 601-607.

Steinberg L., Lamborn S.D., Darling N., Mounts N.S., Dombusch SM. (1994). Overtime changes in adjustment and competence among adolescents from authoritarian indulgent and neglectful families, Child Dev;65(3).;754-70.

Sujata Sahai. (1994). School fright and other student phobias. The Pioneer, New Delhi, February 10, Pg. 74-75.

Sullivan M. and Risler E. (2002). Understanding college alcohol abuse and academic performance. Journal of College Counseling, vol no. 5, issue 10, pp 114-116.

Swearinger, E.M. and Cohen, L.N. (1985). Measurement of Adolescent's Life events: The Junior High Life experience survey, American Journal of Community Psychology. 13, 69.

Symonds, P.M. (1976). Characteristics of Effective Teachers based on the opinion of senior pupils. Assam: SIE.

Synder, W.U. (1947). Do teachers cause maladjustment? J.

Except Child, 14, 40-46.

The Times of India (2004). HC notices to schools on student segregation, Sept. 30, 2004, Mumbai, India.

The Times of India (2005). 'All work and no play for kids at play schools', Sept. 19, 2005.

Thomas A.M., Forehand R (1993). The role of parental variables in divorced and married families; Predictability of adolescent adjustment. Am J Orthopsychiatr, 63(1): 126-34.

Triandis H. C. (1989). The self and social behavior in differing cultural contexts. Psychological Review, vol no. 96, pp. 506-520.

Trillon. Andrew *et al.* (2005). NICE guidance sets new standards for training depression in Children and Young People. UK. www.medicanewstoday.com/medicalnews.

Uma H. (1988). Study of childhood hysteria, unpublished doctoral dissertation, Bangalore University, Bangalore India.

Valerie E., Lee, Helen M. Marks; Tina Byrd (1994). Sexism in Single-Sex and Coeducational Independent Secondary School Classrooms. Sociology of Education, Vol. 67, No. 2. (Apr., 1994)., pp. 92-120.

Van. Voorhees. W. Benjamin. (2005). Beliefs and Attitudes Associated with the Intention to Accept the Diagnosis of Depression Among Young Adults. Annals of Family Medicine. 3:38-46. www.annfammed.org/cgi/content/full/3/1/38.

Vargas, I. (1991). A descriptive study of school induced stressors among inner city Hispanic students. Unpublished doctoral dissertation, Temple University, Philadelphia, PA.

Varshney, N.C. (1979). The Organizational Climate if different types of schools and reactions to frustrating school situations among adolescent boys studying in these schools. Unpublished Ph.D Thesis. Raj Univ.

Verghese, A. and Beng A. (1974). Psychiatric disturbances in children - An epidemiological study Ind J. Med Res 62(10). 1538 – 1648.

Vyas R.P. (1982). Relationship of selected Factors with the teaching success of prospective Teachers in Rajas than, PhD Edu, and RC. Edu. Ajmer.

Wagner B.M., Compas B.E., (1990). Gender, instrumentality and expressivity:Moderators of the relation between stress and psychological symptoms during adolescence. Am J Commum Psychol. 18(3)., 383-410.

Walberg, N. J. (1967). Scholastic Aptitude National Teacher Examination and Teaching success, Jr of Edu, Res. 61:129-31.

Walter R. Gove; Terry R. (1974). Herb Stress and Mental Illness among the Young: A Comparison of the Sexes Social Forces, Vol. 53, No. 2, Special Issue. (Dec., 1974). pp. 256-265.

Website for Indiana Resource Center for Autism. (IRCA aritcles). **http://www.iidc.indiana.edu/irca/IRCAarticles/** fgeneralarticles.html

Werner E.E. (1995). Resilience in development. Current directions in psychological science, vol no. 4, pp 81-85.

Werner E.E. and Smith R.S. (1982). Vulnerable but invincible. McGraw Hill Book Company.

Whitaker A., Johnson J, Shaffer D, Rapoport J, Kalikow K, Walsh BT, Davies M, Bairman S, and Dolinsky A. (1990). Uncommon troubles in young people: prevalence estimates of selected psychiatric disorders in a nonreferred adolescent population. Arch Gen Psychiatr, 47; 487-96.

Whittakar, E. Neil David (1967). Psychological Characteristics of alienated non-conformist college age-youth as indicated by AVL, OPI, ACL and SVIB-M/W group profiles. DAI 1968, 28 (7 and 8). 3055-B.

Wilburn V.R. and Smith D.E. (2005). Stress, self-esteem and suicidal ideation in late adolescence. Adolescence, vol no. 40, issue 13, pp 33.

Worchel, S. and Goethals, R.G. (1985). Adjustment pathways to personal growth. N.J.Prentice Hall, Inc, Englewood Cliffs.

Workshop on learning without burden (1997). organized by school of excellence and S. J public school July 7th and

8th Jaipur.

World Health Organization (1994). Mental Health Programme in Schools. Geneva, Switzerland: World Health Organization.

World Health Organization (1997). Young People and Their Families: A cross-cultural Study of Parent/Adolescent Discord in Cote d' Ivoire, India, and Nigeria. Geneva, Switzerland: World Health Organization.

www.iaae.net/Articles/Alt_ed_Spoiled_Image.pdf

www.jurisproexpertwitnessdirectory.com

www.learningalternatives.net/Alt_Sch_Survey_Understanding_and_Best_Practices.doc

www.malignanselflove.tripod.com

www.nationaleatingdisorders.org

www.openmind.org

www.psychecentral.com

Yash Pal (1993). "Learning without burden" part of national advisory committee appointed to the ministry of human resource department to suggest ways and means to reduce the academic burden of school students. New Delhi.

Zachlod, M. (Sept., 1997). Room to Grow: Giving Children a Sense of Ownership in Their Classroom. *Educational Leadership*.

Zahn, B. (1995). Stress symptoms in 11-16 year old victims of child sexual abuse. Unpublished doctoral dissertation, Temple University, Philadelphia, PA.

Index

D

E

F

G

H

I

J

L

M

N